Inside Out Parenting

DR HOLAN LIANG

Inside Out Parenting

How to Build Strong Children
from a Core of Self-Esteem

bluebird
books for life

First published 2017 by Bluebird
an imprint of Pan Macmillan
20 New Wharf Road, London N1 9RR
Associated companies throughout the world
www.panmacmillan.com

ISBN 978-1-5098-3017-6

9 8 7 6 5 4 3 2 1

A CIP catalogue record for this book is available from the British Library.

Printed and bound by CPI Group (UK) Ltd, Croydon, CR0 4YY

Visit **www.panmacmillan.com** to read more about all our books
and to buy them. You will also find features, author interviews and
news of any author events, and you can sign up for e-newsletters
so that you're always first to hear about our new releases.

For my parents

Contents

SKIN

Introduction

'Oh, for pity's sake!' I silently cursed.

I had timed the nursery run to a tee and for once we were actually on schedule – until my three-year-old daughter, Molly, realized that her new shoes did not have her name label in them. Disaster! I tried to persuade her that this would be fine for one day and promised to stick the labels in that night; I explained that I couldn't do it there and then because we would be late for her nursery (and, more importantly, I would be late for a meeting I was due to chair). But Molly out and out refused to see reason.

So I tried cajoling, then bribing, then threatening her. All to no avail. Ultimately I gave in, impatiently got the name labels and grumpily stuck them in her shoes. But by then it was too late. Molly was digging her heels in and her anger wasn't just about the shoes anymore, but had become an incoherent fury with the world in general. And she was still refusing to put on her shoes. There followed more shouting, this time from me, along the lines of, 'Now I'm going to be late!' Reciprocal shouting and foot stamping from Molly ensued, until I realized that physically picking her up, bundling her under my arm and forcibly depositing her in the car was the only way I was going to get anywhere that day.

This was no mean feat. Picture me shuffling sheepishly down the road to the car, praying not to encounter any of my neighbours, Molly tucked under my arm like a log, kicking and screaming, with no shoes on. Simultaneously, my eighteen-month-old son D (Chinese for little brother, which is what we've always called him), was clinging on to me like an oversized pendant, his arms wrapped tightly around my neck. Assorted nursery-required paraphernalia was haphazardly piled into two bags, which weighed down so heavily on my elbows that they were cutting off the circulation to my fingers, from which dangled the contentious shoes. I must have resembled a demented rag and bone woman with my assorted wares hanging all over me. Meanwhile, Molly's ongoing high-pitched wails of, 'You're hurting me!' advertised our approach to everyone in the neighbourhood.

It was on that day of model motherhood that I decided I should write a book about parenting. If this seems perverse, I haven't even confessed the funniest part of the story yet. About an hour after that little episode, I finally took my seat at the meeting. There I sat, solemnly discussing the effects that 'compromised parenting' has on the mental health of children. Believe me, the irony was not lost on me.

You see, I am a child psychiatrist. Handling Molly's meltdown should have been second nature to me, but it wasn't. After this humiliating escapade, I started to write down the more ridiculous of my parenting moments, because on one level they intrigued me: 'Surely a child psychiatrist should know better?' I kept asking myself.

Before having children I probably considered myself something of a 'parenting expert'. I doled out parenting advice to parents like hot dinners and wore my, 'I know about parenting; I'm a child psychiatrist y'know' badge with pride. It was only when I actually *became* a parent that I woke up to the humbling reality that there is no such thing as a 'parenting expert'. Parenting is, in essence, often a process of mainly well-intentioned trial and error. The well-intentioned part is important because in recent times parents have been taking their role in their children's development much more seriously. We've come a long way from the days when children were seen and not heard; when it was fairly common for them to be farmed out to wet nurses, governesses or boarding school at one end of the social spectrum, or sent up a chimney at the other. We now know that leaving the administration of parenting to others means potentially leaving the outcomes of our children, and the adults that they will become, in the hands of others.

Indeed, sometimes it seems we have gone to the other extreme; there has been such a seismic shift in our attitudes towards parenting. Rather than abdicating responsibility for our children, or being ambivalent, we now have an almost obsessive preoccupation with them. I like to think that this is because my profession has done such a great job at promoting the importance of loving and understanding our children, though cynics might argue that it has more to do with the fact that most of us can no longer afford nannies, governesses or boarding schools. Whatever the reasons, there is no doubt that there is now a genuine interest in giving our children the best possible start in life. And, on a purely selfish level, what could be more fulfilling than being surrounded by a happy, tight-knit, loving family?

What Child Psychiatrists Do

Child psychiatrists, who should not be mistaken for child psychologists, are a rare breed with a unique training. Whilst child psychologists study psychology, child psychiatrists start by studying medicine and surgery. Many, including myself, will also study for a degree in psychology and then practise medicine, surgery, adult psychiatry and psychotherapy before specializing in children. All in all, the training takes a minimum of thirteen years, with a fair few exams along the way. And if you really love the subject, as I do, it will take even longer because you'll take a detour into research, trying to find answers to questions about child development and mental health, as well as trying to treat them. As this was the route that I took, my interests span not only the thoughts and feelings of children and their behaviour, but also how these are underpinned by genetics and the way our brains work. In other words, I know my neurotransmitters from my hormones and am as comfortable with synapses as I am with psychoanalysis. I guess that you could say I know about children inside and out.

But even expert knowledge can wither in the face of a screaming child in full-on tantrum mode. Every new parent worries about how they will measure up. This insecurity is compounded by the fact that many women of my generation are given more advice on handling boardroom tactics than nursery tantrums. And yes, I can confirm that I was one of these women; I certainly wasn't prepared for my transition from high-flier to bum-wiper. Faced with my own inadequacies, as a scientist I reverted to type. I delved even further into scientific papers and started to attend lectures given by world leaders in child development, all in a bid to help me improve my parenting. As well as having an extensive background in working with children, I have been fortunate enough, through my work, to have had access to some of the most fascinating scientific theories regarding parenting around. This is the information I will be sharing with you in this book. This, and the comforting knowledge that even parents who are doctors and scientists get it wrong sometimes.

As a child psychiatrist, my views are influenced by both psychology and neurology and, needless to say, I know my facts and figures on child mental health. These are stark: 75 per cent of adult mental health problems begin before the age of eighteen years, and 50 per cent begin before the age of fourteen.[1] To me, this is clear evidence that if we want to promote psychological well-being, we need to look at what is happening much earlier than adolescence. If we want happy, healthy, successful adults, we need first to raise happy, healthy children.

There is an interesting new development in psychology research which looks at 'resilience' in children. The technical definition of resilience is 'a dynamic process by which individuals adapt successfully to an adverse experience'.[2] Researchers in child development are asking questions like: why do some children who are exposed to the same level of bullying/stress/trauma emerge untarnished, while others are emotionally crippled for life? This umbrella term 'resilience' is likely, in reality, to describe a mixture of factors: 'self-esteem', 'adaptability', 'grit', 'self-worth', 'a can-do attitude', 'strength of character' and a whole host of similar qualities for which I don't think the English language, at present, has just the right word. Let's just call the whole enigmatic lot 'inside stuff' for now. I believe that the stuff that really makes a child or an adult 'who they are' comes from these qualities that are hidden on the inside. You won't be able to see them when you first meet a child, but they are critically important to how that child functions and develops.

But where does this stuff come from? Is it something innate within the child? Is it genetic? Is it developed through the right nurture? These are the kind of questions I will be looking at throughout this book. There is evidence supporting both theories, and nature and nurture are often intertwined. For young children in Western society, at least, the 'nurture' part will relate to their parenting; more specifically, the positive form of parenting in which we are actively involved and interested in our children, in order to raise them as best we can.

From a neurological perspective, I know that the brain is a marvellous organ. At medical school I was once asked why I wanted to study psychiatry. For me this was obvious – it's the brain that makes us human and individual. Joints, bowels and circulation work pretty much the same way in animals as in humans. It is our minds, and their physical manifestation, the brain, that sets us apart and makes us uniquely who we are.

A child's brain begins to form in the first trimester of pregnancy, and rapid brain development continues in the first five to seven years of life, only slowing down in middle childhood, before a second wave of brain development begins at puberty. I know that the brain, particularly a child's brain, has amazing capabilities to adapt. It is common knowledge that young children are 'like sponges' and can pick up foreign languages and musical instruments with much greater ease than adults. I know that the brain is also responsible for the 'inside stuff' – emotional resilience, self-esteem, character – just as it is responsible for learning foreign languages and music. So if music and language can be hard-wired into the brain in these early years of a child's life, shouldn't this also be the case for the 'inside stuff' too? And if this is the case, then the critical part of parenting happens very early on. The years between birth and the age of seven are the time when the crucial blueprints for your child's self-esteem, relationship patterns, ability and attitudes are laid out. The Jesuit saying, 'Give me a child until he is seven and I will show you the man' couldn't be truer. It is in these first seven years that parental involvement can have the most significant impact.

The Power of Good Parenting

Realizing the enormous impact that we, as parents, will have on our children is daunting. And we are made even more confused and insecure by all the current parenting trends buzzing around. Personally, I think that the tiger parents, the helicopter parents, the micro-managers and maxi-organizers, the French parents whose children don't throw food, the Chinese who are all about the tutoring, have been getting their priorities wrong. They've been sweating the small stuff and worrying over the less import-ant aspects of what makes a successful child. Does it really matter if a toddler throws food, eats quinoa or can recite Latin declensions? I call these things the 'outside stuff' – the things that are relatively superficial, whether they are appearances, or manners, or all the other stuff that children can get a certificate for (and parents can brag to their friends about). For me the crux of the matter, the part that you cannot afford to get wrong, the part that will make it all worthwhile in the long run, is the 'inside stuff'. This is the stuff you can't see, but you can *feel* in your child. Typical, isn't it? We make all that effort to help our children to shine, but no one will ever give them a certificate to say they have an A* in self-esteem. Seriously, without self-esteem, a child's achievements will be unfulfilling, their relationships will be lop-sided at best and doomed at worst, and perhaps happiness will elude them for ever.

It seems to me that all the things we parents tie ourselves into knots about – that our children get into 'that selective school', that they get the A* exam grade, give the perfect piano recitals, speak three languages fluently and become captain of the tennis team – are all just the icing on the cake (undoubtedly sweet and shiny, but not much use without the layers of cake beneath). The bulk of our efforts should be spent on what is really important, on what's inside our children: their core and their foundation. We need to start building them up from the inside out, rather than obsessing over the minutiae of presentation and performance on the outside. I am convinced that even with nothing to show immediately for all the effort put in, the long-term pay-out will always be worthwhile.

Of course, if you are also partial to a little bit of window dressing (as I am), you will be glad to know that when they have a solid core of security, self-belief and self-esteem, it is easier for children to thrive socially, academically and creatively. To that extent, the tiger parents are right: parenting to support natural ability can go a long way, not just for academic achievement but for other crucial skills as well, from social ease to creativity. So maybe my frustrated inner tiger parent can get those certificates as well! I am Chinese, after all.

An 'Inside Out' Approach to Parenting

What I am proposing in this book is an inside out approach to parenting. Whilst the outside stuff can be captivating, I believe that the focus of parenting should start with the vital invisible and enigmatic traits at the heart of our children, the inner hard-wiring that will give them 'resilience' against life's myriad challenges. This core is the fundamental basis of our children, and, as I said earlier, it is forged in the early years of life, when brain development is still happening. With the basis of a stable and resilient core, development can be built up, layer upon layer, to form a happy, healthy, well-rounded child.

I will show you how a parent's love, care, attention and affection have the power to actually physically mould a child's brain, thereby profoundly influencing their psychology and transforming their life's path. In this book, I will show you how detailed scientific research has shaped my philosophy on parenting and how I have translated this research into practice, by offering practical tips along the way. As the best evidence for my theories has often been right under my nose, in the form of my own children, I have used many awkward situations I've had to 'solve' with them as examples through the book. Like most things worthwhile, parenting is harder to practise than to preach and by no means do I get it right all the time; as you have seen, even 'parenting experts' resort to carrying their howling children like logs at times.

I am happy to report that five years after 'nursery-gate', after countless more embarrassing episodes, sleepless nights and hours of research, Molly is now a cheerful, bright, bold and articulate eight-year-old, with a love of ballet and swimming who possesses insight beyond her years. She is popular in her class and when she is not pinching her brother, she is making sure to take his hand when they cross the road. My son, meanwhile, is now a creative, analytical six-year-old who loves making crazy inventions by tying bits of the furniture together with Sellotape or elastic bands, or spending hours in his 'lab', mixing together potions made from washing up liquid and paints. Like his inventions, he is clever and silly in equal measure. Of course, part of their transformation is just down to them both being a bit older and therefore much easier to manage. But I also know for sure that some of what I've learned along the way has helped them become the happy children they are – and it has certainly helped me and my husband, Andrew, become better parents. I hope it helps you, too.

CORE

1. The Fixed Core: Genetics

The Egg and Sperm Race

I was waiting at a bus stop when I felt the first contractions that signalled the end of my life as I knew it, and the beginning of my new one as a mother. In fact, my life prior to this had felt like a kind of preparation for this precise moment. My readiness for motherhood almost bordered on complacency: I had a good job, a good marriage, supportive friends; I had ticked all the boxes. The year before, Andrew and I had moved so we would be closer to my family. Before that, I had exhausted my wanderlust by hiking the Inca trail in Peru, photographing blue poppies in the Himalayas, reaching the summit of Mount Kenya, partying in New York, Hong Kong and Cape Town; I was ready to sit at home for a while. As part of my family planning I had even consulted my calendar to contrive delivery in the advantageous month of September,*

---

* This helps you to avoid winter flu in pregnancy, which is a purported risk factor for schizophrenia. It also ensures that your children are the oldest in the academic year at school which provides them with a myriad of advantages. These include the likelihood of being more academically advanced; being larger in size and therefore less likely to be bullied; being more physically developed and coordinated and so more likely to be picked for team sports; being more articulate and socially sophisticated and therefore likely to have more social presence.

and of course during my medical training I had delivered five babies for other people. I felt I knew exactly what this giving birth business was all about. I was ready for this moment.

But of course the parenting story doesn't start at the bus stop. It starts nine months earlier.

The Egg and the Sperm

Most parents believe that parenting begins at the birth of their first child. Child psychiatrists, however, know that parenting begins at conception. A large proportion of your child's destiny (future health, educational level, occupation) is determined before they are even born and if we combined genetic tests, pregnancy and birth histories with a thorough history of your family's lives, I reckon that we could provide a fair estimate of your child's outcome. It's not 'determinism'; it's just probability.

As we all know, the origins of the human race begin with an egg and a sperm. The egg contains information coded in DNA from the mother, as well as a functioning cell with battery and starter pack to kick-start reproduction. The much smaller sperm contains information coded in DNA from the father, as well as a whippy tail to get it swimming up to deliver its information to the egg. What is important is the genetic information coded in the DNA that is contained in the egg and sperm. This is the basis of biological relatedness.

But what is this information and where does it come from? Your DNA (deoxyribonucleic acid) is basically a sort of manual that contains instructions on how to make 'you'. These instructions are coded in your genes. Every single cell in your body: your liver cell, your blood cell, your skin cell; they all contain a full set of your DNA. Thus CSI detectives can pick up DNA from a drop of blood on a shirt, and match it to the victim's DNA to place the shirt-owner at the scene of the crime. The only cells that do not contain a full set of instructions (DNA) are the egg and the sperm. They each contain only half. Within the female ovaries and male testes are the egg and sperm factories. Here, the DNA dances about a bit, gets chopped in half at random, and is then packaged up into eggs in the ovary and sperm in the testes. It is at conception that the sperm-meets-egg story finishes, and, as in the Spice Girls' song, 'two become one'. A new 'instruction manual' is then made for the new individual, based on the combination of information from the father and the mother.

Why are genetics so important in parenting?

Although I think that parenting is vital, as a scientist I would be pretty rubbish if I didn't declare upfront that genetics is also going to have a significant effect on children. It doesn't take a brain surgeon to work out that identical twins (who share 100 per cent DNA and the same womb at the same time) are bound to be a lot more similar than non-identical twins (who share womb environment but only 50 per cent of DNA). For a start, non-identical twins can be of different sex, and their genetic relatedness to each other is no different from any other brother or sister. This is consistently backed up by scientific studies involving twins and adoption. Research over a range of disorders (learning difficulty, ADHD, schizophrenia, depression, anxiety and autism, as well as physical conditions), proves that monozygotic (identical) twins are more similar to each other than di-zygotic twins (non-identical).[1] This is true even if the twins are raised apart. This is such strong evidence for genetic effects that no one really bothers to argue against their importance anymore.

Where debate does continue is on the question of the degree to which environment and genetics play a part in the making of a child. As this is such a moveable and interconnected interplay, I am quite happy to sit on the fence and go with 50 per cent of each. In reality, research is moving towards relative proportions that differ from person to person and over time, with nature and nurture interacting in a multitude of ways – making the simplistic 'nature versus nurture argument' completely obsolete. And the percentages don't really matter; what matters is that genes are an important contributor and they are one contributor that we have knowledge of and control over. Now, when the concept of 'control over genes' comes up, people automatically think about things like eugenics, gene therapy, genetic engineering and designer babies, all of which are expensive, not widely available and ethically questionable. Those sorts of extreme scenarios ignore the easiest and most widely used method of gene selection – the choices we make for ourselves.

The study of genetics has merely given evidence to what we already knew: that the apple doesn't fall far from the tree. From time immemorial, way before IVF and debates on designer babies, dog and horse breeders have been selectively mating animals to produce favourable traits in their progeny. And in humans, the basis of attraction has evolved to reflect the physical traits of health (tall height, glowing skin, good musculature) and social success (fat people in poor countries and thin people in rich countries). In Eastern and Western societies alike, families have historically chosen suitors for their children based on family background, on the reasonable assumption that a child is likely to be similar to their families. These days there is more emphasis on personality and intelligence than health and virility, but the same principle still holds true. If you don't like the personality of your partner and can't stand any members of his/her family, there is a good chance that you might not 'like' the personality of your child. This will be even more the case if you also do not like yourself or any members of your own family.

It might sound politically incorrect, or unromantic and overly pragmatic, but with my behavioural geneticist's hat on, a major step in becoming a good parent is finding the right partner to start with. Not only to love and support you throughout your life, but also to provide you with children who have a temperament and a personality that won't jar with yours. This is important, because unlike a lover or a partner, whom you can divorce and be rid of (society and religion permitting), your children are yours and will remain your responsibility until they are eighteen years old at least, whether you like it or not!

Thankfully, it is not as hard as it sounds to find compatible stock, because most people try to find partners that they actually like, as well as love. It's a phenomenon known as 'assortative mating' – like-minded people tend to marry each other. The process of who you choose to marry or mate with is not a random one, but highly predictable. The 'like' part is important here as whereas a good dose of physical attraction, athleticism, sexual prowess and general lusty desirability can save any marriage, these traits are no good in helping you 'like' your child. If you would enjoy eighteen years of your own or your partner's non-sexual company, then you have at least the best chance in genetic terms of liking your children. Given that conception is now available by IVF from sperm and egg donation, it is interesting to consider whether you would select the same profile for a donor (what you want your child to be like) as you would for a partner (what you want your husband/wife to be like). You might be in for trouble if there is a big difference between the two, because your child is inevitably going to bear a resemblance to your partner. An aggressive, dominating, powerful alpha-male type might be an exciting conquest who offers strong physical protection as a partner, but an aggressive, dominating five-year-old son? That's a recipe for grey hair! A beautiful and passive woman with not much between the ears might be your idea of an ideal wife, but then you should accept that your child may not be a genius.

Genetics and parental expectations

Genetics should always be taken into consideration when you want to get an idea of what to expect in terms of your children's ability. While it's unlikely that you can 'inherit' ability, for example, for needlework, you can inherit traits like 'visual acuity', 'fine motor skills', 'the ability to concentrate and pay attention to detail' and 'low thrill-seeking tendency'. All of these would make it possible for your child to excel at needlework, given the right exposure, passion and encouragement. If neither you, nor any member of your family or your partner and his/her family have anyone with any of these core abilities, your dreams of spawning the next 'World Needlework Champion' aren't impossible, but the odds are much more challenging. Parenting, coaching and education can definitely conquer much of genetic disadvantage, but can they conquer other children who have both genetic *and* environmental advantage? Unlikely. At the highest level of competition, genetics will *always* come in to play, as can be seen clearly by the ethnicity of the line-up at the one-hundred-metre sprint finals at any Olympics.

Whilst I don't believe in ruling out potential in children, clinical experience tells me that ignoring a child's essential nature and natural disposition can be really corrosive to a child's self-esteem; which I see as the emotional backbone of a child. Parents who blindly overly aid and abet their children into academically competitive schools, only for the child to be prematurely confronted with the limitations of their ability, or children who are coerced into competitive sport and laddish behaviour when all they really want to do is read a good book; these are ways to make children feel that pressing the self-destruct button is a good option. This is where knowledge about genetic background can help, as forewarned is forearmed. What, if any, action is then taken will be up to the individual parent to decide.

Genetic loading and spousal choice

During my training, I helped conduct genetic counselling assessments for couples where there was a history of autism in the family. The term autism covers a spectrum of disorders to do with social interaction and communication and there is a probable genetic basis. The most frequently occurring form of autism is thought to be a polygenic disorder, whereby risk is conferred by multiple as-yet-unidentified genes, maybe six or more. In fact most inherited traits, such as intelligence, aggression and attention span, are also likely to be due to multiple genes in combination. A genetic counselling assessment involves taking an extremely thorough family history to look for symptoms of autism and its broader spectrum, getting information from as far back through the generations as possible. The way it works is that the more 'genetic loading' there is in the family (that is, the more family members with the disorder or traits), and the closer they are in relation to the parents (which means the greater likelihood of shared genetic material), the greater the statistical probability that the couple in question will have a child with autism. Parents and siblings share 50 per cent of their genes with any one child. Grandparents, aunts, uncles, and half-siblings share 25 per cent of their genes, great-grandparents and cousins share 12.5 per cent, and so on.

What I didn't expect was that in the clinic, when we told prospective parents the estimated statistical probability that they would have a child with autism, there was a huge disparity in their reactions. When we relayed the same low statistical probability back to several couples with similar genetic loading, most couples felt happy to accept the very low-level risk. However in one couple, the reaction was extreme and unexpected: the wife decided to divorce her husband (where the family history lay). I am using autism traits as an example, but this type of basic genetic loading analysis can be carried out with any trait, such as beauty, height, intelligence and criminality; there is some science behind it, but I'm mainly mentioning it here out of interest, rather than seriously suggesting that this is how you pick your spouse.

The Egg

As we are on the subject of genetic contributions, I thought it would be interesting to share my own family history as a living illustration of this process. Although I like to think that my parenting position is 'highly scientific' and driven by 'evidence-based research', reality is never so clinical. As well as inheriting my parents' genes, I realize that my views on parenting are also influenced by my own life experience, which is in turn influenced by the life experiences of my parents.

I was born in Taiwan, the third and last daughter of a civil engineer and a secondary school science teacher. My dad's family, along with three hundred years of Liangs before him, were peasant rice farmers tilling the land west of Taipei. Taiwan in the 1940s bears no resemblance to the bustling, developed country it is today. Then it was predominantly an agricultural economy, where life for a subsistence farmer was hard and tied to the will of the weather. Growing up, we were forever being regaled with my father's hard-luck stories. If we ever complained about having to go to school, we would be lectured, 'You're so lucky you can go to school. When I was young I had to plead with my mother to go to school, which was a ten-mile round trip. I had to walk barefoot and wear my father's cut-off trousers. My feet were always calloused and bleeding.' We would, of course, mercilessly make fun of this in the manner of a Monty Python skit, replying, 'That's nothing, when I was a lad, I had to crawl naked on my hands and knees through dark underground tunnels to get to school!' and so on.

In my heart, though, and particularly now I am older, I truly respect the effort my father made to give us a better life. He was the fifth of eleven children, and none of his preceding siblings had completed primary school education, but were forced to enter into child labour at a nearby factory where they were physically and verbally abused on a daily basis. On finding that he was to suffer the same fate, my father cried until a neighbour took pity on him. This neighbour, having heard that my father was the brightest child in the class, persuaded my grandmother to allow him to enrol for secondary education, for just a year at least. When the year was up there would be ever more cycles of crying and pleading – 'Just one more year of school' – until my grandmother realized that all this crying and attachment to intellectual study had probably made him too soft for factory work anyway, and he was allowed to continue with his education. Nevertheless, during holidays he had to work on the land or in the factory as a kind of repayment for not taking his share of the family's load. In term time, as his school was so far away, he managed by sofa-surfing in the homes of richer classmates, until eventually he found his way to university to study Civil Engineering. On graduation, he landed a job as a hydraulic engineer in one of Taiwan's harbours, and so successfully climbed out of manual labour and into the professional class. After working hard for ten years as an engineer and saving as much money as he could, he eventually followed his dream: he applied to study abroad, first for a Masters in Holland, and then for a Ph.D. in Civil Engineering at Swansea University in the UK.

My mother, meanwhile, was the fifth child of seven, born to a primary school teacher and a headmaster in Taiwan. Teachers in the East are highly regarded and as such, my mother was more privileged than other children. For instance, she was the only child in her class to wear shoes to school. Despite this, when the school held a maths competition with a pair of shoes as the prize, she won it, and thus became the only person in the school to own two pairs of shoes. My mother had studied entomology at university. This wasn't her first choice – she had not done as well as she had hoped in her exams and therefore didn't get on the course she wanted. She pleaded with her father to be allowed to re-sit her exams, but he told her that as she was a girl, and therefore destined to become a teacher and then ultimately a mother, it didn't make any difference what she studied at university. That's how my mother, an academically and socially able woman, became a reluctant entomologist and subsequently, as foretold, a secondary school science teacher and a mother.

When my mother went into labour with me, my father was already studying in Holland, the country that was to inspire my unusual name. By then, I already had two older sisters and labour was old hat to my mum. She just hopped onto her moped and scooted off to hospital by herself. Through contractions she weaved inbetween the traffic, uncomfortably aware that third children have a habit of flying out rather suddenly, due to the pelvic floor's strength being diminished by prior encounters with large skulls. However, she managed to get to the hospital in time and out I plopped. No doula, no water bath, no family present – just pragmatism. In case I haven't been explicit enough, I am the fortunate beneficiary of genes from two wonderful people.

The Sperm

In the summer of 1997, I took a holiday between completing my Experimental Psychology degree at Cambridge and continuing on to Clinical School. I went to visit my sister in California, who was studying for a Ph.D. in statistics at UC Berkeley. Ever the pragmatist, I had the idea that if I spent the summer learning to play pool this would be a good skill for 'pulling' men on my return to the UK, so my sister and I spent some time over the summer playing pool in the halls that are popular stateside. Back at Cambridge, within ten minutes of utilizing my new-found pool skills in the bar, I 'pulled' my future husband, Andrew; a cocksure postgraduate Fresher, come from South Africa to study economics with dreams of using his skills to bring his country out of inequality and mass poverty. This dream was never quite realized as life diverted him into other careers, but he still holds these liberal and fair values, which is one of the reasons I fell for him.

I never played pool again.

The Progeny

Is it luck or assortative mating that Andrew turned out to be a sociable and intelligent man with an easy temperament, low aggression and blind optimism (qualities that in my children make my life a lot easier)? OK, often his optimism and relaxed attitude is infuriating. For instance, he has a tendency to leave windows and back doors open when going out because according to his relaxed mindset the chances of being burgled in London are low. Even when I call him up and have a go at him about coming home and finding the back door wide open, he can't understand and just says, 'Well, nothing happened, did it?', while I am left shaking the phone, crying, 'But it could have. It could have! Aaaargh!!' The upside is that what I have gained from his DNA is a daughter, Molly, who is relaxed and easy-going. When she broke her left leg falling off a climbing frame (supervised by relaxed dad), after the initial pain had settled, she never complained or moaned once and would cheerfully state, 'Well, my right leg is OK'! Even the headmistress at her school confided, 'Thank goodness it was Molly who broke her leg rather than anyone else in her class, as she hasn't complained or made a fuss at all!' Indeed, sometimes when I am in a tizz about one thing or another, Molly will tell me to 'Calm down, dear!' in the manner of Michael Winner. Annoying, but sometimes useful.

Our son is rather more careful and neurotic. Once, on leaving the doctors' surgery when he was less than two years old, he became grizzly and upset. I was getting annoyed because there seemed no apparent reason for this, until eventually he said, 'My coat.' He had remembered that we had left his coat in the surgery. I could have kissed him because I, too, get distressed about losing things and I blessed his cotton socks that I could retrieve the coat immediately, rather than give myself an ulcer worrying about it later. D wouldn't like the back doors being left open. He clearly takes after me.

And so we are back to genetics, but how does nurture fit in?

The One where Nature and Nurture Stop Fighting and Get a Civil Partnership

Most people are happy to 'believe' that genetics can affect our hair colour, our blood group and particular medical disorders, but when 'personality', 'intelligence' and 'attitudes' come into it, people prefer to see environmental causation. Part of the problem around genetic explanations is in the fear of 'determinism': the thought that your lot in life could be determined at birth and that human will and struggle are for naught. The irony is that 'nurture' – the proxy term for 'environment' – can also have its own form of determinism, with many people struggling to escape from the prison of their family, class and birth environments.

What interests me is the interaction between nature and nurture. It is a wonder how the nature versus nurture debate has lasted so long, because the two are so heavily intertwined. At the most basic level, the success of a gene is based purely on its suitability for the environment. It is a misconception that you can have 'good genes' and 'bad genes'. Gene combinations are like nature's version of trial and error. A new combination is attempted at every conception, and the genes that are successful within a particular environment survive, the ones that don't fall away. Thus the success of a particular gene is purely judged on environmental adaptation. A 'good gene' in one environment may be a 'bad gene' in another. Take, for example, the gene that causes sickle cell. This is generally thought of as a 'bad gene', because it also causes anaemia. However, in some parts of Africa, where malaria is endemic, this sickle cell gene is actually a 'good gene' because it protects against malaria. This concept seems to be more socially acceptable when we are talking about a medical condition, but the same principle applies for genetically determined personality traits.

Take aggression. Elements of aggression are genetically determined. It's useful to look at dogs when talking about this: certain breeds make for better security and attack dogs. No one would ever have a little pug or poodle as a security dog. Yes, of course you can rear a poodle or pug to be aggressive, but not as readily or effectively as an Alsatian or a pit-bull terrier. There's something in the genes. Moreover, these aggressive genes are not in themselves 'bad genes'. In certain environments (the end of the world, lost in a dark forest with wild animals surrounding you, the secret service, competitive sport, a competitive job market) they may be the best genes ever. Selecting or providing the appropriate environment for particular genetic traits in our children can be crucial in maximizing their strengths and minimizing their weaknesses.

Another reason people are sometimes wary of genetic explanations lies in the fears around genetic modification, gene selection and the idea of 'tampering with nature'. People often feel either that this is bound to lead down the slippery slope of eugenics or that there is nothing that can be done about genetic predisposition and you just have to live with it. The thing is: it's much simpler than that. In this day and age, to a large extent, we are able to cheat nature. My genetic predisposition to short sightedness has been environmentally sorted by living in a country with access to an optician. Had this not been the case I would be dead by now, probably having gone to hug a grizzly bear that I mistook for my mother. The most common genetic predisposition in the world – that for having dark hair – is environmentally corrected worldwide on a daily basis, with a bit of bleach from a bottle. Many genetic 'weaknesses' can be vanquished by environmental solutions.[2]

How this impacts our parenting

Given that nurture can impact nature in this way, rather than discussing the question of nature versus nurture we should be looking at how we can best nurture nature. As parents, we are able to drastically manipulate our child's environment, especially their early environment, which is thought to be one of the most important periods of influence. We can do this not only by providing safety and comfort, but also love, warmth and understanding, books, toys, exposure to language, music, models for good social interaction, the right nursery selection, primary school selection, and so on. By understanding our own and observing our children's 'genetically determined' personality traits, we as parents are in a position to shape and manipulate their environments to suit their needs.

Of course, most parents are doing this already. When you select your child's nursery, primary school and secondary school, you are thinking not only about the values you want the school to impart to your child, but also about the particular attributes of your child and how they will fit into the school. It would be short-sighted to send a small, intelligent boy with a love of learning and loathing for sport to a rough and tumble school specializing in rugby. If your child has particular needs, for instance autism, getting their school environment right is by far the most effective treatment, way beyond any medications or other therapies.

And there's more . . .

The parenting that any mother or father offers their child also depends on their child's genetic attributes. Most parents don't like to think that they treat their children differently, but they invariably do. Although it is easy to blame parents for this differential treatment, the fact is that parenting is like any other intimate relationship. It is a two-way process, and often the type of parenting given is in response to the child's behaviour and actions, which may be influenced by their genetically determined nature. If you don't believe me then think about how much you might cuddle an irritable baby who cried round the clock for no reason, and compare it with how you would respond to one who slept peacefully through the night and smiled and chuckled all day. If you are truthful, you know that your response would be different.

Genetically determined traits in children will also lead them to seek out their own environments, with intelligent children joining the chess club and sporty children joining the sports team. As children grow older they increasingly have the power to shape their own environments and choose their own friends. This may not sound like it would have much to do with genetics, but if you agree that 'beautiful people' tend to hang out with each other, brainy nerds tend to befriend each other and jocks stick together, you are admitting there is a genetic component to friendships, because we all know that physical appearance, intelligence and muscle structure are heavily genetically influenced.

What My Parents Did

So how did my own childhood influence my parenting? Well, to give one random example, when D was about eighteen months old, I clearly remember Molly and me crawling around on the floor, barking our heads off like two rabid dogs, while D stood in his cot and belly laughed at us. The reason I remember this so vividly is that even at the time I was conscious that this was a direct recreation of one of my earliest memories, when I had stood in my cot laughing while my elder sisters barked like loons purely for my enjoyment. It's moments like these, of foolishness and fun, that I remember from my childhood. This despite having had a Chinese upbringing with the stereotypical emphasis on academic achievement.

In the early 1980s my mother joined my father in the UK: travelling for her first ever time on an aeroplane with three kids (aged three, five and six years) and arriving in a foreign country without speaking a word of English. I have the utmost respect for her now – I struggle to take my two abroad on holiday, despite being a seasoned and well-equipped traveller. At the start of their new lives in the UK, my parents were not well-off, but our family of five was frugally but happily fed and watered on my dad's Ph.D. stipend. We had very few toys and I can actually remember my sisters and me making a chess set from the cardboard of a cereal packet! We amused ourselves by reading Enid Blyton books, cuddling the teddy bears we got from the second-hand stall at the school fete and begging our friends to share their sweets and chocolates with us. We did not have a washing machine and my mother washed all our clothes by hand on a washboard. She also knitted our clothes, and as shops in 1980s Swansea did not sell 'exotic foodstuffs' like noodles, she would make noodles by hand from flour and water and hang them to dry from broomsticks in the kitchen. At our birthday parties, we had no entertainers or bouncy castles. My mum and dad bounced my friends and me up and down on a taut blanket. We learnt that material things did not matter because we had the most important gift of all: FAMILY. I know that this is something that has heavily influenced me and the way I view parenting, and if I can instil just some of this ethos into my children, I will be happy.

By immigrating to the UK, my parents de facto changed my environment wholesale and therefore my life course. In Taiwan I would have been in the mainstream; fitting in naturally with no need to explain or feel excluded. In 1980s Wales I was the only 'darkie' (as I was referred to) in the class. South Wales to us was amazing as everything was new and different. Our new host country took some getting used to. It was not just the cold, rain and the inability to communicate with anyone (we didn't speak English); it was the food, the music, the culture, the lack of any support network and the fact that everything was unknown. I remember my mother asking me how my first day at school went. 'The ghosts followed me around school,' I told her. Looking back I find this amusing, as I do remember all the children in the class following me around in a line, rather like the closing sequence of a Benny Hill show. They were clearly curious to observe the first 'Chinese' or even 'non-white' person they had ever met. To me, with their pale skin, they resembled ghosts.

Immigrating has a profound effect on people and my father,

who had experienced class discrimination in Taiwan and now racial discrimination in the UK, passed on a life lesson to me: 'As a Chinese person, you will face discrimination, but if you work twice as hard as the others, you will succeed. People will presume that you are not capable, but if you have the certificates to prove it, they will be forced to acknowledge it.' As with other children of Chinese parents, I was subject to many elements of tiger parenting, including high expectations regarding hard work and academic achievement. So there was the time when I was locked in my room at the age of five, until I could recite all my times tables up to twelve. Or the eve of my A-level exams, when my mother took me by the shoulders, looked me in the eye, and said, 'You are our last hope to get a child into Cambridge University.' No pressure, then.

Yet my experience, unlike that of some other tiger cubs, was always tempered with love from my parents and an emphasis on life being about more than work. When my mother taught my sisters and me maths around the dining room table we were taught together and the lessons often descended into chatter and fun. My older sisters were always encouraged to help me. My father gave us projects to do like writing poems, documenting flowers from the garden or sketching bowls of fruit. He would always help us, encourage us and praise us. So learning also came to mean spending time with our parents, which we prized. For much of our early childhood, we laboured at the extra maths work set by my mother under a massive print of the words of a Taiwanese philosopher which said, 'Sometimes be foolish'. My penny-wise parents had saved up a long time for this print and it took pride of place in the house. As it was written in Chinese, it never meant much to me as a child, but now I am an adult I realize this message was so important to my parents because it was the epitome of their ethos – one which they have subliminally passed on to me: although hard work and success are important, they are not the be-all and end-all. Occasionally being free to do irrational things, purely for fun, is just as important; even, or perhaps particularly, amidst the seriousness of adult life.

Whatever genes of ability I inherited were supported by an environment where I was loved and encouraged to be hard-working and determined to succeed. Being a different skin colour to everyone else growing up, and being made to have seaweed in my packed lunches in nori-ignorant times ('Ugh! What's that? She's eating snot'), meant that I got used to being different and sometimes marginalized. It could have gone badly and I could have loathed myself for being different, but the strength I got from my family made me stronger instead: I learnt to accept my difference, give up on conformity and be my own person.

With values of hard work and determination instilled, school was a breeze. We went to the local state primary school, and without the seemingly now obligatory tuition, my sisters and me managed to get places at the local grammar school. A clean sweep of A grades throughout my school career saw me arrive at Cambridge University to study medicine – although this was very much a second choice for me as I had wanted to go to art school. Obviously, this was forbidden by my Chinese immigrant parents. And my initial disappointment at this led to another life lesson: although material things aren't important, financial independence can buy choice and freedom, which definitely are. These attitudes and values made me determined not to completely give up my job when I had children, which would often have been the easiest thing to do.

Chapter Summary

While genes are important, our life experiences will also dramatic-ally shape who we are. Both these factors influence our childhood choices, which in turn continue to shape us throughout our lives. It is this ongoing interaction between nature and nurture that makes us who we are. Whilst in the following chapters I make it clear that parenting is critical, the best parenting is that which is tailored to a child's genetically determined strengths and weaknesses. Therefore I would always encourage parents to put a greater emphasis on understanding their child's genetically determined nature. Burying our heads in the sand to the importance of genetics, the greatest scientific leap of the last century, is counterproductive. Instead of adopting a one-size-fits-all approach, we parents can adapt the environment we provide for our children to the greatest benefit of their nature. And we can certainly be more accepting that, ultimately, our children's capabilities in any arena will be limited by the genes that we have provided them.

This is important, because while we all hope that our children are 'THE BEST' in the class/school/world, the chances of this happening are going to be slim. We would do much better to accept them for who they are and to bring out THE BEST THAT THEY CAN BE. Often, rather than looking at our children, we should be taking a long hard look at ourselves, and that's perhaps why we find it so difficult. In my case, I warned my husband from the outset that if he was hoping for a brood of basketball players or one-hundred-metre sprinters, then he had better rethink his choice of wife, as height and fast-twitch muscle fibres are sadly lacking in my family. In his turn, I was to wipe singing in tune from my list of aspirations for our children. I think together, however, we might have spawned an unstoppable force for Scrabble.

2. The Malleable Core: Self-Esteem

Resilience, Self-Worth and All That Jazz

If my children were chocolates, I would want them to be a Ferrero Rocher rather than a strawberry cream. I know this sounds bizarre, but think about it. The Ferrero Rocher is uniquely multi-layered, with each part providing a different dimension and serving a different purpose. The outer gold paper is not only attractive, but protective; the nutty, outer chocolate coating adds texture and crunch. The unctuous chocolate ganache layer adds a dimension of soft vulnerability, and at its core is the solid, whole nut centre. Awesome.

By comparison, the strawberry cream (always the last thing left in my chocolate box) seems sadly soft, over-sweet and one-dimensional. The true worthiness test comes, however, when you put them both through some kind of 'stress test'. Like blasting them both with a high-pressure water patio cleaner. Although both chocolates look delicious from the outside, only the Ferrero Rocher has a solid and resilient core – the strawberry cream will be obliterated. Ultimately, the ability to survive a high-pressure water jet has got to demand some respect. Of course, some children and adults never encounter stress, mishaps or having pressurized water inadvertently dumped on them in their life, which is why many 'strawberry creams' get on perfectly well, but when life throws you a curve ball and turns on the pressure, it's always better to have a strong kernel of self-belief at your core.

The Solid Nut Core

As a psychiatrist, I have seen how differently people can cope with stress. Whilst genetics will play a significant part in both one's vulnerability and resilience to stress, as I explained in the previous chapter, this is not the whole story. Nurture also has a large part to play. The main part that nurture plays in a child's resilience is in the development of self-esteem. Self-esteem is like the solid core of nut in the Ferrero Rocher; the inner strength, that will get that person through stressful situations without disintegrating. And when I use the term 'self-esteem' I am using it as a proxy for the 'inside stuff': 'a central belief in oneself as a good person who is able to achieve and worthy of love', rather than someone who holds themselves in high regard or suffers from self-importance. The terms 'self-worth' or 'self-belief' also apply. I am being explicit about this because many people who outwardly behave in a self-important way may actually have low self-esteem by my definition, and assessing someone's 'inside stuff' cannot usually be done superficially.

However multi-layered, multi-talented and successful a child is, they also need to be mentally strong, and it is this strength, hard-wired into their core, that will allow them to survive and thrive. Much of self-esteem is formulated in the early years of life and this is why early parental involvement in caring for children is critical. The good news for parents is that this is something that we can directly affect as this core is built from all the love which has been given them through their early parenting.

So, are you saying that 'All you need is love'?
Yep.

Cheesy, I know. But before you slam this book shut and demand your money back, thinking, 'Not another happy-clappy, hippy-dippy, psycho-babbly book recommending we heal the world by all singing "Kumbayah" together', I'll tell you why love is so important and, in terms of parenting, how and why we sometimes get it wrong.

Knowing that we are loved and lovable is at the core of our self-esteem. When I trained in cognitive behavioural therapy (CBT: one of the main recommended psychotherapies for depression in both adolescents and adults), I learnt that early on in a person's life they develop a world view or set of beliefs that although hidden and often unconscious, will dictate their patterns of thinking and behaviour for the rest of their lives. When someone is depressed, their belief system is negative, leading to a lifelong processing bias that views all situations in a negative light. So compliments are not accepted as genuine, achievement is always down to luck and relationships will not last. The aim of CBT is to search back with clients for the one 'core negative belief' that is driving this mindset. You'd think that this belief would be different for different people, right? Yet what I found in practice is that the human psyche is not so unique after all. It is amazing how predictable and limited the core beliefs that cripple so many good people are. The truth is that this core negative belief is almost always an iteration of 'I am not good enough. I am unlovable.'

Why these core beliefs matter

If you have self-esteem, a fundamental belief in yourself as a good person who is able to achieve and who is worthy of love, then when you encounter adversity you will see it as temporary and surmountable. You will believe that you possess the ability to fix any problems and then move on, and that come what may, your friends and family will love and support you through the rough patches. Even if you have no friends or family, a fundamental belief that you are lovable means that you will anticipate the acquisition of love. You will be able to ask for help with the expectation that you will receive it. If this is your starting point, then it is self-evident that you will be able to weather many a storm. If we consider the reverse belief – that you are useless and unworthy of love (low self-esteem/worth/belief) – then all adversity becomes further evidence of your uselessness and compounds your misery. You will feel alone in that misery and not reach out for help because you feel that you deserve to be punished and no one will help you anyway. This is a very lonely mental place to be in, and one which is fertile ground for mental health problems when adversity arises.

When are these core beliefs formed?
In early childhood.
Who contributes to the formation of these core beliefs?
Parents.
How can parents promote positive beliefs about being lovable?
By showing love.

You've Got to Show Your Love

I think that sometimes people forget that 'love' is like heat; it's no good in a theoretical or inaccessible form. Having a radiator that is not switched on, or a heat source at the bottom of your garden, is not going to keep you warm at night; ultimately you need to be able to FEEL heat for it to have value. In my line of work, almost all parents will say that they love their children, and I believe this to be true. Many parents work day and night to provide money in order to give their children the better things in life. Many parents sacrifice their jobs to ensure that their children are driven to myriad tutors and after-school activities to make sure they get the best start in life. Many parents allow their children to do whatever they want in the name of love. However, in my experience, the percentage of children who FEEL that their parents love them is much lower. Maybe they are just ungrateful little sods. Or maybe it is this: it is one thing to love your children. It is another to make them believe/feel in their hearts/know to the core/have no doubt of the fact that they are loved. The former can be done from the office or at the kitchen sink; the latter is much harder work.

I also think that sometimes parents get confused about love. They think it is something that needs to be earned, or won, or is conditional. They think that unconditional love is excessive; an extravagance that will 'spoil' their children. They believe that denying love can motivate their children to work for their approval. They, and in turn their children, come to believe that achievement (or becoming a certain kind of person) leads to love. Many great and successful people have grown up believing this way. It makes sense to them that achievement would lead to 'being worthy of love' and self-esteem is built on achievement and love. Many people's drive for success comes from a desire to win their parents' affection (Model 1).

Model 1:

Achievement
Academic success
Beauty
Sporting success $\longrightarrow$ Self-esteem $\longleftrightarrow$ Love
Popularity
Financial success
Status
Kindness

But there is a second model where a fundamental core of love (which is not conditional on any achievements) can lead to self-esteem in its own right, and this self-esteem, built on the basis of love, can drive achievement all on its own. The acknowledgement of the unconditional love and support of their parents is commonplace in the acceptance speeches of all kinds of award-winners, from the Nobel Prize to the Oscars.

Model 2:

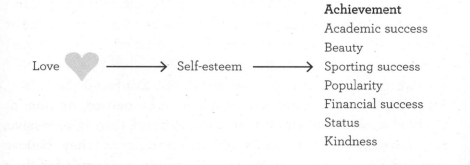

Both models work, and there are many success stories built on people wanting to prove their 'haters' wrong. However, the second model is infinitely stronger than the first. When love is dependent on achievement, it can be a very bitter pill to swallow if your achievements wane and your self-esteem and love (which were dependent on the rocky foundation of achievement) are diminished. This can leave someone, in effect, stripped of everything. This first model might explain why many successful, amazing people can still feel they have nothing or are perpetually 'not good enough'. In the second model, even if your achievements wane and your self-esteem is dented, love is untouched and the source of everything lives on.

Making sure someone feels loved is hard work, so I think it is important to stress that the effort involved in making your children feel loved is front-loaded. It's a bit like when you start a new romance: you swap your old grey bloomers for some fancy new lingerie, refrain from passing wind, frequently ask about your new partner's day, and always make time to go on holiday together. In the same way, 'romancing' your child (putting extra elbow grease into making them feel loved and special) is required in spades at the start. Once a secure loving relationship is established, then inevitable liberties can and should be taken, but if the work of the early years has been solid, then nothing can shake the secure foundations of love.

I am a great believer in the fundamental importance of showing love, and with regard to my own children I always operate on the basis of the second model. I want my and my husband's love to be the fuel for our children's success. (Or failure, we will love them anyway.) As a parent, it is sometimes difficult to know 'how to make children feel loved', as this is not a topic covered at medical school, in a psychology degree or during psychiatric training. There is no scientific paper that will answer this question and you shouldn't let any pseudo-science, pop-psychology book tell you otherwise. What there are, however, are suggestions that have a basis in science. Seemingly unrelated experiments, often tried on animals as well as humans, that point to potential things that we (maybe) should be doing.

How to Show Love: Babies
(Up to Twelve Months)

Many parents see the parenting of babies as purely a matter of keeping them in a safe environment, feeding and changing them. Certainly, for a new parent, it does sometimes feel as if your life has been reduced to dealing with 'input', 'output' and laundry, laundry, laundry! However, for most parents, there is so much more that we are doing without noticing. It is the love and affection we give our babies along the way that are far more important than any routine-based feeding schedules.

Children need a good licking

In the sixties, a psychologist called Harlow undertook a seminal experiment with monkeys.[1] He found that baby monkeys preferred to stay with a furry pretend monkey that gave them warmth rather than a wire-frame monkey that gave them food. This is some powerful evidence that if a baby was given an ultimate choice between warmth and affection or food, it would choose affection. More recent research has shown that in a litter of rats, the pup that is licked the most by its mother turns out to be the most successful rat. The pup that is licked the least becomes the least successful. Some mother rats do not lick their pups at all and these pups turn into adult rats that are more aggressive or withdrawn. When baby rats of mothers who don't give them a good licking are given to a mother rat that does, these pups grow up just fine and are not aggressive or withdrawn. This shows that there was nothing innately 'aggressive' or 'withdrawn' about these pups, or if there was, it was melted away by the power of a few good licks. Similar results have been found in experiments with monkeys, in relation to being stroked, and there are parallels

TOP TIP: CUDDLES ARE GOOD

Cuddles in humans are probably the equivalent of stroking and licking in animals. Surely nothing says love so much as some kisses and cuddles? Forget Victorian repression and stiff upper lips, I'm all for open affection. Often. Get as many cuddles in as you can, particularly in the first year. Dads can be just as good as mums, and the more dads cuddle, the stronger the bond will become between father and child. Mums don't need to be possessive; a good relationship between dad and child means LESS WORK for mums – now and in the future!

with the outcomes of human children whose mothers have had post-natal depression.

In post-natal depression, one of the main problems that mothers encounter is in responding appropriately to their babies. Often, mothers with mild symptoms can still perform the fundamental tasks required – feeding and nappy changing – to the extent that many mothers with post-natal depression go unnoticed and untreated. What is a greater difficulty for depressed mums is a sensitive, timely and appropriate response to their baby's emotional needs. Depressed mothers differ from non-depressed mothers in the number of times their baby is picked up and cuddled, the number of times there are face-to-face interactions with their baby, and the time they take to attend to their baby when it cries. These subtle differences are often overlooked and may even seem irrelevant; indeed it is only recently that their crucial long-term effects on a child's psychological development (depression, anxiety, behavioural problems and IQ) have been documented.[2] If you are worried that you or your partner may be suffering from depression during your baby's first year, then it's really important to seek help, not only for the short-term well-being of the parent but also for the long-term well-being of your child.

The crying game

So we can see that the sensitivity, timeliness and appropriateness of a parent's response to their baby is of critical importance to their child's emotional and intellectual well-being. This ties in with the parenting practice of 'responsive parenting', which means that parents should respond to their baby's needs, whether these are physical or emotional. Where, then, does this leave popular parenting practices such as controlled crying, that dictate the reverse of responding to your baby's needs?

Good research in this area is thin on the ground, because quite frankly, who would want to hand over their newborn infant to a research study? How can you ethically impose controlled crying on a random parent? If you analyse outcomes of children whose parents had chosen to use controlled crying, how can you exclude bias? Bias is relevant because particular parents will choose to parent in this way. Evidence in animals, though, consistently shows that early exposure to stress leads to long-term changes in the hormone-regulating pathways that can affect future development and stress responses (*more of which in Chapter Four*). So, does leaving a baby to cry for prolonged periods count as stress?

As a newborn, Molly was big on crying. She was as good as gold all day but turned into a screeching banshee on the stroke of eleven every night and continued till four in the morning. This lasted for a good three months, at least. Even when she was being cuddled she would scream. Once, after I had been moaning about how shattered Andrew and I were from all the late nights, my mother scoffed at me, saying, 'That's because you don't know what you are doing. Come and stay over on a Friday night and I'll take her and show you how it's done.' Never one to look a gift horse in the mouth, Andrew and I rushed over and joyfully crashed in the spare bedroom, leaving Mum with Molly. We were deep in sleep when at one in the morning there was a knocking at the bedroom door. There stood a frazzled, five-foot-tall Chinese lady, outstretched hands holding a screaming, red-faced banshee, whose whole being shook at every outpouring of indignant rage, drawing breath only to inhale in order to continue the onslaught. 'Molly is *not* a good girl!' my mother declared, thrusting her back into my arms and marching off, defeated. At least there were no more of the 'you don't know what you are doing' lectures.

Soon after this, when Molly was six weeks old, my in-laws came to visit. They encouraged us to try 'controlled crying'. This basically consists of leaving your baby to cry until they fall asleep from tiredness. Certain regimes allow you variations of the number of times you can check on them, but in essence the theory is to teach your baby to go to sleep by themselves by leaving them to it. In effect 'crying until they are so tired that they fall asleep' is rebranded as 'self-soothing'. After forty minutes of continued crying and visual checking, there were still no signs of Molly tiring. I knew she had stamina because she would cry for hours, even when I was consoling her, and in the end I felt so awful that I could not continue with it. Attachment theories and results of animal studies raced through my mind and I abandoned the process. It felt completely wrong to me, anyway, to be attempting to have a polite dinner conversation with her distress so evident in the background. Andrew, however, seemed to have no such problem and just knocked back the vino, while the in-laws kept stating that this controlled crying was exactly what they had done with my husband and look at him, hadn't he turned out OK? Although a psychoanalyst might link self-medicating with alcohol to relieve stress with the self-sufficiency learnt from early controlled crying, I guess this is true enough!

Where all the research done around this falls down is that studies in animals may not translate to humans and even in human research, strategies that appear to have small, significant effects across a population may not tell you anything about your individual child. Your child may be the outlier; the chain smoker that never develops lung cancer. But countering the 'he turned out OK' argument is always easy, because with these arguments one is never privy to the counterfactual – such as how much *better* adjusted Andrew might have been if he hadn't been left to cry. For all the research, a parent must ultimately decide themselves what is best for them and their family. Personally, I could not go through with controlled crying for my baby. While I am sure that it would have worked and Molly would have learnt to stop crying much earlier, it didn't feel right to me that one of her first experiences in life should be to cry alone. As a child psychiatrist I know that babies who are very badly neglected often don't cry. They cry at first, when they still have the hope that someone might come, but when that hope is gone, they stop. They have already learnt that the world is a harsh place and other people can't be trusted to help. They learn to be closed and self-sufficient. This is not a conscious process and they cannot tell you this is happening, but when you meet children who have suffered early

TOP TIPS: RESPONDING TO BABIES AND COFFEE MORNINGS

Respond to your baby's needs When babies cry, they need you to respond. If the hormonal system that manages stress is placed under continuous pressure at an early age, while the brain is rapidly developing, it can become reprogrammed. This can have life-long consequences, leading to a vulnerability to developing anxiety and depression. I am not one for absolute rights or wrongs, but I personally would not advocate controlled crying for babies under six months, although it is probably acceptable for a one-year-old. As doctors we often make 'risk-benefit analyses', and I guess parents must look at the risks and benefits of this themselves. If a single mum with two other children needs to sleep in order to be able to care for all her children, then she should go for it – the risks of controlled crying are minimal compared to the risks of maternal depression. But if parents are able to cope, then I would avoid it. Ultimately, the situation is not cut and dried and although I personally don't believe in controlled crying in young babies, it's not something to get judgemental about.

Take a pinch of salt with you to coffee mornings All new parents struggle with insecurity, and never more so than at parent coffee mornings. Here you will hear other parents regale you with stories about how their babies slept through the night from six weeks old and have never cried. PLEASE don't feel down on yourself if you hear this. Remember that larger, formula-fed babies who have also been introduced to dummies will invariably sleep better, and that there are cons as well as pros to making those particular choices. Ultimately, all babies are different. D was so much easier than Molly that had he been my firstborn, I probably would have bragged about how well he slept, when in fact this would have had nothing to do with my competence – or lack of it.

Being a shrink made it easier for me to weather the coffee-morning gloaters as I know that how people portray themselves is often not the whole truth, just their version of it. I have spent days listening to the woes of people who, if you met them at a party or saw an airbrushed version of their lives on Facebook, would appear pretty 'perfect'. My go-to defence, when someone seems to be gloating, is to presume that they are probably not giving me the complete picture and I find that being incredibly nice in return is generally an effective response:

Gloating mum: 'My baby is so good and she sleeps eight hours every night, I've never felt so refreshed!'

Me (thinking: 'Your baby probably sleeps for four hours, but for some reason you feel the need to exaggerate because of some awful problems in your life that you don't want to share with us,' but saying instead): 'Wow! That's really great. Lucky you, you have a lovely baby.'

It mightn't be true, but it doesn't hurt anyone and it makes you feel a heck of a lot better.

neglect, there is often a hardness and lack of trust that is hard to penetrate. This is not the type of world view that I wished my children to develop.

So I made the choice (and forced Andrew into agreeing with me) that, until their brains had sufficiently developed, our children would not be left to cry. In actuality, this was an arbitrary age

I plucked out of the sky, but it sounded good and was credible enough to get Andrew to play along. Having not been left to 'self-soothe' Molly was sometimes still at the crying game after the age of one, but by then I felt much more comfortable about doing the controlled crying, safe in the knowledge that 'love' and 'responsive parenting' had come first, and had had time to be established before the necessary iron fist of discipline came down. My own view is that controlled crying has its place for older infants, but has no place for babies. D turned out to be much less of a crier and a much better sleeper, so controlled crying was never even mooted with him.

A good kind of brainwashing

Some of our current obsessions with parenting have their root in the theories of John Bowlby and Mary Ainsworth, who showed how much bonding and attachment affect a child's outcome. Their ideas clearly demonstrated that the outcomes of children are directly associated with the level of bonding parents have to their infant children, and the degree of attachment infants have to their parents.

Bowlby's theory goes that in order for parents to develop a nurturing attitude to their baby, they need to 'bond' with them. In my mind, bonding is a bit like a brainwashing programme that makes it seem reasonable to think: 'Yes, I love you so much that I am quite happy to deal with cleaning up your excrement and depriving myself of sleep in order to serve you day and night.' This brainwashing is necessary if we are to become good parents and take responsibility for all manner of infant atrocities. Without the brainwashing, it's likely that we'd grow crazy and resentful – if any other person in the world treated us the way our baby does, even someone we loved dearly, we'd probably have killed them by now. Only if you are brainwashed does it become possible to endure. I would thoroughly encourage parents to submit whole-heartedly to the brainwashing process as it makes the required ordeal so much more bearable. Think of bonding as the corporate induction you undergo when you start with a new employer. Let them brainwash you about their amazingness; for the sake of your own sanity: drink the Kool-Aid.

You can help facilitate this brainwashing by cuddling your baby as soon and as much as you can, particularly in the early days after birth. For some parents the brainwashing is instant, for others it may take some time, but usually it will come. Some people believe that by virtue of having heaved the foetus around with them for nine months, mothers will have an immediate bond. I don't believe that to be the case, but rather that the bond is formed in the same way as any other deep bond; by spending intimate time together. It probably won't take too long, as by the time you've done your first twenty-four hours with your baby, you've had the time equivalent of about twelve dates and have probably already shared a bed.

For me, it took about three days. I remember that when I was pregnant I looked over at Andrew when he was sleeping (creepy women do this sort of thing) and wondered how I could love anyone more than I loved him. Following the birth of Molly, I searched myself for the 'instant bond' I was supposed to feel with my baby, but strangely found that Andrew was still number one. Then, surprisingly, on day three I woke up and cuddled my Molly and looked over at Andrew snoring away next to me. I poked him awake and said excitedly: 'Hey, it's happened! I love her more than I love you!' It took Andrew a bit longer, but at three months, he turned to me and said, 'Ha! I love her more than I love you now, too!' 'Good,' I said, 'just remember that. Because if we were both drowning, I would want you to save her first.'

The Importance of Secure Attachment

The reciprocal love of child to parent is termed 'attachment'. In the first six months of life, babies are primed to seek help from anybody. Pass a newborn around the relatives and that baby will be perfectly happy. As long as they have a warm body cuddling them it doesn't matter to them if it's mum, dad or the postman. They are like the desperate girl at the party who'll sleep with anyone. Between six months and a year, babies become more discerning and will seek to attach themselves to someone special. They will usually choose the person or people who have been there for them; the face that appears when they are hungry, cold or in need; the face that smiles at them, feeds them and plays with them. As a parent, you should really hope that this is you, and not the nanny.

By eight or nine months it will be pretty evident WHO this person is, as the infant will cling to, and only want to be calmed by this person. They will make a fuss if this person leaves them. They have now transitioned to the jealous girlfriend. In Bowlby's era, the attachment figure was always the mother, but in my mind there is no reason why this should not be the father, or indeed both parents. In these modern times of dual career families, I found it useful to make sure my children formed attachment to BOTH parents, so that Andrew and I could be equally as useful and used interchangeably. I know some people who say, 'Yes, we want them to form a strong attachment with their nanny because we are both working,' but this to me defeats the purpose. Attachment figures are for life, not just for Christmas. And if your child forms too close an attachment to the nanny, what do you do when the nanny, as they inevitably will, leaves . . . ? This was one reason I chose never to have a nanny.

This is one of the trickiest dilemmas for working parents and there is no right or wrong solution, only the one that is made to suit the whole family. By the whole family, I mean both parents and the child. In some families, the parents give their careers priority, with the child's needs coming second. Others decide that the child is paramount, often with one parent sacrificing their career. This can lead to resentment and for me, neither of these outcomes are ideal. We, as a society, need to think more carefully about how much we really value family life, and keep pushing for changes in the law to suit modern families.

My own family–career balancing act was a hectic put-together, patchwork job. I was in the middle of my specialist training on one of the best psychiatric training programmes in Europe at the time that Molly was born, with two years left before I could become a consultant. I was keen to complete my training as soon as possible and therefore took the decision to return to work full-time when Molly was seven months. Andrew, meanwhile, had a well-timed job change and was granted three months gardening leave, which allowed us a lovely month-long holiday together as a family before the mantle of childcare was passed from me to him. This all happened between Molly's seventh and ninth months and by the time she started full-time nursery, secure attachment to us, her parents, was already well established.

'Secure' attachment is the most desirable form of attachment. It has associations with all sorts of positive outcomes throughout childhood and even into adulthood. Securely attached children are more resilient. They do better academically and socially and have better physical and mental health. The good news is that typically 75 per cent of children will establish secure attachment.[3] But what of the insecurely attached? These children have poorer outcomes across the board and are more likely to attain less and be more susceptible to mental health problems. If you want to build resilience in your child, secure attachment is vitally important. If you want to promote secure attachment, this will develop in the first nine months of your baby's life. Blink and you'll miss it.

Babies in strange situations

The work of Mary Ainsworth, the other protagonist in attachment theory, can help parents determine if attachment has occurred, and furthermore whether this attachment is 'secure'. She conducted the now famous experiments with one-year-old infants called 'The Strange Situation Test'.[4] The crux of the experiment goes like this: baby is allowed to play in a room with their mother in a new environment, with new toys. Next, a stranger will come into the room and start to try and engage the baby. The mother is encouraged to stand back, and after a while she will leave the room. The stranger will try to encourage the baby to carry on playing, and eventually the mother will return. Researchers taking notes are crammed into the next room, viewing it all through our beloved one-way mirrors. They will be observing how the baby plays with the toys, how they explore the room and the proximity with which they stay with their mother. They will observe if this changes on the introduction of the stranger and how the baby responds when the mother leaves. They will then observe the interactions between baby and stranger, and finally and crucially what happens at the reunion with the mother.

Here's how a securely attached child will behave: on being introduced to a new environment, she will initially stay close to her mother. However, the toys will be exciting and so she will want to play with them. She will tentatively start to play with them, but seek reassurance by looking at her mother or bringing the toys back to her mother to play with. After a while, she will get more confident and independent and explore the room more widely, playing with a variety of toys. When the stranger comes in, she will become shy again and return to her mother and play close to her. When encouraged by her mother, she may engage with the stranger. When the mother leaves, she will get upset and protest. She may cling to her mother and not want her to go. She may cry and have a tantrum; she may pull at her mother. When her mother is gone, she may stand by the door and carry on protesting. Then she may be dejected, quiet and withdrawn. After a while, and with the support and encouragement of the stranger, she will settle down again to play with the toys.

If reading this account sounds familiar to you, it is because 'The Strange Situation Test' is more or less replicated in any nursery settling-in day. This is perfect, because it means that all parents who are intending to send their children to nursery will gain insight into whether their child is securely or insecurely attached. Insecurely attached children may stray immediately away from their mothers or alternatively cling to them when introduced to the new environment. They may play roughly with toys or not explore the toys or room as widely. They may be immediately over-familiar with the stranger or refuse to interact with the stranger at all. They may or may not protest when their mother leaves. However, the main difference between securely and insecurely attached children is in the reunion with mum.

No matter how much or how ferocious the protest was when the parent departed (and I have seen screaming, clinging, door-banging and hair-pulling), the securely attached child will be happy to see her parent again when she returns. She will want to be with her again; all is forgiven and forgotten. The insecurely attached child will be indifferent at best and actively ignore and punish the parent at worst.

So if you have ever had a wet limpet stuck to you at the nursery school gates, refusing to let you go to work, be thankful that this is one sure sign of a securely attached child. If, on your return, they don't know who you are, or are sitting with their feet up on the table, smoking a joint, giving you the evils and saying, 'Yo. Where y' been, bitch?' you might want to start worrying.

How to Show Love: Toddlers (Ages Two to Four)

As children grow, their requirement for physical attention wanes and is replaced by the requirement for positive interaction. Communication, shared experiences and fun times begin to take precedence over comfort. For parents, this should be the easy part because toddlers are such fun, inquisitive, excitable, hilarious little beings. They have the best facial expressions and say the funniest things and LOVE and ADMIRE you so much unconditionally. I have proof; I remember my sisters and me at around this age debating who was more handsome: Dad (think Chinese bloke with a comb-over and a seventies 'tache) or George Michael (in prime Wham! days). We decided Dad was better looking. Such is the deluded adoration of children.

Make time, make memories

Unfortunately, in this day and age of dual career families, giving children our time is often hard. Creating these precious moments is sometimes tricky. Even when great lengths have been taken to clear the diary for a day to 'tick off' the 'making precious moments from childhood so that he will remember I was actually a fun parent' box, the day is usually too pressurized and something

TOP TIP: LAUGHING IS GOOD

What says 'I love you' more than enjoying someone's company? One of the vows I made when I had to work full-time was that I would laugh with my children every day, and we did, and we still do.

spoils it. Although I worked full-time for two years after Molly was born, I was determined that every minute of the non-working day would be spent with her. I stopped working late and my reputation as an ambitious, dedicated, high-flier took a battering. It was tough having to take being bypassed and overlooked at work, and needless to say, my social life went completely out of the window, but it was worth it for the relationship I built up with my children. Thankfully, once I completed my training I vowed to only take part-time work thereafter. As such, I hope that the sandwiches with the giraffes at London Zoo; drenched picnics; swimming debacles; splendid theatre trips; afternoons spent junk-modelling cars, robots and trains; baking biscuits; reading books; singing rhymes; painting masterpieces; acting plays; dressing-up; performing puppet shows, and demented dancing, as well as the follow-up conversations, laughter, in-jokes, nostalgia and reminiscences about these times, have served to grow the seed in my children's hearts and minds that they are loved and lovable, not to mention damn good fun people to hang out with.

In praise of praise

As time passes and your child starts to get a strong grasp of language, what parents *say* as well as do becomes more important, not just in forming your child's self-esteem but in shaping their values and identity. Parents differ on their views about praising children. Some parents praise them for breathing – 'Wow, son, you drew breath; and you've done it again. It's amazing how you can keep doing that.' Whilst for others, drawing a compliment requires Herculean feats. Proponents of the former are often enthusiastic Americans. Proponents of the latter take the view that kids are bright and if you keep praising them for everything, then the praise will be meaningless. They think praise should be used sparingly and reserved for impeccable achievement.

Where do child psychiatrists stand on the issue of praise? Well, definitely in the camp of the enthusiastic Americans. Praise is good and should be shared, not spared! If, as a kid, you ever received genuine praise for a job well done from your parents, then you will know that the warm fuzzy feeling you get from that is GREAT! Children love to make their parents proud; why should we deny them this?

We may have come across parents who praise their child at every tiny step and thought to ourselves, 'Good grief, that's a bit over the top, isn't it? I don't want to be like that,' but often these parents are doing this temporarily, just for show, as they know you are watching. Most parents actually praise too little rather than too much. Constant praising is really hard work, and not many people, even enthusiastic Americans, can keep it up consistently. In our own working lives, praise is limited. When was the last time you were praised for your work by your boss? I can't even remember. Would I like to be praised a bit more? Yup.

Thinking back over the last day, I would say that I probably only praised my children three times each (if that) and even then, the praise would have been a cursory 'Well done', or 'That's nice'. When I remember to, or when there is clear reason to, I do praise more often and more elaborately, but if three times a day is about the average for a parent who knows the benefits of praise and is consciously looking to do it, then I don't think that we as a nation are in fear of over-praising our children. Having a standpoint of reservation towards praise probably means that most days children are not being praised at all.

What mirrors reveal

In child psychiatry clinics, we have the opportunity to view parenting interactions through one-way mirrors. Parents are asked to play with their children in a room with some basic toys provided, and a large group of clinicians stand in the next room poring over their interaction. Each physical contact that is made, eye contact given, supportive gesture and shift of body language is noted and its meaning interpreted. In terms of speech, every tone, choice of word, supportive comment, criticism and praise is noted. And, crucially, the absence of praise when an opportunity to praise arises. It is amazing, but often in a half-hour observation you can learn more about a family, and a child's problems, than in hours of history-taking from the parents. For me, this is the best part of child psychiatry. This is the child psychiatrists' version of a physical examination, of putting stethoscope to chest and hand to skin.

Sadly, in some families praise is just not in the vocabulary. Often these parents have problems and may never have been praised themselves, or they are suffering from depression. I remember a family like this. I had been seeing an eight-year-old boy from a very deprived neighbourhood for suicidal behaviour. On our recommendation, the social workers had organized for him to get involved in an after-school activity, and he had started football. I had heard that he was doing well at it, and that the England football team had visited his club and he had played with them. When he told me this, I smiled and said, 'I'll watch out for you in a few years' time when you're playing for England for real!' It was obviously a joke; I knew the reality of this ever happening was very unlikely. I say this sort of thing a lot in my line of work and in my experience a typical response would be for the child to smile and think, 'Wouldn't that be great?', or laugh, thinking, 'I know you're joking, but thanks for saying it anyway.' Parents would join in, maybe with a supportive comment. Instead, I was met with silence. The deadpan faces of mother and son spoke unanimously: 'That is never going to happen. We are worthless, and nothing good is ever going to happen to us.' It was a really depressing day, and the first time that I physically felt the emotional poverty of what it would feel like to grow up in a vacuum of praise and hope.

So praise is definitely good. Erring on the side of too much praise is better than too little, particularly with young children, and the most beneficial time for unadulterated, hedonistic praise should be in the first few years of life. Luckily, for most parents this comes naturally. (We've all witnessed it: 'Look at his wee nose and those darling eyes, he's the most beautiful baby in the world,' uttered to the most pug-ugly baby you've ever seen.) After that point, there does come a time when praise can and should be used to shape behaviour. Now it may be useful for parents to differentiate between 'esteem praise' and 'functional praise'. The purpose of 'esteem praise' is to raise self-esteem: 'You're so clever,' while 'functional praise' is used to reinforce behaviour: 'Well done for remembering to check your spelling.' The years up to about four are the time when esteem praise should be used liberally, as it will be accepted without question, and its use will peter out naturally until your child reaches adolescence, when it will become an embarrassment. Functional praise should kick in at about two and continue from then on. (*I talk more about this in Chapter Five.*)

What did I do with the eight-year-old boy? Amongst other things, I taught his mother to praise him. I even gave her a crib card full of praises: 'Well done', 'That was really good', 'Fantastic job'. I told her to use as much energy and enthusiasm as she could muster. We rehearsed together in clinic. This took some doing. She was asked to use all the phrases on her card in the next week, slipping them into natural conversation. Fake or forced praise is still better than no praise, and with time, we hoped it would become more genuine. She was asked to dedicate the ten minutes before bedtime to praise each of her children for something good they had done that day. She was asked to encourage each of her children to praise each other. Slowly, slowly, bit by bit, we sought to bring her family some self-worth.

How to Show Love: Children
(Ages Four to Seven)

Once children reach school age, the need for physical closeness and time spent together will naturally loosen (thank goodness – no more dragging children around who are attached to my ankles), but the apron strings should not be completely cut yet. Children should start to become confident at forming relationships and learning new things without their parents, but parents are still required to empathize, guide and advise. While pre-school children can feel like the King of the Castle in the family home, believing they are the smartest, brightest, most lovable kid they know (because they don't know any other kids), what happens to this self-esteem when exposed to other children? When they notice that they actually can't run as fast as Harry, or draw as well as Chloe? Can their self-esteem survive? The work of parents in this next part of early childhood should focus on reinforcing their children's emerging self-esteem and preparing them in a supported way to face their weaknesses and deal with the inevitable failures.

Fixing the Field: Guaranteeing Success

Most parents want to know how they can ensure that their child succeeds. It's easy! As parents of young children we can always guarantee our children's success by fixing the field. The biggest field that we can 'fix' is through our selection of primary school. To a young child, 'school' is 'the world', so the first identity they form of themselves in the outside world will be influenced by this choice. When it comes to developing self-esteem rather than just academic performance, being a big or a medium-sized fish in a small pond is always preferable to being a small fish in a huge, overwhelming pond. It is up to us as parents to try and find the right size of particular pond to suit our particular fish. If you have a very big fish, it will still be a substantial size in a big pond, but if you have a small to medium fish you need to think more carefully. Choosing or paying for a big pond for a small fish to become lost in, in these formative years, may be detrimental in the long run.

Whenever I am asked if an academic child should start school a year early or go into the year above, my typical response is, 'Whatever for? And make life harder and more competitive for him?' Instead, if you have an able child, why not allow them to enjoy academic confidence, intellectual security and plenty of prizes. Use the time to develop social skills, music, sport, creativity and breadth of interest. Able children will always end up in the big pond but I don't feel the need for a rush. I think that schooling decisions should try to take into account self-esteem as well as academics. After all, self-esteem is more important than the precocious age at which children master Latin and trigonometry.

The key to motivation

Another example of how engineering the field for children can be beneficial is with regards to motivation. Children are more likely to persist in activities that they feel they are good at, so it follows that if you wish your child to persist at an activity then you should try to make sure they feel good at it. Even if they are not naturally good at something, picking an appropriate field can engineer the perception that they are. For me, football is a valuable life skill. Not that all children need to be able to shoot penalties and fake dives, but that getting along socially in the UK requires a passing knowledge and ability in this sport, particularly for boys. A boy will have no trouble being accepted into peer groups across the UK, Europe and South America if he is able to kick a ball into a net. Who wouldn't want this guaranteed social acceptability for their child?

D is not a natural footballer, and why should he be? His parents were both goalies on the school team, indicating enthusiasm without skill. He is a fast runner, but his attention to detail, lack of aggression and instinct for the game was evident from the outset. We tried him at a reputable football club but he only managed to frustrate all the other children by such meticulous dribbling that it took him *for ever* to finish the drill and led to a traffic jam of impatient boys behind him, like sports cars behind a combine harvester. D, who could see that he was not as good as the other boys, soon decided that he did not want to play anymore. My ambitions for the next David Beckham, never particularly realistic, were put on the back burner. Yet I didn't want him to drop out completely because then he would never improve and I still wanted him to benefit from the social advantage connoted by football participation. I looked around for other clubs, and found a low intensity drop-in club for children whose parents were using the gym next door. The children covered a random collection of abilities ranging from the very good, to children who had been dumped there by parents who just wanted to have a work-out. This was perfect! Amongst a less able cohort, D was able to score some goals and feel like a champion. He continues to attend quite willingly, which gives him the opportunity to practise and improve. Although he will never be the next Beckham, he remains enthusiastic and passably competent in the playground, which as far as I'm concerned serves the designated social purpose of schoolboy football.

Oh, I think I've found myself a cheerleader . . .

My daughter Molly, on the other hand, was a confident participator. Her assumption going into most activities was invariably that she would be good at it. Such was her self-confidence that I began to view her as invincible, but the job of a parent is never so smooth. Self-esteem in the formative years is dynamic and can vary from day to day, event to event; everybody needs a top-up from time to time. When Molly was in Year Two she came home from school one day excited because her teacher had asked the children to think about ways of visually presenting the class's stories about *The Faraway Tree*. Molly was confident that she could come up with a great idea and enthusiastically set about drawing and designing her plans. 'That's my girl!' I thought. The next day, I took her into the playground and she immediately set about explaining her ideas to two boys from her class. I overheard the beginnings of the conversation:

'That's not going to work.'

'How are you going to do this bit?'

'No, that's rubbish because you won't be able to do it.'

Molly started to explain and seemed to be standing her ground, so I left to take D to his class.

When I returned, Molly was standing by herself in the playground. I came up to say goodbye and she gave me her design. 'Why are you giving this to me? Aren't you showing it to your teacher?' 'No,' she said, 'it's no good.' She was being brave but I could see the tears welling up in her eyes. I had never seen Molly like this before: so deflated.

'Is this because of what the boys said about your ideas?' I asked. She didn't reply, but she didn't have to. All sorts of thoughts raced through my head: Is this how it starts? The erosion of girls' self-confidence by heckling boys with no ideas of their own? Was Molly's self-esteem not as strong as I had hoped? Is she not going to be resilient to criticism? Will this have a lasting effect on her confidence in putting forward future ideas?

'Well, Molly,' I said. 'Those boys aren't the deciding factor. I think you should show your idea to your teacher and let him decide.'

Molly remained unmoved.

'Those boys don't know what they are talking about. Did they have any of their own ideas? It's all very good to tear down other people's ideas, but I bet they didn't have any of their own, did they?'

Molly acknowledged that they had not had any ideas, but this didn't make hers seem any better.

I was running out of things to say. I'd been caught off guard and yet I knew that this was a pivotal moment in my motherhood career and I had to come up with something before the bell rang.

I knelt down to her level and looked Molly straight in the eyes.

'Molly,' I said. *'I believe in you and your ideas.'*

It's cheesy, I know, but it was said with love and passion, and the amazing thing was that I visibly saw the reserve galvanizing in Molly as I said this. It was as if some restorative energy had been transferred from me to her. I think that as adults we under-value the meaning of our opinions to children. For young children, however, we should remember that parents are like immortal deities: what we say *is true* – be it Santa or the Tooth Fairy. We have the power to restore or take away their self-belief with our words and our actions, just like that.

Later that day, Molly told me that she had told the teacher her idea and he had listened and said it was a good idea. They didn't end up using it, but she had been taken seriously and treated well. I was grateful that I had been able to help, and in particular, I was grateful that I had been there to witness what had happened. I have no doubt that had I not been there, Molly would not have talked about it after school. It would have been an experience she would have kept under her belt. She may have taken it in her stride or it may have had a negative lasting effect. What I do know is that I am glad that I was there and I hope that I'll be there many other times so that she will know that, throughout her life, she will always have a cheerleader on her side.

EXTRA TIPS

• **Words matter, so make them count** I recently read an article in the *Harvard Business Review* by Martin Seligman (Psychology Professor at Pennsylvania University) about the Master Resilience Training that is run for soldiers in the US Army. I got to thinking that these principles could also be used for training resilience in children. It shows how there are four different ways that we, as parents, can respond to something our child says, for example: 'I got picked for the choir.'

Active constructive: 'That's fantastic! When do you start? What will you sing? Will there be a performance?'

Passive constructive: 'That's nice.'

Passive destructive: 'Your father's coming home late tonight.'

Active destructive: 'What do you want to be in the choir for? Singing is for wusses.'[5]

It seems obvious we should be aiming for 'active constructive' comments, but I am surprised at how often I can veer towards passive constructive or passive destructive, especially if I've been having a bad day.

• **Those three words matter** I am a big believer in the three words 'I love you'. I think they are necessary even if they are not always sufficient. If you want to engender unquestionable love, why hold back? Go the whole hog. Say it every day, say it five, ten, twenty times a day if you like – contrary to popular belief, if you say it continually to the same people, the power is not diluted. At this age, children may not always understand nuance and behaviour and may not understand situations and emotions. Verbalizing your emotions and intentions helps to bring things home.

When he was three D got a telling-off which made him cry. 'You don't love me anymore,' he said. Since then I have been extra good at verbalizing exactly what I mean and really spelling it out: 'I will love you if you are clever, I will love you if you are not, I will love you if you are fat, I will love you if you are thin. I will love you if you are nice to me. I will love you even if you are horrible to me.

Even when I am shouting at you, I love you. I love you for being you. You will always be beautiful and smart in my eyes. I am proud of you for being you. You will always have my support. I am always here for you. Nothing will change that. I love you.' Said to an adult this would come across a bit stalker-ish, I know, but with young children it's good to leave them with no doubt.

• **Being there is good** I know that I can't always be there for my children but I make sure that I (or my husband) am there every time it matters. School plays, sports days, class assemblies, concerts and parents' days – we've only ever missed one (and there have been many) and even then we sent Grandma. I wave like a frantic loon to ensure that they KNOW I am there. Embarrassing I know, but why take time off work to go if they don't even know I made it?

• **Being *really* there is better** It can't be right just to show your face on the special occasions; part of 'love' is about sharing the mundane. Being around at least some of the time to catch the joke, the thought, the upset in real time. Some things are lost in the retelling. You can love from a distance but can you make someone *feel* loved without really spending much time with them?

• **Understanding matters** What says love more than knowing what the other person is thinking? I often finish Andrew's sentences; I can do this with the children now too. Talking about, listening and exchanging experiences and feelings regularly is the basis of being able to know and understand someone. Children's experiences and feelings are just as significant as adult experiences, even if they might seem less important. A child being told off by a teacher will hurt as much to them as an adult being told off by their boss. We need to show children the same concern and understanding.

• **Respect matters** I don't think you can engender love without respect. This means listening and valuing your children's opinions, even if they are wrong, and never denigrating them. Remember that respect works both ways; always educate your children to respect others, including YOU.

• **There's usually room for improvement** When Molly was heckled by the boys, my first response was to question her self-esteem. However, many parents are fearful about questioning their child's self-esteem. There have been times when friends have asked me for advice about their children's behaviour and when I have questioned their child's self-esteem I have been given the kind of looks that would have been appropriate if I had just stabbed them in the chest and called them 'a bad parent' (for mothers this is probably worse than being called a slut-whore). Luckily, this has not ended any friendships as my advice is genuinely well intentioned. Self-esteem is the core of children and we should always question it because, particularly in the formative years, it is dynamic, and will fluctuate depending on environments and challenges. If we do not question our children's self-esteem, we will never be in a position to recognize when it needs a top-up.

Fixing the Field: Guaranteeing Failure

This may sound counter-intuitive, but failure as a learning experience has become quite fashionable. Psychologists like Martin Seligman and Carol Dweck are researching and improving our understanding about the importance of failure and how a fear of failure can be a real hindrance.[6] In an age where children are tutored to perfection by helicopter parents or have their paths swept clear of adversity by snow-plough parents, they are often not exposed to failure. They are thus denied the opportunity to learn from it, and strengthen their resilience by getting up again after a fall. Never having to fail may seem like a good thing, but if it means never trying something new, never challenging oneself, never opening up, never committing to something for fear of failure, it becomes a bit like never living.

My own first experience of true failure, failing at something that I really cared about, came in my mid-twenties. This was too late, and it meant I spent longer dwelling on it than necessary. Having aced the written component of my exams for membership of the Royal College of Psychiatrists, for my oral exam I was sent to Glasgow to interview an in-patient on a forensic ward. If you are a plummy Londoner and have ever spoken to a true Glaswegian – this was my first time in Scotland and I had yet to learn the wonderful cadences of its accent – you'll recognize that the conversation could go something like this:

Glaswegian: XXXXXX

Londoner: I'm sorry, what did you say?

Glaswegian: XXXXX

Londoner: Sorry, can you say that again?

Irritated Glaswegian patient who happens to be in a Forensic Mental Health Unit for stabbing his mother with a kitchen knife: XXXXX!!!!!

Londoner: OK. Never mind, let's move on to how you felt?

Glaswegian: XXXX

Londoner: #@£%

Thankfully, I was sent to the Home Counties for my retakes.

I am now quite glad of having that failure under my belt, because it meant that the subsequent inevitable fails have been less traumatic. I learnt a valuable lesson from that experience.

Everybody fails

For the period following my exam failure, I told everyone about my ordeal. If I was introduced to anyone, I would say, 'Hello, I'm Holan. I just failed my exams'; I even went so far as to email everyone I knew just to tell them, 'Hello, I know we haven't spoken in years, but did you know I just failed my exams?' My husband found it excruciatingly embarrassing but it was almost compulsive. However, Professor Maureen Marks, an esteemed psychoanalyst who was supervising me at the time, commended me on my coping response: 'That's the best way to cope, because then it's out there and you don't need to carry shame with you like a "dirty little secret".' I liked this idea, and indeed, wearing my shame 'on my sleeve' forced me to accept my failure and move on.

The other interesting and restorative thing that happened as a result of my over-sharing was that many of the friends, professors and peers to whom I confessed, confided in kind about their own failures. Some of the top professors and some of my cleverest friends had also failed one or other exam along the way. Had I not professed my failings, I would never have known this, and would have mistakenly believed that I was the only 'dumb' one. In fact failing, and being able to move on from failure, is a potential marker of success. Many of our oldest idioms recognize the benefits of failure: 'If at first, you don't succeed, try, try again'; 'What doesn't kill you makes you stronger' and, of course, ' 'Tis better to have loved and lost, then never to have loved at all'. So how can we impart this wisdom into our children? How can we teach our children that failing is part of succeeding? That the taking part, the journey, the experience itself, is the winning?

Show your children your mistakes

I think that role-modelling may have a part to play. For young children, role-modelling is such an important way of learning. As well as learning how to talk, what to eat and how to behave from their parents, children also adopt their parents' attitudes and coping mechanisms. It is a fact that children with parents with anxiety, eating disorders or depression are more likely to develop the same disorders, even if genetic effects are taken into account, because children copy their parents' coping strategies.[7] Many parents rush about trying to look 'perfect' in front of their children, hiding their imperfections in order to be 'role-model worthy'. They will show their children the rowing trophy they won when they were sixteen years old, but bury the report card that said, 'Must try harder.' It's only natural to tend to share our successes but keep our failings to ourselves. We suggest activities to do with our children which we are good at. And if we are not good at it, we choose not to participate. Yes, I am talking about the parents who don't risk pulling a muscle in the parents' races at sports day! We even expect teenage popstars to present a perfect image, lest our children realize that all people are human with strengths and weaknesses. In a world where only perfect versions of people are projected, is it any wonder that children have a fear of failure?

My solution was to put my money where my mouth was: to role-model the concept of participation despite ineptitude.

I agreed to ski.

Not having grown up in a wealthy family, skiing every winter was not part of my childhood. By the time I was earning enough money for skiing holidays to be possible, I was happily avoiding them. 'Oh no, I can't come skiing, we are off to explore the temples at Angkor Wat'; 'Oh, sorry, maybe next time, I'm off to climb the Himalayas!' Until kids, that is. Then I started to think about all those independent secondary school and Russell Group university ski tours. All those ruddy-faced chaps called Tristan and Hugo who might invite Molly to a family ski holiday; or blonde, horsey gals called Cressida who might require D to ski down a slope and deliver chocolates to her. Did I want to deprive them of these opportunities? If I wanted them to learn to ski, how could I not participate myself when I encourage their participation in things on a daily basis?

So I was forced onto the slopes, against my will, by my diligent parenting ethos. My ski instruction started with three hours with a private ski instructor. Ski instructors are usually of the buff, twenty-year-old variety so this was no great torture, particularly as I spent most of the three hours being hoisted up and supported by them. ('Oh dear, I've fallen down again!') After that, however, I was left to my own skill (or lack thereof) and my darling husband.

Think of the second Bridget Jones movie and you'll get the idea. Only worse, as frankly, Renée Zellweger would look great in a paper bag. Think instead: short Chinese person dressed head-to-toe in unflattering Michelin-man onesie, with sporadic fits of catalepsy. No button lift was able to keep me upright and even flat terrain was insufficient to guarantee that I could stand. There was the time when a failed turn left me skiing backwards, screeching like a banshee till I fell forwards, leaving a trail of scratch marks in the snow as I desperately tried to stop my downward trajectory, in the manner of a cartoon cat failing to cling on for dear life. Then there was the time my ample bottom fell off the minuscule seat of the button lift, and fearing that I would be left alone halfway up the mountain, I kept holding on, and was dragged on my backside for several metres before I decided I had better let go. Or the time that I fell over for no apparent reason whilst attempting to get on the button lift and couldn't get back up. In true British fashion I didn't want to hold up the queue of teenagers waiting behind me, so heroically gestured, 'Don't mind me', and encouraged them to step over me in the interests of the queue. I won't even mention the slope-side verbal exchanges with Andrew, incredulous at my ineptitude when I tried to put my skis back on with them pointing downhill. Let's just say that I measure the success of my skiing by my ability to descend a slope alive. If no bones have been broken, it has been a successful day.

At least my humiliation was not for naught. As I hurtled down the piste, poles akimbo and at constant risk of entanglement with my skis, heart and lungs in my throat, shouting 'sorry' every five seconds as I cut uncontrolledly across the paths of furious skiers, I glanced sideways to see Molly and D amongst an orderly row of bibbed midgets skiing calmly, gracefully and naturally down the slope past me. Ah, it's all worth it, I thought. I hope Cressida and Hugo will be grateful, and if ever Molly and D fear trying something new and failing, I can always say, 'Don't worry, you'll never be as bad at anything as I am at skiing.'

What better role model can there be for participation over perfection, than a parent who is prepared to put public humiliation, and the safety of their life and limb, above looking good and doing well? Forget all the motivational speakers, surely the biggest impact we can have on children in this matter comes from parents who are not afraid to demonstrate failure and can persevere with a smile? I encourage Andrew to do the same (you should see him trying to ice skate), because if failure becomes family normality, what is there to fear? For me, a proud moment came when I picked up Molly after a cross-country run. Ten metres behind everyone else, she and a classmate came bumbling back into the school grounds, covered in muck but with bright smiles and glowing cheeks. 'It's really strange,' she said. 'Even though I'm rubbish at this, I just enjoy taking part.'

Why Parents Should Have Zero Tolerance for Sibling Rivalry

Sibling rivalry may seem a little off-piste from self-esteem but the issues are related. One of my early papers on depression looked at differences in depressive symptoms between identical twins. Identical twins share the same genes and the same parents, so any differences between them are thought to be due to 'non-shared environment'.[8] Most people take 'non-shared environment' to mean things related to school or outside the home. Being bullied at school, for instance, or getting in with the wrong crowd of friends. But my view was that just because twins had the same parents, this did not mean they were treated the same. 'Non-shared environment' could just as well apply to differential parental treatment. Favouritism within a family has always seemed to me to be a potent toxin, a killer of self-esteem. My patients often describe themselves as being 'the black sheep of the family'.

My suspicions were born out in the data. I found that the difference between the way identical twins felt their parents treated them was a more powerful predictor of depression than the absolute degree of perceived maltreatment. Thus a child who felt maltreated by her parent who had a twin sibling who felt equally maltreated, was at less risk of low mood than a harshly treated child whose twin was treated with warmth and affection. The way that we, as parents, treat siblings, and the way that our children perceive how we treat their siblings, is a point for attention. One way to reduce sibling rivalry and to promote self-esteem in all the children within a family is to foster sibling friendship, and that's why, in general, I have zero tolerance for siblings not getting along.

We are family, I got all my sisters with me

For me, the bond that I have with my two sisters is very important. Even though personality-wise we probably would not have been in the same circle of friends had we been peers, as sisters we are closer than a Philips shave. Even though I rarely socialize with my siblings, if anything important in my life happened, they would be the first people I would contact, and vice versa. I would never be alone in a crisis because I know that they would support me – come what may. Friendships and marriages may come and go, parents will pass away, but siblings are with you, living in your time and generation; for life.

This is not just my view, it is borne out by science. Warm, supportive sibling relationships that lack conflict are related to better psychological well-being in children and into adulthood.[9] The reverse is also true; hostile and aggressive sibling relationships are associated with higher levels of anxiety, depression, low self-esteem and anti-social behaviour.[10] Maybe this is less to do with sibling relationship, and more with genetics? You might expect that argumentative parents always have argumentative children who don't get on and become argumentative and unhappy adults. But this doesn't seem to be the case; in fact, the literature suggests that warm, collaborative sibling relationships protect children from all manner of adversity – including argumentative parents as well as parental mental illness, negative life events (such as natural disaster and death of a loved one), high-risk neighbourhoods, low-income backgrounds and bullying.[11] All in all, the evidence suggests that sibling relationships can have just as much impact on how children develop psychologically as parents and friends.

This makes sense to me. Much adolescent and adult unhappiness comes from feeling alone or unsupported. When I worked as an adult psychiatrist I met many unhappy adults of whom I just thought, 'You know what? You'd be fine if you just had a supportive friend.' That's exactly what a brother or sister could and should be; and whilst as parents we have little or no say in who our children choose to be friends with in adolescence and adult life, we have a lot of influence over whether siblings get along or not. We are perfectly placed to ensure that our children, through their siblings, will always have a strong support network for life.

So why have we as a population of parents come to expect sibling rivalry and discord? When we see it happening, we shrug our shoulders and say, 'Siblings, eh?' We may take some cursory action: 'Don't hit your sister', 'Get off your brother's back and put down that brick that you were using to pummel his head', but overall we assume that this is run-of-the-mill sibling behaviour. In effect, we at best tolerate it, at worst encourage it.

My own childhood experiences were different. My mother came from a family of seven extremely close siblings. Even though they live on different continents, they still go on holiday together and skype each other regularly. They laugh, joke, bitch and support each other as much now as they did when they were children. My mother told me that in her family, when they were growing up the older children were each allocated a younger child to look after. Second Uncle had to piggy back my mother on long outings and my mother in turn had to rock Third Uncle to sleep. I am sure that this instilment of responsibility and need to care for each other fostered an affection that has lasted into their old age.

In her turn, I remember clearly my mother saying to my sisters and me as children, 'You three are best friends. You are all each other have and must support each other.' I remember thinking sulkily at the time, 'I am *so* not best friends with these two. This one has just pulled my hair, and that one has just scratched my face.' But we moved several times as children, first from Taiwan to Wales and then from Wales to London, changing primary schools four times in eight years, and so it turned out to be true. While friends came and went, 'Laurel and Hardy' as I liked to dub them, or 'The Two Ugly Sisters' (to my narcissistic Cinderella, of course), were always with me. And guess what, as adults, we are like best friends.

So what of my own children?

As explained, I take a zero-tolerance view of siblings not getting along. Here are my TOP TEN TIPS for how to support this.

TOP TEN TIPS FOR SIBLING LOVE

1) **Make sure they feel secure** My number one tip is to ensure that each individual child feels loved and secure *in themselves*. Children who have 'secure attachment' to their parents have all manner of better prospects throughout childhood and into adulthood. The more secure a child feels in themselves, the less prone they will be to jealousy, and the more generous they will be to their siblings. So ensuring a child grows up feeling secure from the outset helps a great deal.

2) **Prepare for the sibling** Throughout pregnancy, the prospect of D's arrival was talked about as a very positive thing. 'A little brother for you to help me look after.' 'A little brother to play with you.' Read books together about new babies and about siblings that get along (*Topsy and Tim* books are good for this). Buy your

child a baby doll and play at looking after it together. Be as realistic about this as possible, as this will help your child to role-play and prepare for what is to come. Massively praise any caring actions and discourage rough handling.

3) Allow them to bond with their sibling Parents can be precious about newborn babies, but being overly guarded and excluding a child from their baby sibling can be a lost opportunity for them to bond, and can make the older sibling feel left out. Where possible, always involve siblings. Place the baby on the sibling's lap and help them cuddle and play with them. This is perfectly safe as long as children are well prepped and you are supervising them.

4) Deal with jealousy Jealousy between siblings will be inevitable at times, even with secure children, but how you manage it can dampen or amplify its existence. First, try to anticipate situations where jealousy is likely to occur and notice it as and when it happens. Then, rather than ignore it, address it as soon as possible. For instance, when there is competition for attention, this should be verbalized, acknowledged and resolved. 'I know you want me to play with you, but I am feeding your brother. But tell you what, he will be asleep after this, and then I can play with you.' Or when they get older, 'I know I am spending the day with your sister because I am taking her to see her favourite ballet, but next week, I will take you to the zoo.' Many young children become angry and frustrated when they feel excluded or unfairly treated in favour of another. They cannot understand the reasoning behind it and don't have the knowledge to be able to label it as 'jealousy'. It's up to parents to notice it, label it and explain it. Jealousy is a natural emotion. It is how we handle this emotion that needs to be addressed, rather than attempting to avoid it, or suppress what is a natural feeling. Unaddressed jealousy may lead to lashing out or deliberate misbehaviour in order to get attention, which is never a good thing.

5) Apply behavioural management The tenet of behavioural management is to heavily praise and reward behaviours you wish to see again and to ignore and discourage behaviours you do not wish to see again. If you wish to see caring behaviour between your siblings, you need to reinforce it with praise and rewards. If you would rather they did not bicker and fight, there needs to be consequences each and every time this happens. I know that some parents think that siblings should 'just naturally love each other', and I can be as guilty of 'happy-clappy' sentimentalism as the next person, but even I know that love can be manipulated to some extent.

6) **Us versus them** During my family therapy training I learnt that the only healthy grouping of people within a family is parents versus children. Families that have any other combination are more vulnerable (for example, a family which splits into two, with a mother and son against a father and daughter, or mother and children against father). Keeping the healthy dynamic should always be borne in mind. Using this dynamic, it is possible to foster closer sibling unity as people tend to unite against a common oppressor. Yes, you are the oppressor in this scenario. Don't be tempted to side with the children, enjoy your role as the villain and reap the rewards of sibling cohesion.

7) **Encourage collaboration** Treating children as a team can help them collaborate with each other. Rewards can be given to both children as a team, punishments doled out to both. This will facilitate helpful behaviour and help siblings see each other as partners, rather than competitors. It will also encourage mutual praise.

8) **Promote exposure** I am totally, wholeheartedly in favour of keeping siblings in the same school, especially at primary level where I believe education should play second fiddle to social and emotional development. A close sibling relationship is more important to me than Key Stage Two results. A supportive sibling is there for life, whilst how many of us can remember our primary school grades? I am delighted to hear that Molly crosses the

playground to give her D a kiss and hug when he needs it. Not possible if she is not there.

9) Stoke pride, not competition It's likely that siblings will enjoy the same activities, but it is always hard when one is better at something than the other. Try and anticipate and notice when this happens and acknowledge it and the feelings involved. Encourage siblings to be happy that their brother or sister is doing well at something. It's not easy to manage, but if children are secure in themselves and love their sibling, it is a lot easier. You wouldn't begrudge a good friend a promotion, particularly if you were happy in your own job. D was a precocious reader and was reading chapter books in Reception, whilst Molly had cried her way through reading books at the same age. I was worried that Molly might be envious of his natural ability, but I was wrong. I was rather embarrassed when I heard that Molly had been gloating to all the mothers in the playground that, 'My baby brother can already read chapter books.' But I was also secretly gratified that Molly was happy and proud of her brother, rather than resentful of his ability.

10) Adopt a zero-tolerance policy on siblings not getting on Expecting or accepting that siblings do not need to get on, and that this is 'normal', is the main reason for inaction. So this last point is probably the most important, because action always helps.

Chapter Summary

Self-esteem in a child is the foundation for their resilience throughout life. As parents, our main role in their early years is to ensure that our children start to build an identity for themselves as a person who is valued, cherished, loved and lovable; someone who can withstand criticism and be unafraid of failure. As a baby this means lavishing them with cuddles and prioritizing their needs. As they grow into toddlers, this means having fun with them and praising them abundantly. As they reach school age, it means role-modelling failure, supporting them with the right words and cheering from the side lines.

Getting this core of self-esteem right is fundamental, because just as Karl Lagerfeld would first adjust his model's undergarments if a Chanel dress wasn't fitting properly, so 'fixing' your child's difficulties always involves inspecting what lies beneath the outward problem: looking first at their core layer of self-esteem. However much you stretch, pull or adjust the fabric of an ill-fitting dress, it will never sit quite right if the bra and the corset are missing. Atop a strong foundation, the beautiful external layers can be more easily applied and will shine more visibly and brightly.

FOUNDATION

3. Layer One: Social Skills

Why Some Kids Are Always Invited to the Party

Alpha-Male versus the Boy Next Door

When Molly was in Reception Class, I volunteered to go into her class to paint the children's faces. The teacher asked me to choose the first child to have their face painted, and then that child was allowed to choose the next child, and so on. Whilst painting one girl's face, her male best friend loitered around saying, 'Please choose me next.' Molly had told me that these two were best friends, lived close to each other and did everything together, so I was not surprised when she smiled and seemed to agree. Then, out of the blue, in saunters 'alpha-male', a bigger and brighter boy with better social skills. 'Please choose me next,' he said politely. I smiled, the wicked smile of a child psychiatrist about to test human nature, and asked the girl: 'So, who do you want to go next?'

The answer is as predictable as it is gut-wrenching, but alpha-male wins every time. The 'boy next door' had to wait in line. Social hierarchy in children, it seems, plays out in just the same way as it does in adults – but I was surprised at the extent in which it is already present in four-year-olds. So what destines some children to lead and others to follow? What determines popularity and can this be coached?

In Taiwan, where I was born, academic achievement was synonymous with success and dictated social hierarchy. If you got into the 'Best University' to study the most 'prestigious course' (deemed to be medicine or engineering), you were de facto a Rock God and desirable no matter how 'nerdy' you may have been. This was the mentality with which I was raised, and why many Chinese families prize academic achievement over all else. In this society, it IS the be-all and end-all. Growing up in the UK, I came to learn that the same rules do not apply in the West (although try telling 'tiger parents' that you know better!). Still, the mentality instilled in me by my parents did serve a protective purpose.

When I arrived at Cambridge University, I joined a conversation with other state school-educated children who felt aggrieved because a fellow student had 'looked down' on them, by virtue of being wealthier and privately educated. I ventured that I had had no problems with the girl in question as my conversation with her had gone something like this:

'Which school did you go to?'

'Grammar School.'

'Oh. Well, I went to Posh Private School.' [Haughty voice]

'What are you studying?'

'French.'

'Oh. Well, I am studying medicine.' [Equally haughty voice]

The girl's attempts at establishing a higher social rank than me based on her wealth were completely lost on me, because the social hierarchy markers I had grown up with (based on academics) placed me at a higher rank. Thus we were both kept perfectly happy by our own warped prejudices. However, unless you plan to move to Asia, I actually believe that academic achievement is not the most important trait. There are, for instance, plenty of people with excellent intelligence who somehow don't succeed as well as they might because they find being with other people difficult (or others find it difficult to be around them). And we all know people who may not be the brightest spark in the box, but go far by being affable, cheeky and great fun to be around. Contrary to my upbringing then, this leads me to believe *that social skills are more important than intelligence.*

Social skills, making friends and networking are often dismissed as 'soft skills', yet their importance is critical. Whilst intelligence may give you great ability, social skills allow you to tap into the infinitely greater collective ability of others around you. If you have good social skills, it is pretty amazing what you can access for free: ideas, collaboration, promotion, cups of tea, lawnmower loan, tickets to a gig, people to help you move house, free meals, a bed for the night, people to look after you when you are sick, people to keep you company, protection against bullying, sex – lots of it, free childcare, job opportunities, love, laughter, and of course invites to good parties. Many of these things are money-can't-buy assets and no amount of intelligence, or wealth acquired by intelligence, can give you access to these things. **Social skills are more important than intelligence.**

The funny thing is that although literacy and numeracy are actively taught at school, social ability is not. Children must somehow divine social understanding from what they observe or experience going on around them. Some children are innately expert at this, while others need extra support. I had thought that the development of social ability, social hierarchy and politicking were fairly sophisticated skills that developed in older children, but I was wrong. By watching my own children, I was amazed to find that the differentiation between children's social ability is already fairly developed by four years of age. Furthermore, the battle to be at the top of the social hierarchy was already in full play.

Social hierarchy in four-year-olds

One of the best places to observe social skill in children is at a kid's birthday party. A four-year-old's birthday party is probably the first time that social hierarchy becomes apparent, as it is around this age that children will have developed sufficient social skills to interact in a meaningful way. Also, schools in the UK start when children are around this age, and as the polite convention is for parents to invite the whole class to their child's birthday party, you will be given the opportunity to compare your child's ability within a representative spectrum. Unlike a classroom environment where authority stems from the teacher, a birthday party is like the school playground; it is a social free-for-all. For a child, the birthday party scenario is one of the most challenging of their social skills. Hell, even as an adult, who doesn't occasionally quiver in fear at the prospect of attending a party where you know only a few people? Observing how your child copes with this situation is a real test, and a chance for you to observe not only your child's social skills, but also their pecking order in the social hierarchy. Because sadly, just as in the jungle our primate relatives fight it out to be the alpha-male and highest-ranking female, so all human societies have a social hierarchy, even four-year-olds.

After frequenting many birthday parties and taking the obligatory photo of the birthday child blowing out the candles of their cake, I noticed that in every single picture the same few children, Molly included, were at the birthday child's side. This happened even when the birthday child was not a particular friend of Molly. I began to observe a pattern of 'top table children' at birthday parties, where the same children would be seated around the birthday child, regardless of whose birthday it was. I developed a theory of social hierarchy being played out in the seating of children at birthday parties. I began to watch these 'top table children', and they seemed to be extremely socially aware. For instance, they anticipated exactly when the call to be seated for food was likely to go out, and where the birthday child was likely to sit (usually somewhere in the middle or at one end, depending on table layout). They then sought to position themselves in the prestigious seats – those with closest proximity to the birthday child.

Molly and her friends were experts at this. One summer Molly broke her leg and was required to use a child's Zimmer frame to hop around for a while. At a friend's birthday party, at the all-important call to be seated, there was the usual rush amongst children to sit in proximity to the birthday boy. The table was laid out in one long line, and the birthday boy moved to seat himself in the middle. I was observing Molly. She saw that all the children ran to seat themselves directly next to the birthday boy and there was a bit of a tussle amongst the 'high-ranking' children to gain the prestigious seats. Molly was the first to see that the seat opposite the birthday boy, of equal prestige, was free and hobbled as quickly as she could on her Zimmer frame to get to the other side. Although she was clearly first off the mark, her able-bodied 'high-ranking' friends who had missed out on the prime seats next to the birthday boy had now also seen the free seats opposite, and they raced passed her to claim them. I had to laugh inwardly at this, as it proved my theory: for socially aware children, birthday party seating is a social marker.

In complete contrast, at the same age of four years, D appeared devoid of this social antenna. At parties he would without fail ask to go to the toilet just before the call to be seated for food went out, such that we would emerge from the toilets and he would be sat at the last available seat, a mile away from the birthday child, even if the child was a good friend. Even when he was there at the call, he would stand rooted to the spot until all the other children had sat down before finding the last available seat that nobody else wanted. He appeared oblivious to social hierarchy. The good thing was that it didn't bother him (ignorance of social pressure can be a positive). The critical thing, though, is that I noticed it and marked it out as an area where he might need more support.

Clearly, I have never told my children where to sit at birthday parties, so it is interesting for me to observe the presence or absence of these social instincts in them. This ability, termed

TOP TIP: PARTY TIME FOR KIDS IS RESEARCH TIME FOR PARENTS

As tempting as it is to spend the whole party nattering to other parents and feasting on wine and cheese, it is worthwhile spending some time observing your children at birthday parties. For parents, these occasions are rare chances to observe children mixing with their peers, unhampered by adult mediation. If your child gets into difficulty, try not to always intervene immediately and see how they cope with their own skills. After all, this is what they will rely on in the playground. You can then better understand what goes on in their school day, and judge if your child needs additional support in this area.

social osmosis (that is, learning from social experience rather than actively being taught), is thought to be lacking in children with autistic spectrum disorder. Those with excellent social osmosis and social ability are able to climb to the top of the social hierarchy. Their success is based not on physical dominance, but social dominance – the ability to make friends and influence people.

So, if hierarchy is already being established at four, what can parents do? There are two answers to this. The first is that we should start looking earlier than four to develop our children's social skills; the second is that we can always boost skills as and when we notice the need, because just as prime ministers come and go, social hierarchy is a dynamic system and leaders will frequently be toppled to make way for unlikely newcomers.

The Building Blocks of Social Success
Starting Early: Babies to Three-Year-Olds

Luckily for most of us, evolution has imparted us with specific hardware within our brains to assimilate information about our social world. This allows most of us to understand what is expected of us in any given social situation, or at least, to quickly learn it. Of course, different children naturally (genetically) vary in the quality of their hardware and for some unlucky children this hardware is impaired (for example, in autism). Even in these children though, skills can be taught and developed and in this chapter you will find the science that lies behind these processes, and an array of practical observations and 'experiments' I have used to assess and improve social skills in my own children. While every child is different, this knowledge may help you read your child more clearly and apply what experts know of children's psychological and emotional structures to their needs.

You're never fully dressed without a smile

It would seem that the ability to acquire social skills is innate and develops from an odd collection of basic skills evident from as early as six weeks of age. Children who have difficulties with these basic skills fail to develop 'higher order' social skills in the normal way. By looking at your babies for these early, seemingly arbitrary skills, you can give yourself a heads up if their sociability hardware requires additional support.

Babies will typically smile at around six weeks of age. Isn't it strange that this relatively useless developmental milestone is acquired so early? Not really, when you think about the evolutionary advantages gained by a smiling baby. If you are running from a flood, would you be more or less likely to take your baby with you if it was always smiling adoringly at you? Being able to smile increases a baby's survival prospects more than the ability to tie laces or quote Goethe. Yes, a baby's smiles are evolutionarily engineered to manipulate parents to aid their survival. We parents are such suckers.

Another early developmental marker of social ability is a preference to look at faces, and in particular eyes. The centre of human communication is in a person's face. This is the input and output zone for verbal communication and where non-verbal communication is the most expressive. Most adults can tell what another adult is thinking by looking at their face even if they are not saying anything. Even when the person is saying one thing, the face can often convey a different message. I have received lots of emails where I have been unsure about the meaning (joke – or not joke?) because I have been unable to judge the face/tone of voice with which the email has been written. This exemplifies the importance of non-verbal communication. So common is this problem and so useful is the face, that we now use a face picture in our emails to depict the meaning, hence the birth of the emoji. Typically, developing babies and children are born with an in-built ability to hone their attention to faces because they know this is where the bulk of social context is going to be gained. No one teaches a baby to do this; you either have it, or you don't. Early on as a parent, you can check your baby's sociability hardware by checking whether he prefers to look at your face and whether their eyes follow you Mona Lisa-like around the room.

As babies are primed to attend to your face, they will soon try to imitate it. If you make faces at a young baby, chances are that at some stage you will see the baby trying to move his face to copy your expression. There are hours of fun to be had doing this. This is early social learning – if looking at other people's faces is the fundamental way of developing skills in receiving social information, making facial expressions is the reciprocal skill for communicating back.

Sooner or later, after your baby has got the hang of copying your faces, they will start to copy what you say. Verbal communication makes social skill a heck of a lot easier. 'Motherese' is the legitimate scientific name for the vocal tones and speech repeti-

TOP TIP: BABIES ARE SOCIAL BEINGS TOO

The building blocks for social skills start when your child is a baby. You can encourage the development of these precursor skills by interacting with them as much as possible. You know all those times you thought that shaking a rattle to get your baby's attention was just a dumb, mindless activity? Think again. Joint attention is a fundamental building block to social skills. You know when your partner makes fun of you for spending hours making faces at the baby? Well, you can now legitimately say that you are improving your child's social skills because facial expression and body language are the most universal and powerful forms of communication. A facial expression cuts through any language barrier and can convey all the meaning you need to anyone, from any continent, from any culture. If you don't believe me, watch a bus load of rural Africans watching *Mr Bean* (Rowan Atkinson is the master of non-verbal communication). They hoot with laughter like the rest of us and understand perfectly what is happening without the need for any common language whatsoever. By exposing your baby to as much human social interaction as you can, you are exposing them to more information from which to garner social knowledge. It's the social skills equivalent of providing books to a child learning to read.

tion patterns used universally by parents whichever language they are speaking. 'You *are* a good boy, *aren't* you? *Aren't* you?' and that sort of thing that you swore you would never do because it sounds so banal, but found yourself doing the minute you had a babe in your arms. Again, don't stop! The reason everyone is doing it is because it is the best way to encourage speech

TOP TIP: DADS CAN ALSO COO AND CLUCK

As a feminist, one of my pet hates is how often I hear much of what I have just stated reported in a gender-biased way, for instance: 'Babies are primed to imitate their mother's facial expression.' This should in no way indicate that they will not do this for fathers. Indeed, experiments have shown that baby monkeys will imitate the expressions of human male scientists.[1] This is men enabling cross-species imitation, so I cannot see why men cannot be more involved with cooing and clucking at their own species babies. Babies will attempt to imitate you whether you are male, female or monkey. And don't even get me started on the gender bias in the very term 'Motherese'.

development in your child. Evolution has primed us to do this, and the reinforcement we get when our babies babble back to us keeps us doing it. Research shows that babies exposed to the most Motherese develop language faster.[2]

What happens to children who are not provided with this type of early social interaction? Sadly, we have evidence that they have stunted socio-emotional understanding. When agencies discovered severely neglected infants in Romanian orphanages under the Ceausescu regime, the children were thought to be autistic because their social ability, communication skills and empathy were all extremely impaired.[3] In fact, very few of the children were 'genetically' autistic and some of them recovered fully or partially once they were fostered into loving homes. Early isolation and lack of social stimuli and human warmth had stunted their brain development to the extent that these physical changes could be detected on their brain scans. This is a chilling warning of the long-lasting impact of abuse and neglect on young children.

If in doubt, copy

As your baby grows, joint attention will progress to shared interactions. You can assess early social interaction and turn-taking by
playing with your baby. The typical Peek-a-Boo game (hide your
face, then show your face and make your baby laugh) popular to
all parents and babies is part of the Autism Diagnostic Observation Schedule (ADOS).[*][4] Why? Isn't it just a trick to make your
baby laugh? In fact, it is an early indicator of a child's ability to
take turns, of their understanding of social reciprocity, of the
interaction between two people, as well as a precursor of to-and-
fro conversation, and give-and-take in a relationship. Peek-a-boo
is so much more than a game.

After your baby masters the imitation of facial expressions
and vocal sounds, imitation of speech and complex actions will
follow. Like our animal ancestors, we all have a hard-wired animal
instinct to copy others. There are lots of fun experiments you can
do to try to see this in action. Get into a crowded lift and suddenly
look upwards. The likelihood is that someone else in the lift will
copy you and look up. Copying others or 'imitation' is a fundamental building block of social ability and by and large, it's fairly
effective. If you have no idea what to do in a new situation, copy

---

[*] The Autism Diagnostic Observation Schedule (ADOS) is one of the gold standard diagnostic tools for assessing Autistic Spectrum Disorder. Children and adults
with autistic spectrum disorder have deficits in social interaction and communication (as well as repetitive behaviours and restricted interests). The schedule
involves games and set conversations to be enacted with the child or adult to press
for social interaction and exchange. It is designed so that the assessor initially
allows the child to display their natural social ability, but then allows the assessor
to give staged prompts to get the best ability out of a child if it is not naturally
forthcoming. Scores are given for deficits in social interaction and communication,
and autistic spectrum disorder is suspected once a threshold is crossed. Most typically developing children and adults, even the very socially able, will score
something on the ADOS, and it would be highly unlikely for someone to score 0,
so just because your child has some deficits, it does not mean that they are autistic
or on the autistic spectrum. Despite tools such as the ADOS and the Autism Diagnostic Interview (ADI), Autistic Spectrum Disorder diagnosis remains a specialist
clinical judgement.

what others are doing. This works just as well in three Michelin star restaurants and on business trips to Japan as it does for toddler music group or the first day of school. The children who 'get' this quickly are already one step ahead.

So parents, *watch out*, your toddler will copy everything. One time, Molly started talking to me about beggars. She kept saying, 'Beggar, beggar,' even when there were no obvious beggars about. I thought this was rather a sophisticated concept for a toddler to have grasped and racked my brains for books I had read to her that may have introduced this idea: *The Little Match Girl*? No, we hadn't read that one yet as I always found it too sad. All was revealed when one day she said, 'Daddy says, "Beggar"!' Andrew was given a talking-to that night regarding language, and it was not concerning his portrayal of the unfortunate destitute.

Most infants will be interested in other infants; they will naturally want to join in. If you take your child to a toddler group which involves singing 'The Wheels on the Bus' ad infinitum, you will see that most children will start copying the actions spontaneously. These toddlers have good in-built social hardware that allows them to magically realize that there is an expectation

TOP TIP: THE SHRINK ON THE BUS SAYS COPY, COPY, COPY

If you think that taking the baby to singalongs with inane actions is just about killing time, think again. Exposure to social activity, peer group and joint activity is the basis of learning about society and social skills. It's not necessary to go to an expensive group, you can get together with your pals and their babies or family members and their children and sing the songs together with the actions. This not only allows you to see if your child is developing skills in an appropriate time frame, but also reinforces their emerging skills through repetition.

that they copy the actions, even if no one has told them explicitly to do so. Even if you exclude the children who are anxious, there will still be a few children who will not copy the actions spontaneously, but will do so when told to, or encouraged to. They will remember the next time they go that this is the expectation and will start doing the actions spontaneously. One or two children will need to be prompted again to join in. Occasionally, there will be a child who shows no interest in joining in at all and spends the whole session playing with an electric plug socket. These reactions cover the typical spectrum of social ability in toddlers. As a parent you might want to observe more carefully what is happening with your children if they require repeated prompting to join in, or only play with plug sockets, as they may need additional support.

Playtime can also be study time

As an autism specialist, a first birthday couldn't pass without my children undergoing a simplified version of the 'baby's birthday party' test. This test, which the Autism Diagnostic Observation Schedule uses, is where you set up a dolls' tea party and encourage play. Many typically developing children are able to give a baby doll a pretend drink from a toy tea cup by the age of one, particularly if they see their parent doing it. If your child is not doing this, don't worry; try it again a few months later. If children are able to freely and frequently pretend play you can breathe a sigh of relief that one aspect of their social ability mechanism is functioning. Truth be told, there is nothing magical about a dolls' tea party – another classic experiment uses a banana as a telephone, so don't feel restricted by dolls and tea. Do watch and see if your toddler 'gets' that you are pretending and finds this amusing rather than becoming frightened: 'Daddy's gone mad, he is talking into a banana', or starts to believe that bananas are instruments of communication.

Imaginative play like this can start about the age of one, but may emerge later. The building blocks that lead to social ability will develop at different times during infancy in different children, so don't be too worried if your child is developing six months behind the rest of your friends' children. If they are more than a year behind, then you may want to observe more closely what is going on and consider seeking professional advice. However, most children should have all the fundamental building blocks for social skill in place by the time school starts. This is lucky, because school is like the *Hell's Kitchen* of social ability; the fire in which their skills, hot or not, will get tested.

The Building Blocks of Social Success: Children from Three to Five

When people consider social ability, they tend to think of the confident thespian or the extrovert holding court at a party. Often these people do have good social skills, but social skills comprise much more than confidence, acting and oration. They're about the ability to make lasting friendships, seek help, adapt to new social environments and politely evade confrontation; all the skills that are required to 'get on' with other people across contexts. A sociable child will get on at school better. They will get on with other children in the class, be easier to teach and ultimately be preferred by the teachers. These skills continue to be highly valued throughout life, and there is a reason that, even into adulthood, we are asked to demonstrate our 'people skills', 'ability to be a team player', and 'communication skills' in our careers.

Upskill your child for the start of school

Problems with social ability are currently rarely diagnosed in the pre-school period unless they are severe. This is not because they do not exist but because adults, particularly parents, are extremely obliging in making up for their child's weaknesses, and often aren't aware of their difficulties. Even if a child is gibbering in Alien, you can bet that their parents will know exactly what is being communicated. Playdates at home will be supervised by adults and will involve intervention to make sure that children 'play fair', 'don't leave people out', 'wait their turn', 'be nice', and critically, 'don't beat each other into a pulp'. If another child is 'not nice' to your child, they will not be invited back.

Not so the school playground. There, your child will have to communicate with other children who are impatient, do not necessarily care to hear what your child has to say, have little incentive to include your child in games and may well beat your child into a pulp if they find them annoying. Equally, teachers are human like the rest of us and would rather spend their time teaching than disciplining. It is unfair but true, sociable people get treated better. A friendly, helpful child will be praised and treated kindly which in turn raises the child's self-esteem, confirms the child's belief in herself and in the world being a friendly place full of nice people, which in turn makes it a whole lot easier for her to continue to be friendly and helpful. This is the positive cycle that we all wish our children to experience.

Reverse this cycle and you can see how things can quickly turn sour. An unfriendly, unhelpful child will be scolded and treated with ambivalence or hostility, which will erode their self-esteem and compound their sense of the world being against them, which in turn makes it entirely reasonable for them to continue to withdraw or rebel.

The 'Halo Effect'

Your child's first experience of 'the big world' is usually at the start of school. There is a phenomenon called the Hawthorne Effect or Halo Effect, which basically translates to 'first impressions count'. If people form a positive impression of you, they will tend to see any future positive actions from you as typical of your nature, while they will dismiss your negative behaviour. When I was at secondary school, I liked to skip school to go down to the local McDonald's and eat 'Apple Pie à la Mode'. I used to skip lessons I didn't like, such as RE. I never got caught or reprimanded because I was such a 'good girl' that even if they noticed I was missing, they assumed that it was for a good reason. They were right, in that I was not smoking behind the bike shed, and to this day eating desserts still sounds to me like a good reason to skip RE. Basically, though, what I want to illustrate is that if you want

> **TOP TIP: FIRST IMPRESSIONS COUNT**
>
> A good first impression leads other people to believe in your child's positive potential, the good things your child is capable of. You can help set up this positive first impression by assessing your child and upskilling their social skills before the start of school.

people to see the good in your child and give allowance for occasional weaknesses, it is worthwhile forming a good first impression and investing in upskilling your child's social skills before the start of school.

Assessing your child's communication skills

Spending time playing with your child and conversing with them can reveal if they have any fundamental difficulties with social interaction. Some easy markers for four- and five-year-olds are: Does your child turn to face you if you call their name from behind them? Can your child ask you to pass them something that they need? Can your child look you directly in the face when talking to you or you are talking to them? Can your child smile at you? Can your child smile at you if you smile at them? Can your child spontaneously wave goodbye to you when you leave, shake their head to mean 'no' and nod their head to mean 'yes'? Can your child use gestures to show you how to do something (such as brush your teeth)? Can your child recognize facial expressions in picture books and tell you what they mean? Can your child point to show you something and check that you are looking at the right thing? Can your child make up a story? Can your child feed their teddy bears or make their dolls talk to each other? Can your child understand that other children may have different thoughts and preferences to them? Can your child copy what you do?

Most typically developing children can definitely do all of these things by the age of four to five years. Clinicians are looking for the presence or absence of ability in all the above (and many other things) in a typical autism assessment in a four-year-old. They may sound like an arbitrary list of things to look out for, but they are the basic skills necessary in developing sophisticated social ability. Let me tell you why.

If you do not have a preference for looking at people's faces, particularly their eyes, which are usually the most expressive, you will fail to pick up all the social nuances that a person is communicating through their expression. 'You idiot!' said with angry eyes will mean something different to 'You idiot!' accompanied by a twinkle in the eye. If you are not looking at a person's eyes, you cannot infer their intention and are liable to misunderstand. If your child does not naturally pick up common social conventions (smiling at people, nodding and shaking their head, waving) they will have more difficulty understanding what is going on, because social conventions are so frequently used in communicating instead of speech. Think how awkward you feel when travelling to a foreign country where all the social conventions are different (bowing in the Far East, not using your left hand in India). Your actions may be misinterpreted by others as rudeness and will affect how you get on socially. Similarly, if your child has difficulty understanding that others may have different thoughts, they may not act in consideration of other people. If they cannot understand facial expression, they cannot infer how someone else is feeling and act accordingly. If they cannot ask for something to be passed to them, they may have difficulty communicating other needs in an appropriate way. If they do not

TOP TIP: SORT OUT SPEECH AND HEARING

Speech develops in children at different times, so don't panic. However, be aware if your child's speech is delayed or difficult to understand and get professional help as soon as possible. The same applies for hearing. Many people are reluctant to treat speech and hearing problems, saying, 'Let's wait and see,' or 'They'll grow out of it,' but this position fails to take into account the potential psychological impact this may have on the child's social development. Misunderstanding and being misunderstood is terribly frustrating and may affect your child's emotional and behavioural patterns, as well as their self-esteem.

naturally copy you and what you are doing, they are missing out on the most frequent method children have to acquire social skills, that of emulating their parents and the other adults around them.

If your four-year-old child is struggling with all or most of the above, it is worth considering the four main possible reasons that a child psychiatrist will always consider: hearing impairment, speech and language problems, learning difficulty and autistic spectrum disorder.

The 'mean adult' test

A test of more advanced communication skill is to study inter-actions with unfamiliar adults (such as new teachers and babysitters). It doesn't take much to interact with a parent. Most fourteen-year-olds manage this through grunting alone. Many children with mild autism (de facto, impaired social ability) can also communicate well with a parent who will be primed to be patient, can guess from experience what the child wants, are accepting and willing to invest in understanding the child, and will often allow them to have their own way. Many children with autism prefer the company of adults for this reason.

A less familiar adult will not know or understand the idiosyn-crasies of a child's communication. For instance, when Molly was two, she loved to watch a music DVD called *Fun Song Factory*. At the time, she was unable to enunciate 'Fun Song Factory', calling it 'Bun Song Bactory', or just 'Bactory'. Once, when my mother was looking after her, she kept saying she wanted 'Bactory'. My mother was at a loss as to what she was talking about and it led to frus-tration on both sides. Indeed, my mother decided that she was talking about the 'lavatory' (rather advanced vocabulary for this age group, but whatever), so whisked her nappy off and plonked her on the lav. Needless to say, Molly was not amused. Eventually, my mother phoned me and I immediately knew what she wanted, proving that interaction with a less familiar adult pushes the need for better communication skills to avoid frustration.

In clinical practice, we often see parents who are so good at compensating for their children's weaknesses that they cannot see that their children are suffering from quite severe impairments. They get very upset when difficulties are reported at school and blame the teachers, but the reality is that the level of ability required to interact with an unfamiliar adult is more challenging than interacting with a familiar one. If your child has consistent difficulties interacting with a kind and supportive teacher, the chances are that they will have difficulties interacting with many other people, and are likely to have weaknesses in social ability.

Interaction with unfamiliar adults can be observed easily. Leave your child with a trustworthy friend that they do not know well and see how they behave. You can observe how well your child is able to communicate what they want and extrapolate this

TOP TIP: MANNERS MATTER

Manners are a shortcut to social skills, and that goes for socializing with familiar adults, unfamiliar adults and children alike. But unfamiliar adults, in particular, will fall over themselves to praise your child (and by default you) if they witness good manners. It's the easiest and most effective thing to do, so if you only have time and energy to do one thing, I would do this: insist your child says please and thank you whenever they ask for or are given something. It will initially require you to prompt your children with, 'What's the magic word?' repeatedly, and I did this so much that the phrase would automatically trip out of my mouth every time I passed anything to anyone. It transpires that if you do this while passing your boss water at a meeting, it doesn't go down too well.

behaviour to how they are likely to interact with their new teacher (an unfamiliar adult). If you want to challenge your child's social skills a bit more, you can ask the adult to occasionally disagree with them, or deliberately thwart them (for example, to 'accidentally' knock down the tower they were building), or to contribute a different idea to the game they are playing and see how your child responds. I must be a little sadistic, because I have to confess that I greatly enjoy spending my days being paid to deliberately thwart the games of little children.

Why communication is like tennis

For children, the biggest communicating challenge is in interacting with other children. Children possess immature social skills, so interacting with them is tricky. This is easier to understand if you think about tennis. A child beginning to learn tennis can play with an expert adult because the adult can direct balls at the child and return errant balls. Get two children who are just beginning to learn to play tennis to play with each other and it is much more difficult and frustrating for them, as neither can play properly.

Both Molly and D went to nursery from a young age and so had plenty of exposure to other children. I was able to get good accounts of their social interactions with their peers from their teachers. Most nurseries will be able to tell you if your child is able to take turns, share toys, and join in with other children. Most nurseries will be able to tell you if your child is aggressive in interactions. If your child is constantly victimized (which you will know about because parents are required to sign an incident form at the nursery if their child is bumped/bruised/bitten/scratched or harmed in any way), as well as questioning what the nursery is doing about this, you should question what your child is or is not doing to end up in this situation so frequently. Children who are frequently victimized or frequently aggressive are more likely to need extra attention as they may be vulnerable to difficulties.

Most nurseries will tell you if your child is polite and caring (for instance, how they respond if another child has fallen over). They should also give you information about how they play. If they don't, you should ask about it.

Studying play

The importance of play for children cannot be overstated. It is not only a means of relaxation and enjoyment, but it is through play that children are able to order, comprehend, rehearse and cement their social understanding, as well as be creative. Play is often heavily influenced by what children have experienced in their social environment. It is sad, but no surprise, that following an armed break-in some children I know in South Africa started to play a game of 'robbers', involving tying each other up. Back at home, I know children who play, 'I'm mummy, getting ready to go out to a party'. What these children have in common is that they are all learning about their own social environments and about ways to behave in them. It's no wonder that 'play' with a dolls' house and family characters is the preferred way that shrinks find out what is really happening at home, when we assess children of this age group. If children play mummies and daddies shouting at each other, this doesn't mean a direct call to social services, but it does prompt some questioning and assessment of the parental relationship and what bearing this may have on the child. Observing what my own children play-act when left to their own devices is one of my favourite pastimes, and if they are setting up a school, marking a register and reading stories to the assembled stuffed animals (which they do frequently), I can heave a sigh of relief.

As children grow, re-enacting what goes on around them should progress to imaginative play. Dressing up and pretending to be a princess, a superhero, or both is usually a good sign; in particular if they act out stories that they have generated themselves and if they play this with other children, each understanding

TOP TIP: PRACTISE PLAYING

Before starting school, it really helps children to be at ease with social interaction. Help this by facilitating playdates before school starts, so your child knows some of the other children who will be in their class. Once they start school, give your children a head start in feeling comfortable at school by helping them make friends. If they mention that they like to play with a particular child – arrange a playdate. I have known mums to arrange playdates for their children willy-nilly without taking into account the children's compatibility; or the playdates are arranged for convenience or because the parents are friends. This is all well and good, but if you want to improve your child's social life, playdates should be arranged based on who *your child* likes, not who you like. Of course, there will be inevitable parental preferences, but we cannot force our children to be friends with the people we want. Rather, we should be grateful that children will often select like-minded people (assortative mating again). Despite attending a state school where parents come from all backgrounds, Molly's best friend's dad works in the City and D's best friend's dad is a neurologist – go figure. (So if your child has selected a best friend who you consider a beast, then maybe you should take a look at your own child . . .)

what the other is pretending. Many adults may see this type of play as 'silly', or a waste of time, but imagination and role-playing is the way children rehearse being able to understand how someone else is thinking and how this may affect their behaviour; and how your child negotiates in play (what happens when both kids want to be the Red Power Ranger?) is a good indicator of social skill. It's no wonder that watching children play, and interacting

TOP TIPS FOR PLAY

Act out the issues Role-playing real events with children is a play-therapist staple. If there have been particular events that have been problematic, role-playing these events can help. You can adapt the 'story' if you feel your child will get upset. I often pretend to be Molly or D and act out their difficult behaviour. This usually involves wailing and stamping my feet. They usually recognize themselves immediately and, more to the point, they recognize that their behaviour was wrong. In fact, they often take on the 'parent' role and tell me exactly what I told them at the time. This leads to a good discussion about behaviour afterwards. This type of 'play' is an easier and less tense way of diffusing difficult situations without the need for a lecture. This type of play, however, does rely on an established, good parent–child relationship where the child feels secure and has good self-esteem, because having someone mimic your strop can feel humiliating, rather than funny, to an insecure child.

Engage your inner child Role-playing with children (pretend shops/school/super-heroes/mountain explorer ascending Everest) is a great way to help children develop confidence and social skills. The more imaginative you can be, the more imagination you can pass to your children. The more animated and excited you are, the more you will excite and inspire your children, which will be good for their imagination, speech, confidence and social skills. Channel a CBeebies presenter on drugs and you'll be fine. It may feel embarrassing, but it's great for kids and no other adult need know, so lose your inhibitions. It's great fun. One of my children's favourite games was to pack a picnic lunch and climb 'Everest' (three flights of stairs in a Victorian suburban house) to have a picnic amongst animals (mainly stuffed, one live cat) in the wilderness (messy children's bedroom).

in their play, is one of the main assessment tools in a child psychiatrist's armoury.

Cooperative games, such as hide-and-seek, allow you to observe practical interaction skills between your children. Is your child able to take turns? Will they cry or get aggressive if they lose? Is your child able to follow and understand the rules? How do they react if someone else transgresses the rules? Do they take charge of the game or stand back? Your child's nursery can give you this type of information; otherwise you can observe for yourself when they play with their siblings or with friends.

Children at the top of their game

For the ultimate test of social skill, you need to work in a few spoilers. Most children will be able to display good social ability when everything is hunky dory and going their way. But what about situations when they are required to compromise or negotiate? What about staying out of trouble? Most children are taught compromise when their friends are invited over to play and the 'guests' are given privileges. 'Let your friend go first, because they are the guest', 'Let your friend have the bigger slice of cake, they are the guest' – this type of thing happens all the time on play-dates. If your children are able to accept these social norms, chances are that they will be able to come to terms with compromise. They understand the social rules and etiquette and are able to conform to them. If they always have a tantrum, even when the situation is explained, then problems at school can be anticipated. Good social ability includes understanding that getting along with others is sometimes* more important than the bigger slice of cake.

Other 'spoilers' are not so easily arranged, but these situations will arise all the time naturally and it is often a good idea to stand back and observe how your child deals with them rather than wading in to intervene at the first sign of trouble. When I took Molly to a sandpit one day, I noticed another child who was more boisterous and disruptive playing there. The boy approached Molly, clearly wanting to interact and potentially cause a confrontation, as he had already done by disrupting the play of some other children. Molly turned subtly away and kept her head down, continuing to do what she was doing and saying nothing. The boy got tired of no response and went away to disrupt someone else. Molly had clearly clocked that this boy was trouble but she managed to deal with the problem in a way that was not rude or confrontational and that achieved its objective with minimal fuss. She was able to see trouble coming and avoid it. It may not be the most obvious social skill, but it is a highly valuable one. We all know some children who are 'always' involved in trouble even if they are not the instigators, and I would argue that judging social situations and avoiding trouble is as much a social skill as the ability to make friends. I felt confident that Molly could handle herself at school after this.

But what about D?

D has always been fantastic with adults. He was the darling at his nursery as he was bright, curious and endearing so the staff loved him. Being a working mother with a long commute, I was THAT mother; you know, the one who runs in frazzled at quarter past six, when the nursery closes at six, shouting, 'Wait, wait, don't call

---

* I say 'sometimes' as children who always suppress their own needs for others will have other issues that need addressing, and being the class 'doormat' is also not particularly desirable.

social services, I'm here! I'm here!' One time, I managed to sneak out of work early and arrived at ten to six, only to find D being carried around by the receptionist, who was disappointed that I had deprived her of her usual twenty-minute cuddle with my 'lovely son'. This was when I realized how lucky I was to have sociable children, who people are happy to look after.

When D was two or three years old, he would say things like, 'I love your shoes', or 'I like your hair', and, as you can imagine, this went down a treat with the young ladies at nursery. Then one time when I was in the middle of telling him off for something naughty, he suddenly said, 'I like your shoes.' I almost fell for it and said, 'Ooh, do you like them, they're patent Mary Janes!' but then remembered that I was actually quite furious with him and anyway, what did my shoes have to do with it? It was then that I realized that he didn't quite understand the social situation and was using his stock skills: 'I like your shoes', which he knew usually curried favour, to try and rescue the situation. It worked to some extent because I couldn't help but secretly laugh at the thought that he believed 'I like your shoes' was going to get him out of hot water, but it was nonetheless a misevaluation of the social situation.

Improving Your Child's Social Skills

After I noticed that D was not as adept as his sister in interpreting social situations, I started to play games with them to assess and improve their emotional understanding. We played 'emotional charades', where I would say an emotion and they would have to act it out. We'd start with easy emotions like 'happy' and 'sad', but quickly moved on to more tricky ones like 'guilty' and 'surprised'. Sometimes, I would ask them to act out scenarios instead, like 'act out getting socks for your birthday from your best friend instead of a computer game.' This latter is a bit more sophisticated, as a socially skilled child should be able to act out 'pretending to be happy even though you are actually disappointed'. Children love acting and it turns out that mine were quite good at this game.

Another game we played was, 'What is Mummy thinking?' In this game, the children had to guess what I was thinking by my facial expression. I would make a bored expression by rolling my eyes, or gesture with my eyes at the chocolate that I wanted. Here, I found that while Molly knew instantly what I was thinking, D did not have a clue. He would say, 'What are you thinking, Mummy? You're not doing anything!' whilst Molly would be shouting out the answer, incredulous that D could not work it out. 'It's so obvious, D! Mummy is bored!'

These sorts of early clues made me aware that D struggled more to interpret social situations, while he had no problem in communicating and expressing himself. How would this type of problem manifest itself in day-to-day life? What bearing can such mild problems have on his life, aside from always having to sit at the end of the table at parties? This was soon tested. Since D had started nursery, he had had a best friend called Lucas. The relationship was reciprocal and they hung out together all the time in nursery and referred to each other as 'best friends'. Then, during his penultimate year of nursery, D started to wet himself at school. He had been potty trained early so it wasn't a big deal, but nevertheless it was a regression after at least six months of being dry, so I wondered what was wrong. When asked, he would not tell me anything. He never wet himself at home so I wasn't too concerned, and thought I'd wait to see if it resolved itself. It was a fortunate circumstance that after a few weeks of this happening on and off, I attended a parents' evening at the nursery. His teacher said that something wasn't quite right but she didn't know what. This was enough for me to take the wetting seriously. Two pieces of evidence were enough for me to feel that I needed to get to the bottom of it.

When your child is feeling 'left out'

That weekend, it was Lucas's birthday party and I took D and watched him like a hawk. Whilst Lucas's parents still greeted D by saying, 'Ah, Lucas, your best friend is here!' Lucas himself was busy playing with another boy called Diego. He greeted D in passing but carried on playing closely with Diego. I felt sick for the entire birthday party as I watched D try to join in with Lucas and Diego, but being marginalized. I tried to lead him away to integrate with other children, but he didn't want to give up on his friend and refused to come with me. At one point at the end of the party, D, no doubt tired, hit Diego without reason. D never hits other children, and I knew that this was a mark of extreme frustration.

It transpired that Diego was Lucas's long-term 'out-of-nursery' friend. He had recently started in the same nursery class as D and Lucas and so it was natural that Diego and Lucas would now be close friends in nursery too. Both boys had Spanish mothers and would often speak Spanish to each other in class. As a consequence, D was left out. I don't think he fully understood the situation, or could even understand or label what he was feeling, only that he felt bad and that he wanted Diego to go away. Had I not been observing the situation, I may never have got to the bottom of it. I may have told him off for hitting Diego, which would have made D feel worse. Instead, I took him aside and gave him words with which to express himself: 'D, are you sad because Lucas is playing with Diego and not with you?' With tears in his eyes he nodded, 'Lucas doesn't like me anymore.'

Words like that stab the very soul of parents. I could barely sleep that night amidst nightmares that D was not socially resilient enough to stand life's adversities. I imagined that fifteen years down the line, he would be on his way to a top university, when on the eve of his A levels some callous hussy would dump him, and he'd fail his exams and his life chances would be dashed forever. In these situations I am not in the least bit melodramatic. Thankfully, the long suffering Andrew dragged me back from the abyss: 'For pity's sake, he's only three.'

One good thing about my exaggerated feelings of doom is that they galvanize me into action. I was on a mission to mitigate the negative impact of this situation. My immediate response was one of anger towards Lucas; I wanted to give him a good telling off and a lesson in loyalty. Then I thought about ringing his mother and having a word about it as I was sure that she would make him play with D again. But I knew that neither of these responses was rational or helpful. It was not Lucas's fault that he had a new best friend, and I wouldn't want children to hang around my son because they were forced to by their mothers. So instead, I asked my chief social affairs advisor to give D some advice.

'Molly, do you ever feel lonely?'

'No.'

'But what would you do if you went to school and a friend wouldn't play with you?'

'I'd play with someone else.'

'What if no one would play with you? Wouldn't you feel lonely then?'

'No. I'd play by myself!' [said in the most confident, matter-of-fact voice ever, as if I had asked the stupidest question in the whole world.]

Ah! You see, that's social resilience. That's what I wanted for D.

I think that most parents would have had very similar reactions to me, agonizing, 'How can I fix this situation?' and 'How can I get Lucas to play with D again?' But instead, I think what we ought to be thinking is: how can I make my child more resilient? Because honestly, we have no power to change other people, only to change ourselves and sometimes, our young children.

So what did I do?

1. I went to school and spoke to D's teacher. I explained the situation and she understood. I asked her for the names of other children in the class who would be a good match for D. That whole week at school, D got special treatment and he was encouraged to play with new children.

2. I started to arrange playdates with the children that D's teacher had recommended. I talked about how fun and amazing these other children were.

3. D would continue to bring up his 'best friend' Lucas, but we wouldn't encourage him to do so, like we used to.

D never wet himself at school again. As it turns out, the next year Lucas went into a different nursery class and Diego and D became friends. Still, when D moved on to Reception Class at a new school, I made sure that the teacher was aware that he was a sensitive boy in social situations and to keep a special eye on him in the playground.

Learning to lead, not dictate

Indeed, D was slower in making friends than his sister in Reception. There was a time halfway through Reception when he would say that he did not like school and that no one would play with him. I asked him what was happening and he told me that he would start a game with a friend, but then others would join the game and not play it his way. He would tell people how the game was supposed to be played and they would not listen to him, and so he would stop playing. This was not a big surprise to us as he has always wanted to be in charge and when he was little, we used to sing about him, 'I'm a little despot, short and stout' to the tune of the well-known teapot song.

Technically speaking, I told him that it was not the case that no one wanted to play with him; rather that *he* did not want to play with the other children. I didn't really know what the correct advice to give him was, but went on to explain the difference between a 'leader' and a 'dictator'.

'D, do you know that if I want you to help me wash the dishes, I can do it in two ways. Firstly, I could shout at you and tell you that you had to do it or there would be trouble and then I would watch over you and tell you if you were doing it wrong. What would you do in that situation?'

'I wouldn't want to come and I would shout at you.'

'Or secondly, I could fill a tub with soapy water, blow bubbles and laugh as I dipped plates into the soapy water and marvelled at how clean the plates came out. What would you do then?'

'I would want to see what you were doing and have a go at dipping plates.'

'Well, D, that's the difference between a leader and a dictator.'

'Ah,' said D. 'Now I understand. You have to make it fun.'

I dwelt no further on the subject and had no idea if my advice had been helpful, but the next day after school when I asked him how it was, I got the best response.

'I had a great day at school.'

'Great, how come?'

'Because of what you told me. Because I was a leader, not a dictator. I played a fun game by myself and other people wanted to play too!'

I have no idea if this advice could help other children, but I mention it for two reasons: sometimes I think that we need to spell out social situations to children to help them understand them; and second, that we just need to keep on trying.

At the end of his Reception parents' evening, D's teacher said that D had come into his own over the last half of the year. That he had blossomed in confidence and now had many friends. He played with everyone. Recently, we even went to a party with his old nursery school friends and D sat three spaces away from the birthday girl. A good friend who knew about my theories regarding social hierarchy and birthday party seating said to me: 'I see D is moving up in the world!' and actually, I'm glad to say, I think she's right.

The Building Blocks of Social Success:
From Five to Seven

Once children have settled into school, their social skills will be tested, rehearsed and honed every day. As parents we have the delight of seeing the babbling requests and confrontational biting of our children transform into eloquence and evasion. In this period, parents need to continue to engage with what is happening in their child's social world. There will be spats and fall-outs, loves and losses. They may seem trivial to our jaded adult eyes (because which of us are still bosom buddies with our infant school friends?), but the friendships and social jostling going on for your children at this age are as important to them and as keenly felt as the judders in our adult relationships. Offer support, advice and, where necessary, intervene as I did with D, focusing on improving your child's understanding and social skills rather than solving their problems for them. Try to listen and help because a child that is unhappy socially at school is an unhappy child.

TOP TIPS FOR SOCIAL SKILLS

Harness the power of teachers Teachers are power players in establishing social hierarchy. They will promote 'pro-social' role models. Teachers can also give valuable advice about how your child is doing socially and if alerted to problems can help mitigate them. Unfortunately, teachers are also human and can advertently or inadvertently scapegoat and collude in reinforcing a child's negative image. If possible, it is always worthwhile to get your child's teacher on side; largely this means leaving them alone to get on with their job.

Observe playdates Do your children tend to follow or to lead play? If they tend to follow, encourage them to lead. If they lead, encourage them to follow. Adaptability is key to good social skills.

Take an interest in their social activity Every day, I ask my kids who they played with at break and what they played. Most parents report that they cannot find out anything from their children about what they did at school. In general, I find that this is not because children won't say (this may be different for adolescents, but young children are generally more open, particularly if you have a good relationship with them), but because parents ask the wrong questions. I imagine the standard question is, 'How was school?' That's the adult equivalent of asking a colleague, 'How are you?' The only answer you ever get is, 'Fine.' As parents, if you want a better answer, choose a better question. Luckily, psychiatrists are intrinsically nosy people and have no problems asking questions. Believe me, you will find out amazing things about other people if you choose better questions. With children, I tend to start in the playground because this is neutral territory and usually a place of fun. Also, I already know what the children are learning at school because of the school letters, and I know how the children are doing academically because I supervise their homework. What I don't know is who they are playing with in the playground and what and how they are playing.

Sibling support If you have one child who is better socially skilled than another, you can help the weaker child by harnessing the skills of their sibling, particularly if they are close in age. I often asked Molly who D was playing with in the playground, and also to keep an eye on him and help him out if needed.

> **Improve your own social skills** Getting teachers and other parents on side to support your child also takes a certain amount of social skill. There is a reason that the social hierarchy at the school gates often mirrors the hierarchy within the school walls . . .

Chapter Summary

Social skills are some of the most important skills for children to develop. Much time and effort is spent by parents and education-alists in assessing cognitive performance, but social skills are more pivotal to success and happiness. Your child's social skills can be assessed from babyhood, and supporting your child's social development is absolutely desirable as sociable children will always get invited to more parties.

And who doesn't like a good party?

4. Layer Two: Emotional Stability

Dealing with Tempers and Tears

A little experiment.

1. Get your smart phone and set it on voice recorder.

2. Press record and start talking about your child (do it for each child separately if you have more than one).

3. Talk about your child for a full five minutes, focusing on answering the questions, 'Who is your child?' and 'How is your relationship with your child?', then stop recording.

4. If you start to flag (five minutes will feel longer than you think), here are some ideas of what to talk about: imagine describing your child to a stranger. How would you describe him so that the stranger could pick them out in the classroom or in a playground setting? What are his likes and dislikes? What are his strengths and weaknesses? How do you interact on a day-to-day basis?

5. Keep the recording and we will come to it later on in the chapter.

Tempers or Tears?

Human emotions are a massive subject, the stuff of which fills libraries across the world: jealousy, guilt, love, fear, frustration. How we experience and manage our emotions is a critical component of who we are and by adulthood will be embedded in our personalities. When this goes awry in children psychiatrists refer to it as 'emotional dysregulation', but if it continues into adulthood it can be termed 'personality disorder'. Personality disorders are notoriously hard to treat. If the problem that you are having is due to difficulties in your 'personality', how can you be easily treated because your 'personality' is part of who you are? It is much easier to take action before a problematic 'personality' is developed; that is, in the formative years of childhood. And the process starts with emotion regulation.

I am assuming that having read Chapter One you accept that genetics have a major role to play in your child's emotional state, but I also make big claims for the modifying power of parenting. How else can whole populations become defined by their emotional responsiveness (Latino temperament, British reserve, Japanese inhibition of emotion) if not because of the influence of environment and culture? And in young children, environment is transmitted via parenting. I cannot in one brief chapter cover the whole of this area, but I can try to shed a little light on the main areas of emotion that affect young children: temper (aggression), tears (anxiety and fear) and of course, love.

Temper

Which parent hasn't pretended that they have nothing to do with the kid having the meltdown in the supermarket? 'Who, him? Never seen that kid before in my life. I blame the parents.' Tantrums, meltdowns, hissy fits; all are symptomatic of young children experiencing the emotions of frustration and anger which we all feel, even as adults. I'm sure many of us have felt the urge at one time or another to punch our bosses or slap our partners, but some part of our brains holds us back, reminding us that this is not a good idea. So good have we adults become at controlling our negative emotions that when we see our little ones express their pure and uninhibited rage in all its gory glory we find it shocking and unnatural. The red faces, the flailing limbs, the wretched howling balls of pure anger. Molly can look quite frightening when she puts on her 'face of fury'. (Unfortunately for D, he is still at the cute stage, so that even when he is in this super angry state, he's cute. Strangely, my proclamations of, 'He still looks cute!' don't seem to help.) Most frustratingly, after a show like this, many kids can just switch back into 'normal kid' mode and behave as if nothing has happened, leaving shell-shocked parents heading for the gin and tonic completely bewildered. For me, and probably for many parents, there is a niggle at the back of our minds when our children behave in this uncontrolled way: 'Is there something wrong with him? (Is there something wrong with me?) Is he going to turn out bad? (Am I a bad parent?)'

Let's start at the very beginning, a very good place to start . . .

As with all things related to child development, stuff starts before the kid is born. Just about everyone knows that you shouldn't smoke in pregnancy, but did you know why? Studies have shown that there are over four thousand chemicals in cigarette smoke.[1] Many of these chemicals are able to cross the placenta into the foetus's bloodstream where, due to differing mother and baby physiology, concentrations can build up to higher levels in the foetus than in the mother.[2] Every time you have one fag, that's two fags for the baby. There is evidence that links exposure to smoking in the womb to an increased risk of spontaneous abortion, pre-term delivery, and your baby going on to develop asthma, allergies, breathing problems and even cancer in later adult life.

For unplanned pregnancies damage can be done before parents even know that they are pregnant, so I'll give the right-on medical advice: quit smoking. It is less common knowledge that as well as medical consequences, prenatal smoking has an impact on child development, such as higher levels of aggression, behavioural problems, attention problems, impulsivity, memory, speech and language difficulties and lowered intelligence.[3] If you did already know that, then I bet you didn't know *how* cigarette smoke does this?

Scientists are still hard at work on all this, but their current hypotheses surround the fascinating ideas around foetal programming and epigenetics. The theory of foetal programming is attributed to the late Professor David Barker. David studied a group of mothers who were pregnant during the Dutch famine of 1944–45 and followed the study up by looking at the consequences on the children who were in utero during the famine. These mothers suffered malnutrition and stress, and the children who had been exposed to maternal starvation and stress were found to have a lower birthweight. All of which will be of no surprise. However, despite the end of the famine and a return to plentiful food supply, these children went on to have worse adult outcomes than children conceived just after the famine ended. These negative outcomes included cognitive deficits and the higher likelihood of Type 2 diabetes, heart problems and obesity.

Barker's theory is that there is a mechanism for Darwinian adaptation to environment occurring right there in our swollen abdomens that has probably been responsible for the success of our species. He postulated that the developing foetus could take on information from the mother's womb environment and use this to 'forecast' the state of the environment into which it would be born. It is then able to prepare itself by adapting to how it will best be able to survive the predicted environment (to generate a 'predictive adaptive response'), in much the same way that we might reach for the umbrella, coat and wellies on hearing a weather forecast for rain. Thus, if the developing foetus is unable to get enough nutrients from the mother's placenta, it thinks to itself,

'Bugger, I'm in for it when I get out, if my mother can't find enough food to eat when she is pregnant, there'll be no damn food for me when I am born!' It therefore adapts (or programmes) itself to be small and thrifty (so it will conserve and use minimal resources), in order to be able to best survive the harsh environment it will face on birth.

It was through this mechanism that our ancestors lived to survive droughts and famines long enough to reproduce and eventually generate us. The foetuses that did not adapt themselves in this way would have died in infancy and childhood, not being resourceful enough in their physiology to withstand periods of deprivation. The problem occurs if the forecast turns out to be wrong, as adaptations made at these early stages of development are generally permanent. In the Dutch famine group, conditions improved after 1945 and food became plentiful again. The small and thrifty babies turned into children and adults who continued to store everything they ate. Basically, they became more obese and more prone to obesity-related diseases, compared to children from similar backgrounds born just a year or so later. They are rather like the poor fool lumbered with his heavy overcoat, wellies and umbrella at the beach in 30 degree heat, cursing Michael Fish's dodgy weather report.

Genetics has a trendy younger sister: epigenetics

How the foetus uses the information in its womb environment to affect changes in its development is thought to be via epigenetics. In essence, epigenetics is the study of which sections of DNA get expressed, or 'highlighted'. Imagine DNA is like a large manual for human construction. Epigenetics is like an edited version of this manual, where parts have been highlighted and crossed out and modified so that the final version is streamlined directly to the target audience. (If you had read my first draft of *Inside Out Parenting*, you would understand how much difference this editing can make.) Smoking in pregnancy misdirects epigenetic processes to adapt DNA to cater for a hostile birth environment. In a similar way, smoking pot could have misdirected my editor to cater my work for fairies and hobgoblins (thankfully this did not happen). Epigenetic changes can be inherited and can continue to influence at least two generations of descendants (at least in insects); thus what you do in pregnancy now may not only affect your children, but also your grandchildren.[4]

Understanding how smoking leads to asthma and allergy in this context is easy. A foetus exposed to high levels of toxins prepares itself by bolstering its immune defences. On being born to a toxin-free environment, the baby's now hypersensitive immune system gives rise to asthma and allergic reactions, which are essentially immune responses to normal everyday surroundings. But why should smoke exposure lead to aggression and anxiety? If a foetus predicts it will be born in a hostile, toxic environment, then it will give itself the best chance of survival by becoming vigilant for danger and being able to fight for survival. Aggression, hypervigilance and risk-taking behaviour would be beneficial traits to aid the survival of a toddler in an Armageddon situation, but probably not so beneficial in a three-bedroom semi in Orpington.

So along with genetics, smoking and adversity in pregnancy can contribute to aggression. But what makes a child continually unleash aggression onto others? What is the cause of childhood antisocial behaviour? And crucially, what can we, as parents, do about this?

Anti-Social Children

There is evidence that not all children with anti-social behaviour are the same. Some children may show a phase of anti-social behaviour in adolescence which then passes and they settle down in adulthood. Far more concerning are those children with a lifelong tendency to anti-social behaviour. These children tend to be anti-social from a younger age and their behaviour is more extreme. For most parents it is hard to even conceive of severe aggression in a five-year-old, but I can tell you that I have seen five-year-olds who have used metal poles to beat their pet hamster to death and seven-year-olds who have deliberately set fire to their cat. The murderers of Jamie Bulger were children. And even amongst these children there is evidence of different subgroups. Much research is focused on differentiating between groups of anti-social children to see if we can understand them better.

One differentiating factor is a lack of empathy. Empathy is the ability to share someone else's feelings and experiences by imagining what it would be like to be in that person's shoes. Psychologically speaking, this requires two different types of processes: a 'thinking' part: the ability to see things from another person's point of view; and secondly a 'feeling' part: the ability to recognize emotion in others and to feel it in oneself. People without empathy are described as being callous and unemotional. To be anti-social, violent or aggressive is easy if you do not empathize with the victim, so it is no surprise that a majority of children who display callous or unemotional traits are involved in some form of anti-social behaviour.[5]

Empathy and anti-social behaviour

Researchers have been interested in children who lack empathy for a while now because of their links to extreme anti-social behaviour. In fact the definition of 'psychopathy'/'sociopathy' includes having this lack of empathy. The childhood precursor to this psychopathy label is 'callous-unemotional traits'. University College London professor Essi Viding undertakes research into these traits and has found that if you study kids with anti-social behaviour, you'll find that 50 per cent of them have these callous-unemotional traits.[6] 'These children are unmoved when they are shown images and sounds of others in pain or grief. Their brains show less physical response to these images. In addition, in experimental card games where not playing by the rules generated penalties, they failed to learn to adapt their behaviour to avoid penalties and persevered in flouting rules.

By contrast, the other 50 per cent of anti-social children were able to show empathy. They were just as distressed and saddened as other children when shown pictures and sounds of people in pain and grief. They were also quick to learn to stick to the rules of a game to avoid punishment. However, these children differed from typical children by being hyper-aware of threat and misinterpreting ambiguous situations and facial expressions as being threatening. In a world where every situation is viewed as hostile and everyone is perceived to be a threat or an enemy, it can make sense to be combative, aggressive and violent. This is the bully in the playground snarling, 'Are you looking at me?' when you weren't even looking their way.

Genetic studies have supported this divide, finding that there is a strong inheritance of callous nature, whereas anti-social behaviour without callousness was not inherited, but rather generated by environmental factors such as harsh or inadequate parenting, or an interplay between these environmental factors and genes more associated with anxiety. Evidence of this nature has led to different theoretical models for two groups of children involved in anti-social behaviour.

Group 1: Genetic Predisposition. Anti-social and callous kids: these children are thought to lack empathy as they do not have an aversion to other people's distress and because they are unable to learn from punishment. It is easy to be aggressive and cruel if you are unable to feel guilt and if the suffering of others doesn't readily bother you. It is easy to continue to behave in this way your whole life if you are unable to learn from punishment. These difficulties are often inherited in the brain structure. The adults that these children become are the hardest to rehabilitate.

Group 2: Environmental Causation. Anti-social but not callous kids: these children have abnormal socialization because they have a heightened sense of threat, and view the world as hostile towards them. They exhibit aggression and cruelty as a result of living in unstable and threatening environments which have shaped their brains and psychology to respond in this way as a means of coping and survival. Their anti-social behaviour is often exhibited in the context of a peer group or gang, within which there is support and empathy.

Parenting anti-social behaviour

Whether we like it or not, parents are the first line of defence against anti-social behaviour in society. Most anti-social adults were anti-social children. By better understanding the causes of anti-social behaviour and by understanding our children, we can best adapt our parenting to prevent our children becoming anti-social. All children, including those genetically vulnerable to poor empathy, can be supported by fostering their self-esteem. Vulner-

TOP TIP: HUG A MINI-HOODIE

By the time your stereotypical 'hoodie' reaches an adolescent psychiatrist or youth offending service, you can bet that they will have received a lifetime of messages that they are 'naughty', 'smelly', 'no-good', 'useless', 'stupid' and so on. These messages are not just conveyed in their home, but by teachers and, crucially, other children. As parents of young children we can all do our small bit to help: whenever Molly or D used to proclaim that particular children in school were 'naughty', or even worse, 'smelly', they were told to treat their classmates with respect. As parents, we can always contribute by not judging and stigmatizing children who have more difficulty in behaving, because these children more than anyone need our understanding.

able children, in particular, respond better to being given incentives to act in a pro-social way, rather than to harsh punishment which will not deter them. Wider society has a great role to play in generating or preventing anti-social behaviour, as tolerant, peaceful and accepting societies can offer protection whilst violent, unstable and alienating societies can fuel them. For younger children that society largely means schools.

TIPS TO HELP YOUR CHILD WITH THEIR EMOTIONAL CONTROL

Rather than reinventing the wheel, I must enthuse about the book and parenting programme from which I gleaned many of my tips for this and the next chapter, *The Incredible Years*, based on the work of Dr Carolyn Webster-Stratton.[7] The National Academy of Parenting at the Maudsley Hospital run by the charismatic child psychiatrist Professor Stephen Scott uses this programme for clinical and research studies on parenting and it has a very well-established evidence base.

• **The early bird catches the worm** As with all things pertaining to child development, the earlier you start teaching, the easier it is for the child to learn, and the easier your life will be. If you don't teach a young child to regulate their emotions, they may develop ineffective ways of coping with them. The process of teaching them later on will then require them to break these habits before trying to instil them with newer, more effective strategies and this makes the process ten times harder. Indeed, Stephen Scott's parenting service only accepts children under the age of eight years, because the evidence for parents being able to make any significant change to outcome after eight years of age is weak. I reiterate: it is during the first seven years of a child's life that parents can have the most influence. If you wait too long to enact proper parenting, you'll keep us child psychiatrists in employment, but it's better by far not to.

- **Stability helps** Disruptive behaviour often occurs when something changes in a child's life: moving house, changing schools, the arrival of a new sibling, parental separation. Once things have settled down again, most children will adapt to the new circumstances and settle; usually within six months. However, what if something else happens? What if you live in temporary accommodation and the council shifts your home every six months? What if parents separate and a steady stream of boyfriends/girlfriends start coming in and out of a child's life? This type of ongoing instability has a negative impact on children's emotional adjustment. For parents, consider children when thinking about job changes that require changing homes and schools, or relationship changes. When you think about the impact your decisions may make on your children, plans can be made to limit the effect.

- **Motions and emotions** Having emotions is a natural part of life. Young children are not very good at controlling their emotions. In some ways, this is a lovely thing as we can rarely recapture the uninhibited wonder and excitement shown by children when their emotions are positive. The downside is that the same disinhibition is present for negative emotions also. The National Curriculum does not have SATS for 'controlling meltdowns', and so it is up to parents to coach this.

Parents should view training their children's emotional regulation on a par with toilet training, a vital part of 'parenting duty', but I think most parents don't realize that they are supposed to be doing this, or know what to do. For a baby, controlling emotions is just as difficult as controlling motions. They cannot do it and require parents to sort everything out. By three to four years old, as children start to be able to identify when they need to spend a penny, they also become able to identify feelings. You can help with this by labelling emotions for them. Just as when you see your child crossing their legs and jumping up and down, you might say, 'I think you need to go to the potty', so if your child starts to get cross, it is useful to label it: 'You are feeling angry/frustrated/upset.' Much as you would spend time and effort supporting children to talk about 'needing a pee', time should also be spent encouraging children to talk about their feelings, and maybe 'needing a cuddle'. With support and encouragement to own and independently manage their emotions, children's tantrums should peter out (just like bedwetting) as they mature.

- **Talk about feelings** The more you talk about your own emotions, the more children will understand about their own emotions, and using emotional language in general. Your openness will give your children permission to share their emotions and for this to become a natural part of their life. Talk about both positive and negative emotions and how you handle them, but always make sure that what you are saying is appropriate for children. Although talking about emotion is positive, make sure you don't *burden* your children with your own emotions. Children are your children, not your partner, friend or therapist.

Children should also be encouraged to talk about their own feelings and it is important to listen and be understanding when they do. A stock shrink question is, 'How did that make you feel?' If emotional language is not forthcoming, the shrink follow-up is to label it for the child: 'If I were in that situation, I would have felt really sad/angry/jealous' and so on. Not only does this label the emotion for the child, but it normalizes it, in case the child is feeling embarrassed or ashamed of feeling the way they do.

Feelings should be disconnected from behaviour. It is always fine to have feelings; it is the choice of behaviour used to express the feelings that is sometimes inappropriate. It is OK to be angry, not OK to smash up the TV. Avoid advising children 'not to get so angry/worried/sad'. It's better to acknowledge their feelings and encourage them to express them verbally instead of acting them out. Ask them to imagine playing reverse charades, where instead of acting out their emotions without the ability to speak, they are not allowed to do any actions but must speak instead.

- **Show them how it's done** Ideally, parents should model a preferred response to frustration as role-modelling is one of the best ways that children learn. This is trickier than it sounds, but put it this way: if you respond to frustration with anger, guess who will copy you? I hold up my hands to this one. Molly and D are great at shouting, sulking, but then coming back a few minutes later and saying sorry. I really can't say where they got that from . . . Needless to say, the preferred method is to remain calm, state your frustration, go somewhere to calm down and think of a more rational response. Then, come back and enact the response in a level-headed manner.

•   **Teach children how to deal with their emotions** There are several techniques which are useful for this. Firstly, children can be encouraged to tell themselves what they might say to a friend if they were in their situation. We all tend to be experts at giving our friends good advice, but rarely do the same for ourselves. When a friend is dumped, which one of us wouldn't say, 'It wasn't your fault,' or, 'You deserve better.' And when a friend is getting angry, which one of us would not say, 'It's OK, just calm down,' or 'Just walk away, it's not worth it.' Learning to give *yourself* good advice like this is a skill and if it is taught in childhood, the benefits can last a lifetime. Children can be encouraged to talk kindly to themselves. If a child has difficulty in thinking in this way, stock phrases can be learnt and used: 'I can calm myself down,' or 'This is not worth getting angry about.' I use this 'positive self-talk' as an adult; my self-help phrase to ward off frustration is 'Water off a duck's back'. This reminds me to just let things go. Encouraging children to recite these phrases to themselves in difficult situations can be really helpful.

•   **Help them to solve problems and develop strategies** The ultimate goal of parenting is to equip children with the tools for independence. This means, ultimately, children solving their own problems. The snow-plough parents who wade in to clear their children's path of problems deny them the opportunity to learn to do this themselves, often creating a herd of hapless and helpless adults with little ambition, motivation or ounce of nous about them. Rather than wade in with your cavalry, it's better to provide them with the armour and strategies to help them fight their own battles.

If, like Marty McFly, your child constantly loses it in the same situation (for example, being called 'Chicken'), then time spent talking with them about and thinking through their triggers and responses is time well spent. Encourage children to explore as many different ways of responding to the situation as possible and then talk through the consequences of each action.

For instance, in the scenario where Biff challenges your Marty to a road race and calls your Marty 'Chicken', you could brainstorm different responses with Marty and talk through the consequences. One solution might be to engage in a dangerous road race and have a catastrophic accident leading to the end of your rock star aspirations and the start of a spiral of demise that only space-time travel can resolve. Hopefully, Marty will also come up with some better solutions such as 'reverse the car and drive off'. Your child will start to get the picture that some solutions are better than others, and if they don't, treat them to watching the *Back to the Future* trilogy.

• **Temperature thermometer** One of the cognitive behavioural therapist's favourite tools is the temperature thermometer. This gets children to gauge their emotion on a scale of nought to ten. It can be done with any emotion, but we will use anger here. The object is to establish a scale of things that they notice happening within their bodies at each stage of the ten-point scale, from mild irritation to explosive rage. This will allow the child to recognize when they are mildly irritated and to understand that this is the best stage to act to change the situation, rather than wait until they are really cross, when emotion may overwhelm and get the better of them.

• **And breathe . . .** If anger has already developed, help children to learn strategies to calm themselves down. Strategies such as taking three deep breaths or counting to ten have helped my children. The idea is to instigate literal breathing space between emotion and action to allow consideration of strategy options, rather than impulsive knee-jerk reactions which may be ill-considered.

• **Behavioural management always helps** As I have mentioned earlier, behavioural management is a therapy based on praising and rewarding behaviour that you wish to see again and ignoring or penalizing behaviour that you do not. It therefore goes without saying that destructive and aggressive behaviour needs to be actively discouraged and attempts to control temper and aggression need to be noticed and praised.

Tears for Fears: The Science of Anxiety

Most people are aware that stress and anxiety are not good for pregnant mothers. Not only can stress lead to miscarriage and premature labour but scientists have found that a mother's anxiety in pregnancy can influence her child's psychological and behavioural outcomes. There is now a well-established literature base linking a mother's anxiety in pregnancy to anxiety, attention deficit hyperactivity disorder (ADHD), cognitive problems, aggression, conduct problems and even schizophrenia.[8]

The first evidence came from animal studies. Researchers found that rats and monkeys exposed to stress in pregnancy produced offspring that had long-term difficulties with attention, motor behaviour, aggression, and memory, and that showed 'hyper-vigilant behaviour'.[9] Hyper-vigilant behaviour in animals is a proxy for human anxiety. It incorporates being alert to potential threat with corresponding changes in body systems to prepare to respond to threat. Think about how you would have felt travelling to work on the underground the day after the 7/7

London bombings of 2005, and this would be an example of a human 'hyper-vigilant' state. Darting eyes on the lookout for suspicious bags with no owner, or people with oversized backpacks, slight tension in muscles, slightly increased heart rate and breathing rate, a little bit more perspiration than usual, and if someone were to pop a balloon behind you, you'd probably have been ready to run. Hyper-vigilance is a good thing if you are in a stressful situation. It has served me well on many a walk home from the night bus stop. But if you are continually hyper-vigilant, or hyper-vigilant in non-threatening situations like social situations or on aeroplanes, it can be very problematic and is called 'anxiety'.

It is relatively easy to conduct experiments to find out what is happening inside animals because you can wire them up to measure muscle tension, heart rates and perspiration fairly unobtrusively. Even better, you can take blood samples and measure their levels of the 'stress hormone', cortisol. By doing these experiments, scientists have been studying the various effects of maternal stress on animal offspring and among several suspected outcomes, they found pretty conclusively that in animals, stress in pregnancy and early life causes changes in the development of the stress regulation system, the Hypothalamic-Pituitary-Adrenal-Axis (HPA), resetting it to be on heightened alert.

The HPA axis

The HPA axis is a network of parts of the body that communicate with each other through the release of hormones in order to regulate certain bodily responses, including the stress response. In its function to regulate stress response, it works pretty much like the emergency fire service. When you see a fire, you pick up the phone and dial 999. This puts you through to a national call centre, where you are asked which emergency service you would like. Once they realize that it is the fire service you need, they contact the regional fire control centre, which contacts your local fire brigade, which sends out an engine to where you are. The fire-men hopefully put out the fire and call back the fire brigade centre to report that the job is done, which then feeds this information back regionally so that the case can be closed. Alternatively, if the fire has got out of hand, they can report regionally or nationally depending on the extent of the fire to request more engines to help.

The hypothalamus (a region in the brain) is like the national call centre. When the eyes see threat, they alert the hypothalamus. This lets the brain's pituitary gland (regional fire control centre) know that there is a threat and a stress response is required. The pituitary communicates with the adrenal glands that live atop the kidneys (local fire brigade), which then provide the stress response: the steroid hormone cortisol (fire engine). The fire engine goes out to sort the problem. Cortisol does this by going to the heart and making it pump harder, it goes to the lungs and makes them breathe quicker, it goes to the sweat glands and makes them produce sweat, it goes to the muscles and makes them tense and ready for action. All so that you can either fight or flee the threat.

If a city undergoes a heat wave and there is an increased risk that fires will start and burn out of control, the fire service will probably request that more resources are on standby and it would probably be on heightened alert to send out more engines. More engines than needed might be sent out to small fires to ensure that they did not catch and turn into large fires. This is precau-tionary and helpful in the short term, but is an overreaction if continued long term, beyond the time of realistic threat. The same thing happens to our body's emergency response system. If there is a history of heightened stress, the body responds by increasing the base level of cortisol in the bloodstream and increasing the amount of cortisol released in response to stress. This is not a problem if there is continued threat, but if the situation calms down and the body does not regulate down its stress-response system, the result is persistent anxiety.

Why a stressed mum can mean a stressed baby

In animals, at least, it has been shown that the babies themselves do not need to have been exposed to stress for their bodies to be placed on heightened alert, they merely have had to be exposed to their mother's heightened alert system in the womb. Thus in animal experiments, giving pregnant mothers injections of cortisol-equivalent substances can cause their offspring to have higher base levels of cortisol and heightened cortisol response when they are born, which continue to have an effect into adult life.[10] These animals go on to display a range of long-term behavioural and cognitive impairments. This can be thought of as part of Barker's hypothesized foetal programming (as explained with the effects of smoking), whereby the foetus exposed to high levels of maternal stress hormone predicts a stressful environment and prepares itself by adapting its HPA axis to best cope with an impending fight for survival. Where the resulting environment is stressful (such as war-torn Syria), the child will have an advantage; where the environment is actually not that stressful, the HPA axis is now maladaptive and leads to a range of dysfunction.

Stressing humans to study anxiety is rather unethical. Shockingly, it used to be allowed and 'Little Albert' is a classic case in psychology literature. Little Albert was a nine-month-old boy who was not afraid of rats and who had been given a rat to play with. A dastardly psychologist called John B. Watson wanted to see if it was possible to cause a phobia of rats. Every time little Albert touched the rat, a man stood behind him and banged a piece of metal with a hammer, making a loud noise that scared little Albert. Needless to say, after a while of this Albert became afraid of rats and stopped going near them, proving it is possible to induce a phobia. No wonder experimental psychology has a bad name!

These days, we are thankfully not allowed to do such things, but it does mean that extrapolating results from animal studies into humans is harder. We have to rely on stress that occurs naturally in the lives of pregnant women rather than purposefully causing stress in order to study its effects on offspring. Natural and man-made disasters have been used to study the effects of gestational anxiety.

Babies born at times of crisis

Studies of children who were in the womb of mothers affected by 9/11 showed that they were born with lower birth weights (even though they were born at full term) compared to children conceived following 9/11.[11] Infants whose mothers were pregnant during the 1998 Canadian ice storm, that led to electricity and water shortages for up to five weeks, scored lower on mental development indices and tests of language development compared to other children, even after taking into account birth complications, birth weight, gestational age and post-natal depression.[12]

It is not just extreme stress such as a national disaster that can cause these effects. Studies have also used questionnaires that ask pregnant mothers about their levels of stress at varying times during their pregnancy and then studied their children at varying ages from newborn to adolescence. In general, the link between maternal stress and impaired offspring outcome is borne out, sometimes even with a direct dose-response effect.*[13] Results from different studies vary as each study is different in terms of the stress they are measuring (some studies ask for work stress, bereavement, marital stress, criticism from partners, or just how anxious you feel), the time in pregnancy the stress occurs (studying stress in the first, second or third trimester), and the outcome and age of the children they are studying (some studies look at language and development in the first year, others look at ADHD symptoms in childhood and yet others look for anxiety and

---

* A dose-response effect is when the greater dose of something purported to cause a particular effect will cause a greater effect. For example, if sun exposure is linked to tanned skin, a dose-response effect would mean that more sun exposure leads to a deeper tan. Finding a dose-response effect is good (but not necessarily definitive) evidence that a causal link exists.

conduct problems in adolescence). Despite this, the majority consensus of all the studies is that maternal prenatal anxiety can produce a significant negative and lasting effect. In this way, it is not just your DNA that is biologically influencing your child's outcome, but your environment, via biological mechanisms. This is epigenetics again, the new buzz in child psychiatry research.

Is this a *real* effect or is it because mothers with stressful lives are more likely to experience stress during pregnancy and more likely to have difficulty raising children, and it is these factors that are causing the psychological deficits seen in her kids? In animal studies this is easy to exclude; the newborn pups or monkeys are cross-fostered so that once the baby is born, the mother who was stressed in pregnancy is replaced by an unstressed mother. The results remain the same. It is not possible to do this with humans, although in the majority of human studies attempts are made statistically to take account of markers of stressful lives (social class, post-natal depression, maternal education, to name a few) and the results still significantly bear out the theories.

What about the effect of genetics? It is possible to argue that a mother genetically predisposed to anxiety is likely to be anxious in pregnancy and to pass on her anxiety genes to her offspring, thereby causing them to be anxious. You can see how hard it is to prove anything in science, yet clever researchers continue to try and get to the answers. In a masterstroke of research design, scientists turned to IVF children to compare associations between prenatal stress and child outcome in those who were genetically related to the mother with those who were not (that is, those conceived through egg donation).[14] They found there was an association between the mother's stress in pregnancy and the child's symptoms of anxiety and conduct disorder, even in the unrelated mothers.

So, the best advice is to try and prevent anxiety in pregnancy as far as possible. There are obvious factors here: being in a stable, loving relationship, having a stable financial and employment situation, feeling as if you've lived child-free life to the full and are ready to face pregnancy and motherhood in the optimum possible position. Of course, this isn't possible for everyone, but the age-old advice to 'take it easy' when you are pregnant always holds true.

Early Signs of an Anxious Child

So we've looked at some of the causes of anxiety in children and seen that genetics, epigenetics and a wonky HPA axis caused by prenatal and early-life stress are possible biological factors. But how can a parent identify if their young child is at risk of anxiety and what can they do about it? If you are worried that your child is anxious, firstly remember that anxiety is a normal and natural emotion, a useful and life-preserving reaction evolved to allow our bodies to prepare for fight or flight in response to threat. Children who feel no anxiety are abnormal and likely to face an early grave as they scoot fearlessly down steep inclines, jump down from high places and challenge that muscle-head Year Six kid to a fight, with no thought of the consequences. If your child has mild symptoms of anxiety, think yourself lucky that they do not have the reverse problem. Anxiety is the most common emotional problem in children and it is usually readily treatable.

Some common manifestations of childhood anxiety are the following:

Talking about worries. This is the most useful and well-adapted way to signal anxiety. If your child is able to tell you about their upset, they have taken the first step to getting help and support. In all cases of anxious children, the task of therapy is to get to this stage where the child is able to talk openly about their worries. The onus is then on the adult to help problem-solve and support the child to either overcome or tolerate their anxiety.

If children are unable to recognize that they have a worry or they can't express themselves verbally (this will depend on the child's age, intellect and emotional awareness), their worry is often expressed in other ways and it is up to adults to notice and recognize that these may be symptoms of anxiety.

Crying and temper tantrums. Although extreme temper tantrums are frequently considered to be bad behaviour, sometimes it is fear and anxiety that is driving them. The first thing that a therapist will ask parents to do when helping with temper tantrums is to document the incidents in detail, including what led up to the tantrum and what happened after. Sometimes there is a pattern. A typical scenario goes like this: the child has a tantrum about going to school and refuses to go, kicking and screaming. When the parent gives up and says the child can have a day off, the tantrum resolves and the child is as happy as Larry. On further investigation, it is found that the child is being bullied at school/ has a spelling test/has PE that day which they hate/is frequently being told off by a strict teacher. Punishment, chastisement and behavioural management in response to tantrums that are due to anxiety will not work and therefore understanding the emotion behind tantrums is important.

Clinginess. Some children respond to anxiety by becoming a barnacle clinging to your side and never letting go. The more you try to prise them off, the tighter they cling. They find separating to go to school hard and can even follow you around the house. It's immensely annoying for the parent. I know, because I was a barnacle on my mother's side for a time after we moved to the UK. Immigration is a stressful event even for adults, so you can imagine how a four-year-old feels, starting at a new school in a new country where they know nobody and cannot speak the language. For a period of six months I cried insufferably every day at school, to the extent that my mother had to sit in the back of the classroom for months. Sometimes I followed my mother around at home, or worried that she might die if I was not with her. This is typical separation anxiety. Luckily for me, and my mother, it resolved after I got used to England (or more accurately, Wales) and, crucially, learnt to speak English.

Becoming mute. Some children stop speaking when they are anxious. Usually, the anxiety is related to particular stressful environments, such as school or somewhere outside the house. This is called selective mutism and is fairly common in childhood, although not later on in life.

Tummy trouble. Children are much more likely than adults to describe emotional problems in physical terms. For some reason, the preferred target area for symptoms is the gastro-intestinal system. Anxiety should always be considered in cases of tummy ache or constipation which are ongoing, without obvious medical cause. For children that have tummy aches that miraculously resolve themselves at weekends and in the school holidays, one must always be suspicious of an anxiety involving school. For some reason, in late adolescence and adulthood, the target of psychological pain turns from the tummy to the head, and adults with emotional problems will more commonly complain of headaches and neurological pain. But for kids, it's all about the tummy.

Bedwetting. Once children have been continent for a year, any return of bedwetting symptoms can be indicative of anxiety. Whilst immigration led me to a brief period of separation anxiety, my sister suffered from a brief spell of bedwetting. Again this is a common sign of anxiety in children. Like my bout of separation anxiety, my sister's problems resolved when she became more settled in our new country. A return of other toileting problems (daytime wetting, soiling) in children who have been continent for over a year may indicate more extreme emotional problems if no medical cause is found.

Babyish behaviour. Any reversion to babyish behaviour that had been long outgrown (thumb sucking, hiding, speaking in a babyish voice, requiring a comfort blanket, requesting an adult for help with things that they could previously do, such as wiping their bottom or tying their shoe laces) is referred to as 'regression', and can be a sign of anxiety or emotional distress.

Rigidity. Children who are anxious may become increasingly rigid and unable to adapt to change or to the unexpected. They may become controlling and preoccupied with getting things right (perfectionism), the way things are arranged, the way things are done, the food that they eat. The child is trying to re-establish order and control over a life that they are finding unpredictable, overwhelming and difficult. These are potential warning signs for vulnerability to disorders that overlap with anxiety: obsessive compulsive disorder, eating disorder, depression.

In children under seven years, full-blown psychiatric disorders of anxiety, depression, eating disorders and OCD are quite rare, mainly because the stress that children are under at this young age is usually not severe. However, if your child shows a tendency to respond to mild stress in an anxious way, it may indicate that they might respond in a similar but more extreme and prolonged way when the major stressors of adolescence come online, and even develop a full-blown disorder in adolescence or adulthood if the problem is not addressed now. It is typical in adult psychiatry that when you look back on a client's history, the seeds to their current conditions were often already evident in childhood. This time in early childhood is an opportunity to intervene.

TOP TIP: GET PROFESSIONAL HELP

If you suspect your child may have problems in this area, get professional help as soon as possible. If you can spend time observing your child's skills as I have described above, then you will be alerted earlier to potential difficulties. If you can, try to clearly document examples of the struggles that your child has had. Accessing the right help can be difficult, but by providing detailed examples of any difficulty observed, professionals will be better able to help.

TOP TIPS FOR HELPING CHILDREN WITH WORRIES

• **Encourage talking about worries** As mentioned, much of the therapeutic work for anxiety is to get to the stage where children can talk openly to you about their worries. The work of art therapists, play therapists, psychologists and psychiatrists will usually start by establishing a safe environment and trusting relationship so that children feel able to talk freely, knowing that what they say is in confidence, they will not be judged and that they will be handled sympathetically. It therefore helps if on a day-to-day basis you promote your home as this type of safe environment and family members are sympathetic and non-judgemental. This means things like not going mental if they bring home a bad school report, or setting up a parents' evening to discuss why no one will play with your son.

• **Contain your anxiety** Once your child has admitted their worries to you (they are being bullied, they think that they are a girl trapped in a boy's body, they are worried you will die), however worrying their worries may be, there is no point in you joining in. Your first job as the adult is to contain the worry. You might need to seek advice to help you with this, but in general, the more sanely and sedately you deal with the problem the less worrying the worry will become. If you become hysterical, this will only add to your child's worry.

• **Always take your children's worries seriously** Try not to dismiss them. If a child is worrying about it, it means that it is serious to them, even if as an adult we can see that it doesn't amount to a hill of beans. If a child is genuinely worried about something, off-hand remarks such as, 'Oh, don't be silly,' or 'There's no need to worry about that,' can serve not to relieve the worry but to fuel the idea that they shouldn't talk to you about their worries. This might not be a problem in childhood, but come adolescence when worries can become serious, that communication and trust is paramount, and if it is lost in childhood it might never be reclaimed in adolescence. Reassurance can, of course, be given, but make it genuine and not dismissive.

• **Help your child to solve their own problems** Talking through the worry with your child, the potential courses of action and their likely consequences can help your child see that there is a route through their problem. Demonstrating that you will be on their side throughout the problem can help. Sometimes, as the adult, the problem may be yours to fix. For instance, problems of school bullying in young children absolutely require parent and school intervention and no child can handle this alone.

• **Help your child to accurately assess the situation** Sometimes children (and adults) can misinterpret situations or the likelihood that they will happen. Many adults have stopped flying because of stories of planes disappearing from the sky. The reality is, though, that air travel is safer than car travel. In cognitive behavioural therapy for anxiety, psychologists and psychiatrists often ask children to research the facts about their worries (the likelihood of a terror attack, or of being bitten by a dog) or carry out surveys of what other people think. This allows them to see that sometimes their worry is out of proportion to reality.

• **Help your child to tolerate anxiety** Often anxiety-provoking situations cannot be avoided, for instance anxiety over spelling tests, dogs, going to the dentist or getting onto a plane. In these instances, a parent's natural reaction may be to help the child avoid these encounters, but this is grossly counterproductive and will make the problem worse. Unless you want your child to be illiterate, never to walk in the park, have rotten teeth and never go abroad, it is much better to be able to 'teach' your child to tolerate the stress. The best way to do this is with education, support and graded exposure. Most parents, teachers and psychologists are very good at the first two steps, but the third step, graded exposure, is the make or break and even many therapists fail to do this well.

At some point, anxious children or adults must face their fears to truly overcome them. The best therapists are excellent at this and my favourite story is of the psychologist David Clark, who treated a patient with social anxiety. His patient developed a phobia about social interaction because he was hyper-aware of his anxiety and worried that he would start to sweat a lot and then other people would notice and he would look like a fool. David poured two glasses of water on his shirt under his own armpits and made his patient go with him in this state to a pub, where he ordered drinks and socialized in a nonchalant way. The psychologist styled out 'man with excessively sweaty armpits', and the client was able to see that no scene was caused and the world did not end. The next step was, of course, to make the patient do it himself, and lo and behold, he did, and was more or less cured of his social anxiety.

I was emboldened by this great story when I was first called upon to treat a boy with severe OCD and symptoms of social anxiety. After a few preparatory sessions where I discovered that his fear was related to being stared at, I marched him into King's College Hospital A&E and by the time we left, we had both performed the 'YMCA' song in the waiting room. This was a boy who had been out of school for a year, partly because of his fear of being stared at. He had had two rounds of unsuccessful therapy prior to seeing me, but previous therapists had never made him face his fear. Within a few weeks, he was back in school. Frankly if you can do an impromptu 'YMCA' in front of a bunch of strangers, how difficult is school? With appropriate support, our children can be braver than they, and even we, think.

Fear and Phobia in Children: What Do Children Find Frightening and Why?

Children's fears typically vary depending on their age and intellectual capacity, moving from an almost 'instinctive fear' in babies to sophisticated, abstract fears in adolescence, which require more elaborate thought processes. For babies and toddlers, whose cognitive capacity is still basic, fear is more of an 'instinct'. Evolution has honed humans to have brains that are hard-wired to fear certain things because this has served our ancestors well in the past: for instance loud noises, which could have denoted a falling tree, an earthquake or a sabre-toothed tiger. If you make a loud unexpected noise next to a baby, they will most certainly startle and start crying. There is also a biological predisposition to fear animals like snakes and spiders, things that caused our ancestors harm. Research shows that it is easy to induce a phobia of animals (as with Little Albert), but more difficult to induce phobias to guns and cars, which are more likely to be a threat in the modern age.

At a young age, babies (at least baby monkeys) are also primed to fear what others fear. This evolutionary trick allows them to quickly pick up on the dominant threats in their environment, because if other monkeys fear something, it will probably be wise to learn to fear it too. Scientists Cook and Mineka showed this clearly in Rhesus monkeys, who were laboratory-raised and did not fear snakes.[15] After showing the monkeys videos of wild monkeys showing extreme fear of snakes, the baby monkeys became afraid of the toy snakes in the laboratory, despite never personally having had an unfortunate encounter with a snake themselves. Babies and young children are also primed to attend to their parents' fear. I acutely remember breastfeeding Molly while watching a horror movie late one night. At one point, I held my breath in anticipation of something horrible happening on screen. It would have been imperceptible to most people as I did not move or make a sound, and yet Molly stopped suckling,

TOP TIP: KEEP CALM AND CARRY ON

Because children will copy your fear responses, make sure that you do not pass on your own fears to your children. If you show a fear of passing dogs, it won't take long for your young children to also become afraid of dogs. I have an intense hatred of mice and am that typical woman climbing on the furniture, shouting at my husband for help if they dare venture into my vicinity. Since having children, I am conscious of not passing on my own defects and we have invested in a cat. Although I still detest mice, I am careful to hold it together emotionally if they ever surface, and I alert my husband or cat through urgent gritted teeth rather than full-blown, arm-waving hysteria.

tensed and looked at me. She could not yet sit up, walk or speak, and yet she could sense my fear.

As toddlers grow into infants, they begin to develop cognitively. With this development comes the beginning of their understanding of the world and of their imagination. They can start thinking about things that could happen beyond their own direct experience. At this age 'the dark' and 'monsters' are quite common fears. Often the child's fears are completely unrealistic and may come from the strangest of places. When I was a young child, I couldn't sleep one night and came downstairs to find my parents. They were watching the movie *Jaws*, and I happened to walk in at an inopportune moment when someone got munched. For several nights after this, I had nightmares that 'Jaws' was going to come through my bedroom window and munch me. My parents found this hilarious and at the time I didn't quite understand why. Recently, my own children's fears have been a source of interest and amusement to me, although I try to take them seriously and not be amused in their presence. Molly, while having no problems with the Maidmashing and Bonecrunching giants in

Roald Dahl's *The BFG*, refused to continue with *Matilda*, for fear of Mrs Trunchbull. Several nights of disturbed sleep for Molly and disturbed evenings for us lay at the hand of Mrs Trunchbull. D, on the other hand, took grievance with Violet Beauregarde from *Charlie and the Chocolate Factory*. For some reason, being turned into a blueberry was the stuff of his nightmares. Violet's return to normality by means of juicing only served to fuel, rather than quell, his fear.

At this age, what parents fear for their children is often poorly understood by children themselves. The ever-present fear of parents, 'How will my children cope if I die?', is not at all a concern for young children. They neither comprehend death nor a realistic meaning of time. Once, when I uttered aloud my fear, 'What will happen to you children if I die?' Molly, to my chagrin, in typical matter-of-fact style replied, 'Oh, it will be fine, we will still have Dad.' By the ages of five to eight, however, children come to understand the meaning of death and fear of death and illness becomes more common.

The middle childhood years (between six and twelve), are the peak age for acquiring fear of animals. Dogs and spiders are pretty common fears for children. Sometimes, a child will develop a fear because of a specific experience with an animal, but other times, they may have a fear even without a direct upsetting experience. Evolution has predisposed our brains to accept that animals are potentially dangerous. As children reach adolescence, their fears become more similar to those of adults: fear of failure, of humiliation, of rejection; fear of war, terrorism, illness and crime come to the fore. Whilst on one hand these fears are more 'realistic' than the bogeyman fears of infancy, one can also make the argument that actually many adult fears are unrealistic too.

Remember that fear is a useful survival mechanism

It should always be remembered that fear is a natural response that helps to serve a vital function. Without fear, our species would probably not have survived, because we would have been putting ourselves in the direct line of danger without regard for the consequences. The fear response allows not only the body to prepare for fight or flight, but also the brain to respond by avoiding trouble. People who show low levels of fear often show high levels of 'risk-taking behaviour', and end up in trouble one way or another, whether it is in a high-speed car accident, audacious robbery or in bringing down the banking sector. However, fears should be based in reality and psychological treatment for anxieties and phobias includes anchoring these fears in reality.

As parents, we cannot shield our children from all adversity and helping children to understand and deal with anxiety and fear is part of our role. Teaching children to accept and have the confidence to know that they can handle fearful situations when they arise is more important than preventing fearful situations arising or promoting gung-ho 'fearlessness'. Security and reassurance is the key; but sometimes this is easier said than done.

If at first you don't succeed, try again in a different way

When Molly was in Year One, she studied Edward Jenner and smallpox at school. The idea of smallpox put the fright into Molly like nothing before. Not only was her sleep disturbed, but even during the day she would get tearful thinking about the family being killed by smallpox. This went on for a week, and despite my reassurance that smallpox no longer existed in England, she was still tearful and upset. I eventually went in to see her teacher and told her of the situation. When I picked up Molly from school that day, she declared to me that she was no longer afraid of smallpox.

'How come?' I asked, having given her reassurance all week, to no avail.

'Because the teacher told me about the smallpox vaccine.'

'Er . . . haven't I been telling you about that for the past week?'

'Yes. But she knows about this, she is a teacher.'

Guess that medical degree doesn't count when you are just a mother.

Lessons Learnt about Love via Death

And finally I will end with the most important emotion of all: Love.

I have already waxed lyrical about the importance of love for developing children's self-esteem in Chapter Two, but what I want to bring home here is that this experience of parental love also shapes our children's ability to love others and bring love into their life. Strangely, my views on the importance of love were concreted by two experiences I had of death.

As a house surgeon I had been looking after an elderly gentleman with prostate cancer. The results of investigations were bad. The tumour had spread and surgery was out of the question; this admission would be his last. At medical school we had been coached in 'breaking bad news'; there is a particular body language and tone of voice that is to be recommended. There is a note between scientific certainty and sympathy that needs to be struck – so as not to give false hope where it will be sought, whilst remaining concerned and compassionate. Surgeons hate this sort of thing as they prefer to fix things, and as I had made it plain that I was to be a future psychiatrist, I had been singled out to break the bad news to the patient's only family: his son and daughter-in-law. Facts gathered, scans in hand, tissues in reserve, I led the family to a quiet room to deliver the news. My rehearsed tone of voice, body language, and eye contact were at the ready as I delivered the painful words: 'Cancer is widespread,' 'We can't operate,' 'It's terminal.'

What I didn't expect was the response.

'Can you sign this form for me?'

'Huh? What?'

I looked at the form. It was for the annual renewal of his father's Disability Living Allowance.

'I don't think you fully understand,' I said. Maybe he did not understand what 'terminal' meant. 'Your dad won't be coming back to you. I'm sorry, he is going to die.'

'That's why you need to sign the form now, so I can get this renewed for another year before he dies.'

I guess for some families, defrauding the benefits system is more important than the death of a parent.

The second story does not involve a patient of mine, but a patient in Side Room One of a bustling ward at the Norfolk and Norwich Hospital where I was working in cardiology. It started with a slow trickle. A middle-aged man and his wife. A middle-aged man, his wife and three children. Another family with children in tow. A young couple with a baby, American accents and suitcases in tow, like they had just stepped off a plane. An elderly man being pushed in on a wheelchair by a teenager with middle-aged parents in tow. A student in a leather jacket. A pair of twin girls and their 'Mam'. An old lady using a Zimmer frame. A couple with a toddler. One by one, these people disappeared into Side Room One. There were greetings, hugs and reunions heard. Knowing the sizes of the side rooms, I could not fathom how they all fitted in, but they did; making room for each other, because it was important. The door was always ajar, but I didn't intrude on their privacy. Then there was a silence that lasted longer than was normal. Then out they spilled, one by one, with tears streaming down their faces, old and young alike. The older comforted the younger, the younger consoled the older. Sombre, terribly sad, yet united. I never knew who the patient was in Side Room One. Male or female, young or old. But I knew one thing; I wanted a death like theirs – surrounded by a family that loved me and loved each other.

The only way I can explain the differences I witnessed in the manner the two families responded to death is this: love, and the lack of it. Children who have experienced love are more able to understand, express and show love. They are more open, generous, forgiving and tolerant to others. I believe that the love that we show our children will be repaid in kind in their adulthood. If it is indifference that we give, can we expect more than indifference in our own times of need? Children are 'needful' of us most in the first seven years of their life. In this time we are fortunate enough that they are programmed to love us 'come what may' because at the most basic level, they need us. This will not always be the case; come adolescence, they will be primed to pull away. You will find that parents can abandon, neglect and even abuse young children and they will still come back to love that parent. However, taking advantage of this is a mistake and a ticking time bomb. As soon as the 'need' is gone, children have to 'want' to love their parents to stay engaged with them. If parental love wasn't shown or felt, be ready for the, 'You were never there'; 'What do you care?'; 'You always preferred my brother' fights. They can get bloody; even more so if there is a lot of truth in the accusations. Furthermore, as parent-child relationships build the blueprint for all a person's future love relationships, it is important that we get our priorities right and focus on making this first relationship a successful one.

The measure of love

As 'love' is extremely difficult to measure scientifically, child psychologists and psychiatrists instead measure the expression of love: 'Warmth'. Love without warmth can still leave children cold, so warmth can be a better predictor of outcome than love. Parental warmth can be measured in several ways. At the start of any clinical assessment, the 'preamble' or small talk a clinician has with the parents is their first step in getting an idea of parental warmth. They will also monitor parental warmth in the parent's body language, in every touch of the child, every eye contact made, every tone of voice and big or small behaviour towards the child throughout the assessment. These observations are time consuming and in large research studies often not possible, and so the five-minute speech sample is used as a proxy. Here, recordings of parents talking about their children for five minutes are listened to and coded by researchers looking for specific indicators of warmth. Reductionist and imperfect, I know, that the entirety of your love for your child could be judged in a five-minute tape of you talking about them. But the evidence shows that when accurately scored, the results tally well with longer and more in-depth interviews and observational assessments.

How did you do?

If you took part in my little experiment, you can play your voice recording back now and I will let you be your own judge and jury. Here are a few things that I would be listening for clinically:

- The opening statement should be positive. I'm hoping that you didn't start your tape with, 'My no-good kid is good for nothing and I hate him.'

- Parents who are able to talk at length without difficulty about their children tend to know them better; the more detailed and the more subtle and intimate knowledge that is described, the more it is evident that the parent 'knows' the child well. My children's piano teacher had a story about a student he had been teaching weekly for several years. On one occasion, he called the student's father to ask why his son had missed his piano lesson that day. The father responded: 'Oh really? I didn't know he played the piano.' This is clearly not a winner.

- Positive comments should always outnumber the negatives by at least three to one. This does not mean that weaknesses should not be mentioned, as identifying weaknesses and having thoughts about strategies to help overcome them is also a positive, showing awareness of a child's struggles and a willingness to support them. For instance, 'She's dumb. I've always known she was stupid from the day she was born,' is clearly not good, but what about: 'She has always struggled with learning, but *she's come along really well* over the last few years. We've done a lot of work at home and with the school and *we're really proud* of the progress she's made. *She's even starting to learn to read now*, something a year ago we thought she'd never be able to do.' Although this latter comment is addressing a weakness, it is laden with positive comments and is clearly from a warm parent.

- Parents who openly criticize and use strongly emotive negative language score poorly for warmth. Generalized criticism is seen as indicative of hostility. So while 'He doesn't like to tidy his room' might be a fair comment to make and would not indicate lack of warmth, 'He's a lazy bastard' would. Blaming and scapegoating, 'His sister is fine, so it's not us. I know it's something wrong with *him*,' is also indicative of low warmth.

- Parents who use too many positive and superlative adjectives may be earmarked as being overprotective. Anyone who comes out with anything along the lines of 'my darling diddums' or 'my perfect angel from heaven' will have us reaching for the sick bag. A parent who can realistically and sympathetically appraise their child will be rated much more highly.

- If parents start to talk mainly about themselves (their own problems and the sacrifices they have made) or another sibling ('If only he could be like Jack, our eldest,' or 'Oh, she doesn't cause any problems, but our son, now he's a right little devil . . .') may indicate that the child in question is rather forgotten.

Chapter Summary

Helping your child to understand, express and control their emotions is pivotal for their future stability and an essential tool for parents to teach. Being able to manage their emotions not only allows your child to enhance their social skills (previous layer), but also reduces their behavioural problems (next layer). How we help children to deal with frustration, fear and worry now will help them be braver, stronger and kinder in the future, and may even prevent them developing mental health problems in later life. The love that we express in the warmth of our relationship with our children will be carried in them and flow from them for a lifetime. It will not only form the blueprint for their future love relationships, it may also ultimately provide us with solace in our own times of need.

5. Layer Three: Behaviour and Self-Control

'Lord of the Flies' and Alice's Cake

I am really looking forward to going to nursery. My mum has bought me some lovely new shoes and I am looking forward to showing them to my teacher. I am now ready in my nursery uniform, standing by the steps, waiting for my mum to help me put on my lovely new shoes. 'Here they are!' she says cheerfully as she takes them out of the box. They look lovely, but then I peer inside them. Usually, my mum puts a nice rosy red sticker on the inside of my shoes with a ladybird and my name written in nice big letters so that everyone will know that these smart new shoes belong to me. But today she hasn't. 'Where's my stickers?' I ask, pointing at my shoes. 'I didn't get a chance to put them in,' she says, 'I'll do it tonight. I can't do it now because we need to leave now or we'll be late for nursery.' But my shoes *always* have my name in them. How else will people know that these shoes are mine? Also, the teacher gets cross if clothes are not labelled because she doesn't know which clothes to put on which child. What if she puts someone else's shoes on me and my lovely shoes get lost? No, it won't do. School clothes need to be labelled.

I can't say all that though, because I don't know this is why I am feeling the way I do and I'm not clever with words yet.

I know. I'll refuse to put these shoes on until they are correctly labelled. Why doesn't she just go and fetch the stickers, instead of trying to foist these shoes on my feet? OK, Mum's gone to get them now, but what is she getting angry at *me* for? It's not my fault she forgot to do it yesterday. She should have been more organized. Now she is stamping her feet at me! Well, two can play that game! Why should I be in trouble because of her lack of organization? I don't like being shouted at and if she thinks I'm going to put those shoes on now she's got another thing coming. I'm going to show her my face of fury and see how she likes that!

Oh what? I'm being picked up? This is a disgrace! It's so unfair that she's bigger than me and can do this. Put me down, you big bully! I'm going to kick and scream until she puts me down. How *humiliating*!

It's All about Frustration

If Molly could have told her own version of the tragic parenting moment that led me to write this book, it would have gone something like that. Thinking about it from Molly's point of view, I feel even more ashamed of how I behaved. If Molly had been able to tell me that she was worried about losing her shoes, I would probably have immediately fetched her name stickers and we would have been out of the house in time for her nursery and my meeting.

What's clear, then, is that so many of childhood frustrations and tantrums can be avoided if children are confident in expressing themselves, and can articulate their thoughts and feelings in the same way that adults can. This is why, although as parents we generally focus on children's behaviour, it is their self-esteem, ability to communicate and understanding of their emotions which are more critical to their development. With well-developed self-esteem, social skills and emotional understanding, we would all be more effective at getting what we want and less likely to resort to anger, aggression and tantrums. So if by chance you have just flicked to this chapter without reading the preceding ones, with the hope that I will offer up some magic beans to miracle away your child's tantrums, please go back to the start because the first steps in improving your child's behaviour are always to improve their self-esteem, social skills and emotional understanding. Time spent improving these aspects of your child will *always* improve their behaviour and make the tips in this and the later chapters work much more effectively.

That said, even with solid self-esteem, social skills and emotional stability, life isn't perfect. Frustration is a fact of life, and children, just like adults, need to learn to live with it. The better we are at preventing or coping with our frustration and controlling our aggressive instincts, the better. No matter how sociable, attractive and intelligent a person is, if they cannot control their actions, and in particular their temper or frustration, they will at some stage come a cropper, whether through severed friendships, lost jobs or domestic violence. Self-control in the face of frustration is a really important lesson for any child to master, because if they don't the consequences in adulthood can be severe.

Aggression (and learning to control it)

Many people think that babies are born angels and that society turns them to violence, when the reverse is actually true. Babies are born with aggressive survival instincts and it is society that civilizes them. William Golding's classic depiction in *Lord of the Flies* of a group of boys left to their own devices on an island, without any adult supervision, who descend into violence, is as horrifying now as it was in the fifties; mainly because it is a perfectly imaginable scenario. Aggression is as natural an instinct as sexual drive or fear and is hard-wired in us all, to a greater or lesser extent. Aggression is partly responsible for the survival of our species. Although some children are genetically predisposed to be more aggressive than others, aggression is inside us all. Society (which for very young children is their parents) can act like the 'eat me' cake in *Alice in Wonderland* to grow aggressive instincts, or it can be the 'drink me' potion that shrinks them.

The first time a toddler experiences another toddler snatching a toy from them, particularly if no adults are around to intervene, she will probably try and snatch it back. If this is not effective, she may try to hit/push/bite the other child. At a young age this does not signify a deviant child, but is fairly run of the mill. Aggression is a natural instinct; if you frustrate toddlers enough, most of them will resort to biting. However, after a few rounds of adult intervention and reprimands with the message that hitting, pushing and biting others is unacceptable, most children 'get it'. They are then taught (or learn by experience or by watching others) more socially acceptable ways to get what they want (which at this age mainly involves being a tattle tale and crying to alert adults to the injustice). They actively inhibit their aggressive nature and these instincts get weaker. They quickly adapt to the needs of their environment, learning which behaviours will lead to the outcomes that they want.

If toddlers are left to their own devices without appropriate adult intervention for long lengths of time, the child that hits the other children will end up 'King of the Hill', with all the toys he wants. He and the other children watching him may learn that hitting and biting others is an effective way to get what you want. In some environments, aggression is not just permitted but actively encouraged by adults, consciously or unconsciously ('Show them who's boss', 'Fight back', 'Get in there and tackle him'), and these children may grow into adults who view aggression as a positive thing and actively develop this side of themselves further. Adapting or changing behaviour in response to particular environments happens in adults too. I am pretty sure that if I were to be thrown into a high-security prison tomorrow, I would quickly learn to toughen up, adopt more aggressive responses, do away with received pronunciation and stop asking if my gruel could be served gluten-free.

As a parent, I experienced the impact that environment can have on aggression in a subtle way at Molly's first nursery placement. As a new parent, it is really hard to know the difference between a good and poor nursery and I had to learn the hard way. In Molly's first nursery, which was brand new and housed in a beautifully refurbished Victorian town house, full of all mod cons and designer children's toys, Molly was bitten or scratched by other children in her class at least ten to fifteen times during her eighteen-month career there. Other children in her class were also being bitten and scratched and we parents almost had to form a line to sign the incident book when we collected our children. We would be told that a new toddler had been admitted to the class who had not yet been 'socialized' by the nursery, but they would get the child under control soon. Only then, it seems, they would admit another 'un-socialized' child. I know it is normal for toddlers to bite, and although I was exasperated, I figured that this was run of the mill for nurseries. Eventually I had to sign an incident form saying that Molly had bitten another child (although she had never bitten anyone at home), and to tell the truth, I was rather glad that Molly was retaliating rather than always being a teething ring for the other children.

The seeds of dissatisfaction were sown, though, and when I found out that the nursery had received a 'Satisfactory' rating on its first Ofsted inspection (rather than 'Good' or 'Outstanding'), I decided that Molly should transfer out of there. Once Molly moved to an Ofsted-rated 'Outstanding' nursery she was only bitten once and scratched once in a period of twenty-eight months. She didn't bite anyone. D, who has only ever known the 'Outstanding' nursery, has never been bitten or scratched and has never bitten anyone at nursery. He has bitten his sister at home, though, so it is not as though he is a particularly placid, non-biting child. Although biting and scratching are natural instincts in toddlers, on witnessing how much less this type of aggressive behaviour was occurring at a well-run nursery (more experienced staff, less staff turnover), I am pretty sure that the environment had some impact on the levels of toddler frustration and aggression.

Can't behave, won't behave

I am often asked for the best way of managing aggressive behaviour in children. This is one of parents' biggest challenges, but the 'magic' advice that most seek unfortunately does not exist. Improving your child's behaviour is a long, hard slog. Most Western evidence-based parenting programmes consist of 'behavioural management'. (*The Incredible Years*, 'Triple P Parenting Programme' and TV *Supernanny*'s strategies are all examples of this.)[1] Behavioural management tries to spell out what is and what isn't desirable behaviour and suggest strategies to tip the balance of choice towards the desirable. Well-known strategies include the 'reward chart' for positive behaviour and 'ignoring', 'the naughty step' or 'Time Out' for negative. If you want to read up on behavioural management, an excellent book is *The Incredible Years* by Webster-Stratton, which I have already raved about in the previous chapter. Many of the tips I suggest are from this stable.

Behavioural Management (and Does it Work?)

The answer, in theory, is unequivocally, 'Yes.'

But, alas, so often in practice, 'No.'

This is because behavioural management is easiest to implement when your child is 'typical' and has no other problems, and you (the parent) are brilliant, have no problems and are super-consistent in everything you do, both with your co-parent and with the school. Which basically means 'no', or only 'partially', because how often does such a perfect scenario ever exist?

There are two main reasons why your child may not be 'typical':

1. Neurodevelopmental (brain development) problems

2. Emotional problems.

Back to the brain

Neurodevelopmental problems, and in particular learning difficulty, can heavily impact behaviour. In young children, aggression and temper tantrums are typical responses to frustration, but by school age, some control should have been gained over these. If a child is developmentally delayed, then their ability to behave should be compared to their developmental age rather than their chronological age. A ten-year-old boy with the developmental level of a four-year-old (with speech, reading, writing, numeracy, emotional and social understanding at the level of a four-year-old), can be expected to behave in line with a four-year-old. For a four-year-old, temper tantrums and hitting out are common responses to frustration. But being hit by a ten-year-old boy in a temper tantrum is very different from being hit by a four-year-old. Unfortunately the child 'can't help' responding in this way. These children often become clients in the child mental health services as parenting children with severe learning difficulties can be extremely challenging.

Other neurodevelopmental disorders also cause behavioural problems. Children with attention deficit hyperactivity disorder (ADHD) cannot listen to, or follow, instructions as well as other children. They will tend to act impulsively and without thinking and do things that they regret later. Children on the autistic spectrum may have behavioural problems, as they have difficulty in understanding what is expected of them and their poor social understanding can lead to many frustrations on a daily basis. Standard behavioural management may not work with these groups of children and needs to be adapted to their particular difficulties. In general, it is much harder to implement and has more varied results than in children without neurodevelopmental difficulties. Even within 'typically' developing children, traits such as intelligence, impulsivity and attention are on a spectrum and children with higher intelligence, lower impulsivity and better attention span will tend to be easier to manage. As children grow older, their intelligence, impulsivity and attention span also usually improve, which is why you see fewer teenagers rolling around the floor in the supermarket.

So, how can we assess this in our children?

I will talk about assessing cognitive ability in the next chapter dealing with intelligence, and will focus here on impulsivity and attention span.

Don't touch!

It is very easy to observe a child's impulse control, or largely, lack of it! Most adults are able to control their immediate urge to do something in order to avoid punishment or hold out for a greater reward. For instance, most of us are able to save money in order to buy something expensive, or to wait our turn rather than push into a queue (particularly if we are British). Most toddlers are not able to do this, and if you put a new 'toy' in front of them, they will try and grab it even if you tell them not to. Parents of one- and two-year-olds quickly become dextrous at clearing a big radius around their table when they take their kids out to a restaurant.

Sometime between toddlerdom and adulthood, the ability to control impulses develops and strengthens. The earlier a child develops this impulse control, the better they will be perceived, because they will be less likely to do things such as touch things they shouldn't, shout out in class, push in to queues, interrupt other people and run across the road without looking. People tend to like children more if they don't do these things.

You can easily observe your child's ability to control impulses by taking them into a fancy department store or, if you are more daring, a china shop. Immediately, you will be telling your child not to touch anything. Then see how long they last. If you really want to test them, you can mix it up a bit. Say, 'If you don't touch anything, I'll buy you some chocolate on the way out,' and see if they fare any better, or you can up the ante on the temptation front by taking them to a sweet shop and expecting them not to touch. That would be very cruel indeed!

Cruel, though, is what researchers often are when in the pursuit of answers, and they actually do this test in their labs. They leave a cupcake directly in front of the child, on the promise that they will get two cupcakes as a reward for leaving this one alone and not eating it. As expected, older children find this easier. This test is very easily replicable at home for anyone who wishes to be so mean (or who has plenty of cupcakes to be eaten). Repeated exposure to this type of scenario, where there are clear rewards for waiting a tiny bit longer for something, can help to train your child's impulsivity. The earlier and more frequently children are encouraged to wait, the better they will learn that it is possible. They will learn that they can tolerate the wait, that they can cope with it and that good things often come to those who wait. Once they learn this, they will be better motivated to hold out and control their impulses the next time.

Attention, please!

Children's attention span increases with age. Have you ever felt a mixture of boredom and bewilderment watching *Teletubbies*, when they play their weird tummy tellies and the same video clip is shown on a loop? This is because you (parent, or student on drugs) are not the intended audience. For a littl'un it's fascinating, because their attention span is so short that by the time the clip plays again, they see things that they missed the first time and it seems totally new. An easy way to get an idea of the average attention span of a child at any particular age is to look at school lesson lengths. Educationalists through the years have structured lesson times to try and match the attention span of the children in their class. Thus, in Key Stage One (four- to six-year-olds), activities are likely to change every ten to twenty minutes. By Year Three (seven- to eight-year-olds), lessons will be between twenty and thirty minutes, by Year Six, thirty to forty minutes. At Year Six (ten- to eleven-year-olds), some pupils will be sitting for 11+ exams, which require attention and concentration for up to sixty minutes in an exam setting. By eighteen, A-level students are being treated to the joys of triple maths or triple French, which are a whopping one hundred and twenty minutes each.

You can easily observe your child's attention span by trying to engage them in a task they should enjoy and seeing how long they last. Which of us parents has not spent ages getting out the painting equipment only to find that the child has wandered off after five minutes and we are left painting by ourselves? Next time you do this, time how long your child is actually engaged in the task and then at least you can console yourself if they last a little longer at the next attempt, while you tidy everything up yet again. Ideally, attention span should be tested over a variety of activities, for instance drawing, painting, puzzles, board games and crafts, as well as more academic tasks.

Attention span can be trained. Around the time that D turned one, I read somewhere that children who were regularly read stories from an early age started school ahead of the class. I was already regularly reading to Molly but had not started as early as twelve months with her. Since no one ever tells you exactly when you should start reading to a child, I decided to try it with D. On the first day, it was a disaster. Practically after page one of *Dear Zoo* he was off, despite my attempts to encourage him to sit for longer. I could have just given up and thought, 'He's too young – it's a waste of time at this age,' but for some reason (probably the article that had extolled the benefits of regular reading) I tried again the next day. To my surprise, he lasted two pages! This intrigued me enough to continue and I found that by the end of a week or so, he lasted for the whole book. In effect, his attention had been trained.

During infancy the brain goes through massive growth. Children build circuits and connections in response to their environment at a rapid rate. It is thought that training (by reinforcing particular circuits) at this stage in their development is likely to physically affect their brain development (the interconnections between different parts of the brain) and have a larger impact on them than training at any other time in life. Similarly, we know that at the other end of the lifespan continued mental activity (such as playing chess) can slow the inevitable decline of the brain in old age. Strengthening connections can prevent them from getting lost.

Scientifically, there is growing interest in the idea that attention span and impulse control can be trained. Researchers are now developing attention training computer software to be used as a preventative treatment for children at risk of ADHD. The computer program rewards babies who give sustained attention to a target (such as a picture of a butterfly) by making the butterfly more colourful and interesting the longer the baby looks at it. Repeated exposure to this program encourages and reinforces the brain pathways required to sustain attention, and also links these sustained attention pathways with those for reward.[2] In order to impact brain development to help it deviate away from the ADHD trajectory, the training has to be targeted at babies (less than a year old), whose brains are still plastic and malleable. The BabyLabs at Birkbeck University are trialling just this type of treatment on baby siblings of known patients with ADHD. We may be at the dawn of new preventative programmes for the most common mental health problem in children, which could potentially obviate or reduce the need for the most widely prescribed drugs for children. How great is that?

But why wait for a computer game to be developed to do this when parental interaction is much more fun and rewarding and works on a similar principle? In actuality, many parents are doing this already, instinctively, while interacting with their children in activities – encouraging, supporting and helping their child stay focused to complete something fun, just as I did by reading to D. Now you can confidently start when they are even younger, and continue doing these things with your baby in the smug knowledge that you are not just passing the time, or playing a game, but also potentially improving the physical pathways in your child's brain.

What lies beneath?

Children who are experiencing emotional problems may also have difficulties with their behaviour. Emotions and behaviour are inextricably linked. When we feel down or stressed out, our behaviour changes. Some of us reach for chocolate, some for alcohol, some become withdrawn and unsociable, others irritable and angry. It is important to assess the emotional aspects of your child's life if their behaviour changes or deteriorates. Children may not always volunteer their states of mind to you. They may not be able to label their emotions, or express themselves. They may be afraid to talk about their difficulties. So their unhappiness and frustrations are displayed in their behaviour, instead. It is your responsibility as a parent to notice, to ask, to label these emotions for them, and to give them the words and the permission they need to talk about them. Make an educated guess or do some investigation by asking around teachers and friends if nothing is forthcoming from your child. Maybe they are being bullied at school, maybe they are picking up on the stress in your marriage, maybe they are unsettled by the arrival of a new sibling, or maybe it's something trivial. If you don't notice and/or enquire about it, you won't know what is going on and will see it just as 'bad behaviour' or 'acting out'.

In these cases, behavioural management will not work well. Rewards will feel irrelevant, ignoring and punishment will feel like persecution, negative attention will be better than no attention and rejection will be a confirmation of their own self-loathing. Finding out what is wrong and offering security will work better here. Unattended emotional problems in children can have a long-term negative impact on their personality and encourage the development of 'bad behaviour'. This can become habitual and 'part of' a person's personality that can no longer be easily mended.

I repeat again, as I set out in the previous chapters, getting to the root of your child's behaviour is always the first step in managing it. Always make sure that what lies beneath is sorted first, then you can think about tackling it with simple behavioural techniques.

'My Bad'

In children who have neither brain development issues nor emotional problems, the factors limiting good behaviour are usually down to the parent rather than the child. Here's a list of my 'bads'.

Lack of sustained motivation

In the defining clinical trial for children with ADHD, where they compared medication to behavioural management (The MTA Study), behavioural management achieved equal outcomes compared with medication.[3] But wait, in this study the highly funded behavioural management programme used highly trained psychologists to work with highly motivated parents and teachers to obtain this outcome. Real-life trials, using existing services and patient groups who weren't selected for their motivation, have looked at the efficacy of community parenting and behavioural management programmes and netted unimpressive results. It is not that children's behaviour cannot be managed; it is that the resources of society and parents are insufficient.

I know this all too well. Molly has a weekly spelling test. On the weeks where I've got my act together, we sit down and learn the words and I test her every day so that at the end of the week she gets full marks and I can reward her for this attainment. This is behavioural management in action: co-working towards a set goal that is achievable, achieved and rewarded. This works fantastically well, thumbs up and smiles all around. Only once she has done this for a few weeks, I get complacent and think, 'Well now, maybe I can just give it a rest this week. She and I can both relax a bit and we'll just have a quick look at the words the night before.' Guess what? She makes a couple of mistakes. That's basically my anecdote for behavioural management. It genuinely works until one day you can't be bothered, and it all goes a bit wobbly again. The limiting factor is me, not Molly.

Parental problems

Wobbles also appear in my behavioural management when I am stressed or distracted. One time when I was very stressed, waiting for a phone call regarding a job offer, the children were extremely badly behaved – 'for no reason'. I was snappy and shouted at them and they just wouldn't do what they were told; it was as if they knew exactly when to wind me up. Eventually, the phone call came, and I had got the job. That afternoon, they were extremely well behaved. The change had been in me, not them, and their behaviour was merely reflecting my distracted state of mind and parenting capability.

Expectation

When we talk about 'bad behaviour' we all mean different things. We all have different thresholds as to what constitutes 'bad'. Some friends and relatives come by our house and make 'tutting' sounds when they see our kids glued to the TV, leaving the table at meal times on a whim to dance around the kitchen, helping themselves to the food on the table, whacking each other on the head with cushions and generally shouting at each other and at me. To me, this is not bad behaviour – this is just life in our madcap, shouty household! My kids have perfectly adapted to what is acceptable in their home. Equally, I raise a brow when I see children who never say 'please' or 'thank you', or who run away from their parents on the street. This is behaviour which would not be tolerated in my house, but it doesn't seem to bother other parents in the least.

When parents complain that their children 'will not do as they are told', the severity of the issue rather depends on what they are being told to do. If they will not do sixty minutes of piano practice every night, that is rather different from refusing to stop watching TV, and 'good' and 'bad' behaviour is sooo dependent on the parental and school expectation. A normal child in a school with high behavioural expectations may be deemed to exhibit 'bad behaviour'; a normal child in one culture may be deemed badly behaved in another. The behaviour is relative and in order to assess behaviour properly, it is important to first evaluate whether the expectations are reasonable. There is a limit to how much a child can 'change', and they will not even bother to try if they feel that the bar is being set too high.

Inconsistency

One of the main saboteurs of a good behavioural management programme is 'other people'. Such as the well-intentioned – or not so well-intentioned – other half who disagrees with what you are doing. By not supporting you, they are de facto sabotaging your behavioural management plan because children are such buggers that they can spot disagreement a mile off and work it to their advantage. Much like MPs claiming expenses or benefit fraudsters, they are not averse to trying to get away with as much as they can. Playing one parent off against the other must be a favourite game for children. In my opinion, parents who want to succeed at behavioural management need to get on board together, or not bother at all. A similar situation exists with the school. If children are told one thing at home and another at school, the 'authority' of 'the rules' is undermined. It is a good idea when implementing behavioural management to discuss your plans with the child's school so that the same message is delivered to the child across the board.

TIPS FOR BEHAVIOURAL MANAGEMENT

• **Relationships matter** It's simple: the better the relationship you have with your child, the more likely that they will do what you ask. If your relationship is not great, and your disapproval is insignificant, then your influence on your child's behaviour will be weak. Working on the positives of your relationship with your child, such as love, warmth, self-esteem, fun times and respect, is the first step in behavioural management. The gold standard would be to get to the stage where a saddened look and the words, 'I'm disappointed in you,' are the highest punishment that you need invoke to bring about a positive change in their behaviour. Improving your relationship with your child requires an investment of time. Time spent playing, talking, having fun and getting to know them.

• **Praise him, praise him** I have already extolled the virtues of esteem praise, so now a little on 'functional praise'. Remember that praise works better if you have already established a great relationship, because if your children love and respect you, they will seek your approval and your praise will have more power. Praise can and should be used as a reward for behaviour that you would like to see repeated. It does not need to be reserved for the Nobel Prize. 'Well done for brushing your teeth without a fuss' is more likely to ensure this is done again. An attitude of 'Why should I praise him for doing something he should be doing anyway?' won't increase the likelihood that he will do it again, but praise just might. Praise is one of the main tools in changing behaviour in children.

The most effective way to use praise is to be genuine about it, then to make the praise specific to the achievement. So, 'That's a brilliant picture of me! That really looks like me, and I especially like the way that you did the bags under my eyes!' is always better than, 'Well done.' The former shows that you paid attention to exactly what the child has done, and so the praise sounds more genuine. Crucially, it sets in place exactly which behaviour was good, so that that specific behaviour can be repeated again. If you don't believe this, think how much better you would feel if your boss said, 'Well done, I really liked the professional way that you handled the client's concerns and came up with an innovative solution,' rather than a cursory, 'Well done.' Pre-emptive praise can also be handy in influencing behaviour. If your boss said to you, 'Well done for always being at your desk on time every morning,' what are the chances that you'll rock up late the next morning? Well-timed praise can help reinforce the continuation of positive behaviour. When Molly and D were first trusted with carrying a glass of water alone, I would say, 'Well done for being so careful by carrying that with both hands and not spilling any water!' after they had taken only one step, just to see them through the next ten steps.

- **If at first they don't hear, shout louder** I'm still talking about praise here. Some children find it hard to accept praise. They will reject it and continue to be negative about themselves. 'That picture's really good.' 'No it's not, it's rubbish.' D says this all the time. Rather than stop praising, praise more and praise louder. Some children just need more convincing. Don't give up, because these children, even more than others, need to be convinced.

- **Praising others** The top of the praise tree is to encourage children to praise others. A child who is able to praise others genuinely, graciously, happily and without envy will be given the shrink's 'secure child' sticker. Secure children know that recognizing strengths and abilities in others does not diminish their own abilities. Children who can praise others will win friends and grow warmth. How to encourage this? Praise children that praise other children!

• **Annual bonus** Andrew tells me frequently about bankers who quit their jobs over the size of their annual bonus. It is a fact of life that most people are motivated by rewards, so why deny our children this? Rewards for children can be anything from attention and approval to a yacht and a pony. For the majority of us mere mortals, I suggest operating as much as possible on the attention and approval end of the reward spectrum. For young children praise, attention and smiles will most definitely suffice, although as children grow older, they will inevitably require a more tangible reward. I recommend starting with the cheapest options and stringing these out for as long as possible. Stickers are cheap and effective and will last till around six years old, often longer. If you can't afford stickers, I have often just drawn a picture of a smiley face or star and these have been enough to satisfy young children. The fuss that you make when giving the reward is often more important than the actual token at this age.

Once children fail to be motivated by this, move on to crisps and chocolate buttons. If at other times these are forbidden fruit, you will be surprised how much a child will do for a single prawn skip. Once these rewards die a death, all manner of free 'privileges' can then be used, such as 'fifteen minutes of TV/computer time' or 'a playdate' as a reward. Birthday parties and school discos or anything that your child wants to go to or do (and you had every intention of letting them go to anyway) can be dangled. If more expensive toys are requested, then I suggest that you print out a picture of the object, chop it into bits and offer a bit of the picture each time you reward their good behaviour, only purchasing the object when all the pieces have been collected. For the past twenty weeks, D has been collecting parts of a picture for a

Ninjago LEGO set, earning a piece each week from his piano teacher. He has ten more pieces to collect, and by this means, a twenty-pound LEGO set looks set to ensure good behaviour in piano lessons for the best part of a year, which I would say is a fair deal.

The specific behaviour required in order to gain the reward should be set out clearly. Rather than a generic, 'I'll give you a star if you behave all day', a reward works better if the desired behaviour is meticulously spelled out: 'You'll get a piece of the Ninjago LEGO picture if you listen to your piano teacher and do what he asks for thirty minutes.' The reward should be given straight away, and indeed, D's piano teacher often awards him the picture piece at the end of his lesson. Above all, the target set should be easily achievable for the child on a good day. There is no point offering a reward for the impossible.

- **Ask nicely** OK, we can't always ask nicely. The point is that if we want our children to do something, the instruction should be given calmly and clearly. If your child has difficulty with listening, instructions need to be given one at a time. If the child is not obliging, it is advisable to give two warnings, or 'reminders' of what they should be doing. The second reminder can be annexed with a consequence of what will happen if they do not comply, for example, 'If you do not turn off that TV by the time I count to three, then you will not be able to watch TV tomorrow.' Make sure that if you have issued a consequence you absolutely ALWAYS follow through on it. If your child complies, then make sure they are praised for doing what they were told.

- **Ignore irritations** There is too much stress for parents in life already for us without getting het up about whingeing, whining and foot-stamping. Given that children who do this are not really causing any harm, it's not worth laying down the law over. Rather, protect your blood pressure and learn to ignore such highly irritating but harmless behaviours. When I say 'ignore', I don't mean 'allow'; what I mean is an active withdrawal of attention; the 'getting along with your day as if the other person did not exist' type of ignore. This is in itself highly irritating, especially for children who crave attention, who invariably soon crack after a bit of the 'silent treatment'. As soon as they start to comply, your attention should be given back to them immediately.

•   **Carry out threats** Although we would all love to be 'carrot' rather than 'stick' parents, most parents (the ones that are human rather than droid, or drugged) at some stage will resort to threatening their kids with a loss of privileges to get them to conform. If you do resort to this (and I have done many a time), it is imperative to follow through with it, otherwise your kids will see you for the spineless, empty-threat-making person you are and never do what you ask them to do again. So only make threats that you are willing to follow through on! Once you do this a few times, they will see that the force is with you and comply. Ever since we had to stay indoors on a perfectly lovely day which had been earmarked for the Zoo, not to mention cancel the playdate in the soft play centre, Molly and D know that my threats are good.

•   **Boundary setting** 'Setting boundaries' is one of the most important aspects of raising functional children, and yet the term is bandied around as if we all know what it means. What it means is letting your child know what *is* and what *isn't* acceptable behaviour and enforcing this. My list of unacceptable behaviour consists of 'hitting/scratching/kicking/biting or in any way physically hurting another person' and 'purposely damaging/breaking/potentially damaging something that does not belong to you'. It's good to have a short and succinct list of the unacceptable, because lists that are too long become hard for children to remember. Try to focus on the things that a child would really get into trouble for as an adult. If you put whining on your list of 'unacceptable', you'll be doling out 'consequences' every hour of the day. Transgressions into the unacceptable result in a direct 'Time Out'. This is where the child is transferred to a designated spot to calm down and *The Incredible Years* bible suggests that they remain there for two minutes after they have calmed down. I am quoting from *The Incredible Years* here, because I'm a 'Time Out' flop (*see end of chapter*).

• **Teaching and learning** The goal of behavioural management is not to become a 'Time Out' expert, but to be in a position where 'Time Out' is no longer necessary. Most children exposed to 'Time Out' that is delivered correctly and consistently will soon get the idea that breaking rules is futile and 'Time Out' is a bore. We can help children to come to this conclusion more quickly and help them find better ways of letting off steam or getting what they want through role-modelling and teaching them problem-solving, as discussed in Chapter Four.

• **Independence day** If your children are taught how to get themselves a cup of water, they need never bother you or whine about wanting a drink again. Much of children's frustration is due to not having direct access to their desires and needs. Upskilling a child in independence prevents future frustration. In addition, it is worth teaching them about 'natural consequences' – for example: if you do not put your dirty clothes in the laundry basket then they will not get washed; if you smash up a toy then it will not be replaced; if you break something that does not belong to you then your pocket money will be used to pay for it to be repaired; if you do not eat your lunch then you will go hungry until dinner. As children approach Key Stage Two, parents need to start backing off from doing everything for them and allow them to see what happens as a result of these natural consequences. This is all part of gaining independence, and its flipside, responsibility.

• **Keep calm and carry on** Managing children's behaviour is no walk in the park. Personally I find managing a clinical team of doctors and psychologists in an underfunded NHS way easier and far less stressful. Still, try to remain positive and keep going. Enlist family and friends to help so you get a break from time to time, and remember that tomorrow always begins as a new day with no mistakes.

Spare the Rod
(and You *Won't* Spoil the Child)

OK, so I have talked about boundary setting: how to let your child know what *is* and *isn't* acceptable behaviour and how to enforce this; but when it comes to the practical application of this, the 'enforcing' part can get rather shady. Before I had kids, I told people to 'set boundaries' all the time, but I didn't have a clue how to actually do it myself! I thought that I would be able to just tell my children what the boundaries were and they would say, 'Great idea, Mum, I'll do that from now on.' How little I knew. One of the reasons for this ignorance is the lack of open conversation about this aspect of parenting: disciplining.

Programmes like *Supernanny* are great because they bring behavioural management and discipline techniques into the mainstream, but their entertainment value lies largely in the opportunity for middle-class parents to feel smug in their belief that they do not have children with such extreme behavioural problems, and therefore have no need for the attendance of Supernanny. Whilst parents of children with severe problems are often desperate to seek help and advice and are happy to talk about their problems, the rest of us often clam up when it comes to the subject of discipline, lest we be judged 'bad parents'. The problem then becomes compounded, as without peer reflection on what is and isn't appropriate, and without the support and advice of our friends, we are left to our own devices to muddle through. Often we feel isolated in our ineptitude, and a need to pretend that our children never misbehave, or that we never lose our rag.

This is a fairly new phenomenon as up until recently, physical discipline was widely accepted. The majority of my generation were probably hit at some stage by our parents. There is even a story of a wooden spoon being broken on the backside of my brother-in-law. Children used to be caned at school, pulled by the ears and made to stand in the corner wearing a dunce's hat. These days smacking, and indeed any form of physical punishment, is most definitely not recommended. Firstly, it is not particularly effective as a means of long-term boundary setting; secondly, it may instil fear and aggression in your child; thirdly, it may have the unwanted consequence of teaching them that 'might is right'. As a child psychiatrist, I was determined that there would be no physical disciplining in our household. That said, have I ever *felt like* hitting Molly and taking D over my knee for a good smack of the bottom? Hell, yes. And these are really good kids.

However educated, civilized, gentle and kind you are, I don't think anything ever prepares you for the incessant whingeing, nagging, wailing, and general annoying-ness that a child in full tantrum can exhibit. Pair this with the expectation that parents are responsible for presenting children to school on time, fully-clothed, fully-fed and with well-scrubbed teeth and you have a recipe for extremely stretched nerves. If you are lucky enough to have a placid child, good for you, but not all children are temperamentally like this. I totally take back all the furrowed brows and superior looks I used to give to parents in my clinic when they admitted using smacking to discipline their children. I now totally understand their sentiment. Still, the fact remains that smacking is not a good option for boundary setting, and in child psychiatry clinics it is good practice to keep records of families using physical discipline, as a proportion go on to overuse it, which constitutes physical abuse.

How, then, do you set boundaries? I'm not pulling any surprises here, just repeating the programme that Professor Stephen Scott's National Parenting Academy clinic at the renowned Maudsley Hospital favours: *The Incredible Years*. Stephen's clinics are great fun to observe, because techniques are taught to parents in vivo. We, 'the learned Professionals', sit behind a one-way mirror and observe the interactions between parent and child playing in the next room. The parent wears a bug in his ear, into which we issue live parenting instructions: 'Say: "Well done, for helping me tidy up" '; 'Pick him up and put him back on the chair'; 'Look him in the face and smile now'; 'Give him a cuddle now.' By subtly manipulating parenting, the differences made in children's behaviour and family stress are incredible. If you want to know more about behavioural management please buy/beg/steal/borrow *The Incredible Years* by Carolyn Webster-Stratton. There is no secret formula and much of what she describes is also used by Jo Frost (*Supernanny*) and other behavioural management programmes. I have read *The Incredible Years* cover to cover and it's good common sense. That said, even armed with clinical experience, an array of books and 'expert knowledge' there can still be implementation problems, even for shrinks . . . Here is my account of my less-than-optimal use of 'Time Out', one major method of boundary setting:

'Time Out' (and how not to do it)

From around three years of age, Molly was introduced to the 'naughty mat', the designated place for 'Time Out' (in our case, a cheap circular bit of carpet from IKEA). Many experts do not recommend you call it 'naughty' but rather a 'calm-down' or 'thinking' mat, but somehow 'naughty' still caught on in my house (failure number one). It is probably not ideal to use a common brand of household accessory as the 'naughty mat' either, lest you wish your child to enter someone else's home and declare, 'Oh look, they have a naughty mat too', as happened with Molly.

The idea of the mat or other designated place is that if the child breaks a set boundary (such as hitting), they should be taken to the naughty mat to calm down. Molly got the idea pretty quickly after being taken there once or twice. There was some initial fuss but in general it worked like clockwork. Sometimes when she was naughty, threatening her with the naughty mat was enough to stop the behaviour, and once or twice when she had been naughty, she actually walked there and sat herself down (success number one). The best thing about the naughty mat was that it allowed *me* to calm down as well. Sometimes, caught up in the fury of the situation, you also need a minute's peace to calm down, collect your thoughts and think about how to manage the situation more calmly. So the child is supposed to sit there either for a few minutes, or until they are 'calm and quiet', although the description in our case would more accurately be 'till they stop wailing like a banshee'. Many a time it was very calming for me to know that I could get on with the washing up or laundry without disturbance, as often this wailing would go on for some time.

The naughty mat was such a success that when D came of 'naughty mat' age, he also started out using it without a problem. The first few times he was told to go, he literally ran there and sat bolt upright with a big smile on his face, delighted to be grown up enough to finally 'be allowed' to sit where he had seen his big sister so often.

The one where you resort to desperate measures . . .

Unfortunately, that's not the end of the story – some time around the age of five, Molly began to tire of the naughty mat, and realize that she could fight back. She was now significantly bigger and stronger, so fighting back was becoming an effective strategy. Here on in, she would stray from the naughty mat and follow me around the house stamping, wailing and hitting. Thus not only was she not on the mat, but I was unable to get enough peace to calm down. Each time I took her back to the naughty mat (as per protocol) I became more and more physical in response to her increased kicking, pushing and physical resistance. This started to feel very uncomfortable. Most experts do not recommend physical restraint to get children into 'Time Out' (failure number two).

To avoid this man-handling, I changed my strategy. After sending her to the naughty mat I would start going into her bedroom. Molly would then follow me, at which point I would quickly run out and slam shut the door, thereby trapping her in her room. Generally, using a child's bedroom as the 'thinking place' is not recommended because the bedroom is an interesting and stimulating place (failure number three). Interestingly, when Molly was in this situation she never went off to play with the myriad toys in her room. Instead, without fail, she would try to leave the room in order to follow me around, still hitting and wailing. This happened a few times.

Now, most of the suggested techniques do not mention 'locking' children in a room when they are sent to one. However, I am unsure how else a parent can get their child to stay in there. Presumably if the door was not locked, the kid would just walk out. In any case, none of our interior doors have locks, so this was not even an option. Initially, I stood on the other side of the door, holding it shut. However, as I mentioned, it can take Molly up to forty-five minutes to 'calm down' and standing holding a door shut whilst a raging child does their utmost to huff and puff it down can get pretty tiresome. I therefore came upon the ingenious idea of tying her bedroom doorknob to the bannister with a dressing gown cord, thus preventing it from opening more than a crack. I sat next to the door, periodically repeating calmly (as per protocol), 'You can come out as soon as you stop crying'; boring, but at least I got to sit next to the door and read a magazine in the interim (success number two). I was dubious as to whether the experts would actually recommend this strategy. It reminded me of having to put violent patients into 'seclusion' – basically a padded cell to calm down – when I worked in adult mental health wards. Here, staff need to stand right next to the door and do regular observations on the patient until they calm down. This felt very much like what I was doing with my kids . . . I wasn't sure if this was a good thing and wasn't sure who to ask. The occasion never arose to ask other school-run mums if they were tying their children into their rooms using a dressing gown cord.

Anyway, this strategy was quickly abandoned when it dawned on me that all the things experts such as Carolyn Webster-Stratton highlighted as being negatives for physical discipline also applied to incarceration by whatever means. Two incidents led me quickly to this conclusion, despite it having been effective while it lasted. 1) D, on encountering this situation for the first time, shouted from behind the door 'When I am big, I am going to lock you in your room!' This sent shudders down my spine, with visions of my elderly self being subject to elder abuse by my traumatized son, now twice as big as me. 2) Molly grabbing my dressing gown cord and saying she was going to tie D into their room because he had been naughty towards her (failure number four).

After this, I adopted an ignoring and self-incarceration technique (not detailed in behavioural management manuals). Given that the children were too strong to be taken to the naughty mat and incarcerating them clearly was not working, I took to barricading myself into the toilet to escape being hit. I am fortunate that my children do not destroy property so this was a fairly safe option. However, rather than feel like a cowed victim being chased by my kids into the toilet, I would walk there calmly, grabbing a magazine on the way, and have a good catch up on the fashion pages while they howled and hit away at the door. 'I am not coming out until you stop crying . . .'

I am still not sure what the experts would make of this.

The only blessing I have found is that child development and brain maturity at some point clicks in. That, and to some extent (I hope) my ongoing work on the core layers of self-esteem, social skills, emotional understanding and independence. Molly has now graduated to slamming doors and going to sob dramatically on her own bed. She very rarely has tantrums now and never hits me anymore. When I reminded her of her past tantrums and asked her why she stopped, she said, 'I just grew tired of them and they didn't get me what I wanted anyway.'

D, on the other hand, tended not to have long tantrums or hit out and he never required me to barricade myself in the toilet. When put in his room, he quickly realized that this was a good opportunity to read that book or play with that set of LEGO and would calm down within five or ten minutes, re-emerging sensibly and apologetically. I mention this disparity in particular to highlight that our parenting is to some extent shaped by our children.

Had I only had D, I might have swanned around the place pro-claiming my expertise at behavioural management when in actuality I was just blessed with a genetically unaggressive child.

Many parents who resort to physical disciplining have chil-dren who are more aggressive and difficult to manage. The causality is bi-directional – it works both ways – so it is unfair to judge too harshly parents who use a tougher disciplining style. Whilst I love my children, have a negative view towards harsh punishment and would regard myself as not particularly aggres-sive, even I resorted to incarceration as a punishment for Molly. However, without a doubt aggression begets aggression. Setting up a vicious cycle whereby aggressive child evokes aggressive disciplining, which perpetuates more aggression in the child is not a winning formula for parent or child. At some point the adult needs to recognize this, behave like the adult they are and plan a better way forward. Usually this involves working further on the core of the child: their self-esteem, social skills and emotional understanding.

Our IKEA mat, long outgrown, has now gone into the skip. I am much relieved, although I am sure there will be worse chal-lenges to come and that one day I will be yearning for the days of dealing with tantrums with a simple naughty mat, rather than whatever my teenagers will be getting up to in the future.

Chapter Summary

Difficult behaviour may be the manifestation of developmental problems, poor self-esteem, ineffective communication skills and/or emotional problems. For these children, behavioural management involving punishment ('Time Out'/removal of a privilege) may not work. A focus on improving the inner layers of these children (their self-esteem, communication and emotional understanding), and incentivizing (rewarding) pro-social behaviour will yield better results.

If these problems are excluded, behavioural management delivered consistently and well will definitely improve your child's behaviour. However it is by no means a magic wand. It will take hard toil, stamina, guts, persistence and tears. The good news is that you will be rewarded with balanced, likeable human beings. As parents, none of us is perfect and I am hoping that by putting my flawed account out there others will feel more able to talk about their own experiences of disciplining. I think it is a really tricky territory to get right and there is not enough discussion out there on the subject. Parents often fear being judged a 'bad parent' by others. I think we should all be a bit braver in talking about our difficulties. In doing so, we can constantly question ourselves: 'Is it OK?', 'What can I do differently next time?' and maintain a willingness to keep thinking about the problem, changing tack if required, asking for advice and learning by our mistakes. If we do all this, at least we can say that we are 'doing our best'; which at the end of the day is all that can be expected.

SKIN

6. Layer Four: Intelligence

Why Tiger Parents Are Not All Bad (But Tigger Mums Are Better)

The Subtle Hum of the Tigger Mum

Tiger parenting is the bane of my life. For those who have not read the book that coined the phrase, Amy Chua's *The Battle Hymn of the Tiger Mother* recounts the strict disciplinarian parenting style and relentless focus on academic and musical achievement of a Chinese parent.[1] If Molly plays a piano recital well, I have to wither away rather than swell with pride, as I face the arched eyebrows of other parents, knowing they are thinking, 'Ooh, but her mother must make her practise for hours every night.' When word got out that D was reading chapter books in Reception, I wanted to duck for cover from the playground mutterings of 'typical Chinese pushy parent'. If ever I want to ask the teacher a question relating to how well my kids are getting along at school, I have to cajole Andrew to ask, as he is not Chinese and therefore able to ask these things without prejudice.

It all gets rather tiring.

Amongst Western parents, tiger parenting has started to get a bad rep; calling someone a 'tiger parent' has become an insult. For people brought up in the Far East, it's different; tiger parenting is the norm. I'm not saying it's normal to timetable your children's free time so that they work all day and collapse exhausted at night, or to emotionally blackmail them into four hours of piano practice a day, but the tiger parent ethos of heavy involvement in their child's education and emphasis on scholastic achievement is part and parcel of Chinese, and many other, cultures.

In reality, I don't think that this is so far removed from Western values. There are many Western parents who 'expect' their children to achieve; the difference is that they often 'expect' their child's school (particularly if it is fee-paying) to deliver on this, rather than get personally involved. To this end, if Johnny does not get into 'the best school/university', the teachers can expect a parental rant, whilst for the Chinese parent, either the child would have delivered on the expectation (due to the parents' support) or the parents would be the ones feeling like complete failures and blaming no one more than themselves. Chinese parents find the Western attitude of abdicating responsibility for education to the schools rather strange. For them the school (however good), is only one arm of the education battery, not its entirety.

Chinese parents take their child's education seriously. This usually involves extra work at home, lots of educational outings and plenty of educational conversation (from full answers to any questions asked, to grilling of times tables, to 'What's the capital city of . . . ?' games). Often this interest manifests as an extreme nosiness concerning their child's academic performance in relation to other children (whereupon, if there is a hint of not keeping up, efforts are redoubled). When test scores come back less than perfect, there is a focus on the mistakes made rather than the correct answers given, not necessarily because anything less than perfection is acceptable, but because the parent is trying to understand where the child requires additional help so that they can provide it. All this is, quite frankly, a lot of hard work, but a Chinese parent will feel a failure if they do not do this (to a greater or lesser degree) because it's practically in their blood.

Understanding these cultural differences

Understanding where this parental drive comes from is important, because it is a classic case of Darwinian adaptation to environment – survival of the fittest at its purest. Historically in the East, as was the case in Jane Austen's England, the future of your family (and therefore your situation in old age) was dependent on securing either a good job for your son or an advantageous marriage for your daughter. In the West, where these advantages were achieved mainly by birthright, children were encouraged to look down on lower social classes and indoctrinated to sit up straight, know their soup spoons from their dessert spoons and make genteel conversation lest Mr Darcy be in the vicinity. In other societies, where attainment has been valued more than class, where a peasant with a Ph.D. is better regarded than a banker's son without one, having academically accomplished children has become an economic investment.

Generations of positive selection for successful 'tiger mothers' has led to a society where tiger parenting is now the norm. Interestingly though, now that the job market is becoming more global and our children are up against worldwide competition, who your parents are, or which school you went to, has started to pale into insignificance compared with obtaining a good university degree – even in the UK. And I am starting to witness more and more British tiger parents emerging. For example, in my children's Mandarin class (where I sent them to get in touch with their cultural identity), half the children in the class were European, sent to learn Mandarin before they were four in order to give them a 'competitive edge' in the future jobs market. My children have since given up Mandarin and so these European children are likely to speak Mandarin better than many British Chinese. There are also plenty of stories of parents camping out overnight to be the first in line to obtain application forms for those sought-after academic schools or gymnastics classes. So I think it's fair to say that tiger parenting is definitely alive and kicking in the UK, and not just amongst the Chinese population.

My view is that achievement is important. Achievement, by which I mean your child 'developing to the fullest' and 'achieving *their* potential', is a ratified right in the UN Convention on the Rights of the Child (alongside the right to healthcare and education). Furthermore, encouraging a sound work ethic in children in order to obtain that achievement is not a crime. To this end, then, I fully put my hands up to being a tiger mother. I am deeply involved in my children's academic performance. Do I check my children's homework? Do I stress the importance of getting all their spellings right? Do I make them do ten to twenty minutes of a workbook each day on top of work set by the school (exact amount of time being age-dependent)? Do I supervise their reading every day? Do I coerce them to practise piano for ten to twenty minutes at least four times a week? Do I insist (with varying success) that this continues in the holidays? Do I express disappointment if I do not think they have really tried? Do my children think that my favourite hobby is doing workbooks with them? Do I pack a 'Make your own volcano kit' in our suitcase for a holiday to Sicily, because I know we will be going up Mount Etna and I want to explain how it works to the kids? When I go to the children's school, do I scrutinize the work of other children in the class and compare it to that of my own kids?

Yup.

In the past, this would definitely have been seen as the mark of a tiger parent. Nowadays, it's becoming the new norm. Parents of all nationalities seek to emulate the 'success' of tiger parents. Overall, I think it's a good thing that parents get more involved in their children's education. But I do think that some parents (and not all of them are Chinese) need reminding that scholastic achievement is not the be-all and end-all for success. The layers inside your child that I have already highlighted in the previous chapters are by far the most important. This opinion was borne out to some extent when I heard that in the UK the Chinese population outperform other ethnicities in school exam grades, yet continue to underperform in terms of employment thereafter, when you take into account their academic qualifications.

All work and no play makes Jack a dull boy

In 2011, the *Guardian* issued a report on the findings of the Equality and Human Rights Commission, which stated, 'British Chinese youngsters are the highest performing ethnic group in England at GCSE', and, 'British Chinese men and women were twice as likely to be in professional jobs as their white British counterparts. But average earnings remained around 11 per cent lower throughout the population than for those classed as "white Christian"'[2]. I would argue that the employment underperformance of the British Chinese is in large part due to the fact that during their critical period of development (childhood) they had to focus too much on academic attainment, at the cost of their interpersonal skills. Playdates, parties, drama club, debating teams, sports teams and the like afford children regular opportunities to practise their social skills. What better way to learn the diplomacy and politics of the boardroom than those years in the locker room? Whilst attainment alone will to a large extent get you into a top university, it is interpersonal skill and political savvy that will get you into the Western boardroom.

Furthermore, there is a cultural focus on respect for elders, authority and hierarchy which is indoctrinated in strict Chinese homes. Compliance and submission to a tiger parent's regime are expected to a degree that seems to inhibit the qualities that are often rewarded in the Western workplace: creativity, free-thinking, the challenging of norms, stepping outside the chain of command. I know quite a few Chinese people with impeccable grades who failed to get into the best universities or to attain the most prestigious jobs because they just couldn't get through *that interview* or obtain *that reference*, where their social skills, rather than their technical ability, were being tested. Just as women struggle to get to the top because they are excluded from the golf, squash and lap-dancing clubs that provide fodder for the banter in the pub, it can't help if you are not even invited to the pub in the first place.

So it seems as if 'intelligence', 'academic achievement' and 'success' are not synonymous. Intelligence is significantly genetically influenced while academic achievement is significantly modified by hard work. Hard-working children of average intelligence can achieve more academically than lazy, intelligent children. Unless you believe that Chinese people are intellectually superior (which I don't), you must subscribe to the notion that on average they work harder, given that they typically outperform other racial groups in standardized exams in the West. It is this belief that has propelled scores of non-Chinese parents to emulate the Chinese work ethic, thereby further fuelling the current generation of hot-housed kids. Conversely, we also hear stories of children being prepped by teachers and tutors to succeed academically, who then revert to being intellectually useless once the spoon-feeding stops. This has led to protests from universities and employers about the meaninglessness of examination score cards. Intelligence and academic achievement are not always the same thing.

Being perceived as successful is different again. Premier League footballers are amongst the most successful people in the world, yet few admire them for their intelligence or academic achievement. Sir Richard Branson and Lord Sugar's successes lay not with academic achievement, but with natural intelligence coupled with the critical internal layers I have already described: self-esteem, sociability, determination, emotional strength. I will say it again: high grades and academic achievement are not the be-all and end-all when it comes to success.

Furthermore, although 'success' is paramount to the tiger parent, this is often measured purely in terms of academic or financial success. What of 'happiness', my preferred measure of success? In psychiatry you have the rare position of seeing the mess that lies behind the veneer of many a successful person, and you soon realize that 'happiness' or 'contentment' is a much better yardstick of personal success. Of course, achievement and money contribute to 'happiness', but self-esteem, integrity and a robust personality will always take precedence. For me, before the workbooks and the volcano-making kits, my attention was directed to giving my children affection and fun. Not only will this make them stronger, but I know that with their secure base I am able to push them harder in school. To this end, I aspire to be a Tigger mother. A tiger none-the-less, who remains fanatical about involvement in her children's education and achievement, but one who is optimistic, cuddly, not too serious, and full of fun (although probably, like Tigger, quite a bit annoying).

But what's it all for?

Competitive school psychosis? Take a chill pill

There are few subjects that divide parents as much as the type of education they decide for their children. This is not helped by the British school system being so multi-tiered. No one-size-fits-all Scandinavian model here, but public schools, private schools, grammar schools, faith schools, free schools, comprehensives, even home schooling. And even then, many parents have no real choice in the matter, but are dependent on the quality of their local school for their children's academic success. It's no surprise that many people would like to give their child a bit of a leg-up when it comes to education, but the way some parents get exercised about it almost borders on madness. I have seen many in tears – in my opinion, so not worth it.

Where I live, there is assessment fever for 4+ and 7+ entry into prep schools, to the extent that three-year-olds are invited to 'play-dates' to practise cutting paper and doing worksheets with each other (I kid you not). But for most of the country assessment-mania is targeted at the 11+ entrance exams. These are exams that determine entry to the academically selective schools which tend to deliver the best exam grades and therefore more students into Oxbridge. This arbitrary educational barrier is enough to turn the gentlest quinoa-eating, yoga-hippy parent into a crazed, time-tabling psychopath. In my neck of the woods, the transition from sane to psycho starts to surface at around about the end of Year Three. Even the parents who have previously protested against any homework whatsoever, endlessly repeating their 'let children be children' mantras, suddenly become rather quieter as they haul in their army of tutors.

The feeling I got from playground chatter appeared to be that it is substantially harder to get your children into a decent secondary school these days than at any other time in history. However, I am sure most generations felt like this (just as every generation of teenagers feel like they invented sex). Parents justify their anxieties by equating them with current concerns (which can be realistic – it's down to the baby boom – or steeped in prejudice – 'tiger parented' immigrants are taking all the best places). I've heard some crazy notions, such as if you are sending your child to a state primary school, you have 'no chance' of getting into a selective grammar or independent school, unless they are receiving private tuition from at least the beginning of Year Four. Or that you need to have their name down with the best tutors from Year One, because elite tutors (the only ones who can guarantee your child any future success) all have mile-long waiting lists. I have even heard it mooted that children really should have tuition from *Reception Class*. This is the madness that pervades the air (at least in London) at the moment. And if you cannot afford private tuition, then you should, at the very least, be taking them to Kumon (for the uninitiated, this is an after-school maths club).

Maybe if your child is not academically excellent, you could try and sneak them into an outstanding secondary school by way of a music scholarship, in which case, investment into private music lessons would have been a requirement from well before Year Four, because to audition for a music scholarship at a prestigious school can require a distinction at Grade Five. I mean, seriously? Someone's got to say enough already!

All in all, one wonders about the truth of these rumours. Maybe it's all a big ruse to boost the nation's economy and employment levels by increasing consumer spending on 'must have' educational add-ons. More worryingly, if this is the case, then where does it leave all the children from less well-off families who are unable to afford extra tuition and music lessons? Molly is not quite old enough for me to have to face these dilemmas yet, so I am currently holding a position of scepticism, believing that none of this panic is required. It may be ignorance for which I will pay later, but my faith in the notion that most kids (including 'bright' ones) will end up where they should be, regardless of tutoring, is based partly on my own experience of the system and partly on science.

How it happened in the eighties

My sisters and I attended a local state primary school in Wales. This school had not been checked out beforehand by my parents and was one of those state primaries where Year Three were charged ten pence to watch the Year Sixes snog each other in the playground. My mother taught us maths after school every day. Since she could not speak English, she did not teach us English but attempted in vain to teach us Chinese. Both my parents encouraged us to read in English and took us to the library to borrow books every Saturday. They also encouraged us to write stories and poems in English, which were all fantastic, given that my parents couldn't read them.

When I was eight years old, my parents moved to London where both my mother and father had found employment. Our financial circumstances improved, but my mother was now working full-time at a Taiwanese company, so we no longer had her additional educational input outside of school, although there was still constant encouragement and an expectation of us to work hard and achieve. At the time we moved, my eldest sister was at that important secondary transition stage. Contrary to the at-length planning of most parents these days regarding secondary transfer, my parents, uninitiated in 'the system', took a 'pitch up and see' attitude. My eldest sister was enrolled into the local comprehensive as my parents could not afford private school and she had missed all the entrance exam dates and procedures for the grammar school. Here she whiled away many a happy lesson making wooden pencil cases and large clay sculptures of birds of prey, whilst effortlessly coming top in every academic subject. My second sister and I were sent to the local primary, which to this day remains happily at the bottom end of the primary school league tables. We spent many lessons relearning how to read and write English with the largely 'first language not English' class.

In contrast to the current parental angst over school decisions, my parents took the oft-forgotten-in-current-times view that if it all went a bit 'Pete Tong', we could always change schools. Within the year, both my older sisters had passed entrance exams to the local grammar school, one at common entrance, and the other for Year Eight entry because a free place had come up. I was transferred out of the local state primary to another state primary in the more distant, but much wealthier suburb next door. How? My parents just applied. Children leave good schools all the time for all sorts of reasons and if you play the waiting game, chances are you'll get a place without the hassle of making out that you live on the school's doorstep at common entrance. You might think from the hype that this would be impossible nowadays but despite openly atheist, or non-Christian parents regularly attending Anglican church services for years, or renting two-bedroom flats on the doorstep of the local 'outstanding' state school, there are often places going spare in the older classes. Wait a year or two and you can probably get your child in wherever you want.

It was my parents' intention that I should follow in my sisters' footsteps to the local grammar school. Their utter naivety of the education system meant that they saw this as a foregone conclusion. It didn't occur to them to get me a tutor, or arrange music lessons, or even order up some past papers; they couldn't have afforded to do these things even if it had. I remember being called out of class one day by my school's head of secondary transfer, who was shaking a yellow form at me, saying, 'Your parents have put down a highly selective school as the *only* option on your secondary transfer form! What if you don't get in? They must put down alternative options!' To which my genuine response was, 'But they've already bought my school uniform.' I had no idea that entrance heavily depended on my performance, it was just a FACT that this was the school I was going to and I just had to go and sit an exam and attend an interview to formalize the process. Thinking back, this is probably not the best strategy for parents to adopt, as it would have hit me hard if I had not followed my sisters into that school, but my parents trusted that I was bright and were blissfully ignorant of the fierce competition. One positive consequence, though, was that I felt under no pressure whatsoever.

I nearly did blow my chances of going to the grammar school 'for Young Ladies', as it was then called. In those days, following the Maths and English paper, you were subjected to an interview with the headmistress. She was exactly the kind of headmistress one would imagine for a school purporting to educate 'Young Ladies'. An upper-class lady with portly stature, and portentous demeanour, she was all blue rinse and pearls. I had to describe a painting by Braque that was presented to me on a postcard. I had to read aloud a passage of written text about rainfall. It contained the word 'percolate'. Here the headmistress requested a definition and I was at a loss. Trying to garner as much information as I could from the surrounding text, I may have offered a paltry and clearly wrong definition, or frankly confessed to not knowing. No matter, the headmistress took it upon herself to educate me on the meaning of the word 'percolate'. 'You know, when you make coffee, you must let the water filter through the spaces between the coffee grounds to get the flavour. You have made coffee before haven't you?' 'Yes,' I said. 'I put a spoon of the granules into the cup, add hot water and stir. Is that what percolate means?' I like to think that my old headmistress was bored of being shown the Grade 5 cello certificates, gymnastics gold medals and Houses of Parliament crafted from toothpicks and it was a novelty for me to turn up, pretty much saying, 'I don't really do anything extra-curricular, but I'm good at maths and I make a mean Nescafe.' Whatever the case, I was in.

The moral? Have faith that the school that is right for your child will appreciate who they are, just the way they are.

The Science of Intelligence

Intelligence can be defined as 'the ability to reason, plan, solve problems, think abstractly, comprehend complex ideas, learn quickly and learn from experience'.[3] The majority of research bases 'intelligence' on performance in standardized IQ tests, so when I refer to intelligence in this chapter, this is what I am refer-ring to, as opposed to the ability to be 'streetwise', 'sensible' or 'emotionally intelligent', which are also great qualities to have. Standardized IQ tests are generally not very accurate at measur-ing intelligence before the age of six, but as children get older they become more and more accurate and are quite stable in adulthood.

I am lucky enough to have co-authored a paper with Professor Robert Plomin, one of the world leaders in intelligence research. He and other great researchers have been studying intelligence not only because of its association with academic achievement and success, but because it is linked to many other positive out-comes, including your future occupation and even your health (intelligent people live longer; if you don't believe me, google the Darwin awards – given to people who die from their own stupidity). For decades geneticists have been studying twins to understand the genetics of intelligence. More recently, with their newly developed ability to genotype all the genes in any individ-ual, geneticists no longer need rely on data from twins but can compare the genes of anybody. This has meant that researchers have been in 'big data heaven', wallowing in thousands, nay millions of gene sequences to study, with techniques such as Genome-wide Complex Trait Analysis. The first studies using these new techniques support the evidence found from twin studies:

1. Intelligence is inherited; it is more heritable than any other personality trait. Intelligence is determined by many multiple genes acting together, each with small effect, but together with large effect (think of the number balls in the national lottery, each valueless alone, but worth a great deal if found in the correct combination).

2. Intelligence genes are generalist genes.[4] Thus the as-yet-unidentified handful of genes that underpin intelligence are not specific; that is, there aren't three genes for maths, three genes for languages, three genes for memory, but a bunch of genes for 'intelligence' as described above.

3. Changes in IQ are mainly driven by environment but the influence of environment wanes over time.[5] Conversely, intelligence genes are stable over time; children are born with these genes and they act throughout their lifespan. As the influence of their environment wanes over time, the effects of their intelligence genes are amplified. Genetic contribution to intelligence has been found to be approximately 20 per cent in infancy, 40 per cent in adolescence and 60 to 80 per cent in adulthood. Or put another way, environmental factors (socio-economic status, school and so forth) become less important in predicting intelligence in adulthood (when IQ tests are also at their most accurate and stable).

How this is relevant for parents

Two clever parents are statistically more likely to have an intelligent child than two less intelligent parents. If you desire an intelligent child, your best chance is to be intelligent yourself and seek an intelligent spouse. If you want even more assurance, you should ensure that your own and your spouse's entire family and extended family are intelligent, thereby ensuring that the entirety of their and your genetic stock is laden with only intelligent genes. I hope that no one in reality is such a cynic, but assortative mating (*as discussed in Chapter One*) is frequently at work in choosing a partner and research finds that 'intelligence' is one of the most highly matched traits in spouses (more than height, weight and personality).[6]

I was really interested in the discovery of generalist genes for intelligence. Firstly, it concurred with my own observation from Cambridge that the majority of 'clever' people were good at everything else. Infuriating as it was, I was awed to find that the Cambridge Geography student was also a music prodigy, and a brilliant watercolour painter. That the English student who directed movies had an A in A-level Maths and Physics. That fellow medical students were writing and performing in Footlights plays. Secondly, it concurred with my clinical experience of IQ tests where there is typically consistency between verbal and non-verbal components of the test (some children will have a skewed and varied profile, but these are the exceptions, not the norm). The implications of the generalist genes are important because I have met many verbally intelligent adults who define themselves as 'not a maths person', when in fact the genetic findings suggest that for the majority, if a person is intelligent, they will have had equal potential across the board in maths/languages/literacy and that it is *environment* (parents and schools) rather than genes that has dictated that they have become 'not a maths person'. You will see later on in this chapter that I have a bee in my bonnet about this!

The implications of the fact that by adulthood intelligence is largely genetically determined can be interpreted in different ways depending on whether you are a tiger parent or not. If you are a tiger parent, rather than seeing the 80 per cent genetic influence at adulthood, your eyes will have leapt to the 20 per cent at infancy and the 40 per cent at adolescence. In the mind of any tiger parent it's obvious that there is an 80 per cent of 'environmentally aided' intelligence to play for at four years old, and 60 per cent to play for at the 11+ and university entrance. Herein lie the woes of university departments and employers faced with strangely average, hot-housed students and employees who were taken on for their exemplary academic grades. A tiger parent can absolutely aid and abet their children into the best institutions. If the not insignificant social signifier of a world-class university is important to you, go right ahead and push your child in there. Be wary, though, in case your child is not emotionally robust enough to handle it when their not-so-impressive genetic intelligence is outed. On the other hand, if tiger parenting is not for you, it should serve as a relief that no matter how much you cock up in parenting and school choice, intelligence, if it is in there, will prevail. My father's life story, as described earlier in the book, can attest to that.

Cutting the booze may reduce tutor fees

Before we stop with the science, I must add that whilst I've harped on about schooling and parenting as environmental contributors to intelligence, these are essentially fine-tuning. Their effects are trivial compared to the biggest environmental influences on intelligence which happen in pregnancy and early infancy. Any biological insult (such as alcohol exposure, viral infection, maternal stress hormones, traumatic birth or seizures) that happens in pregnancy, birth and early infancy, while the brain is still developing, can have effects that range from minimal to devastating on your child's intelligence. Foetal alcohol syndrome and its milder spectrum is the world's leading cause of intellectual disability, something that is wholly down to alcohol exposure in pregnancy. Before women are solely blamed for this predicament, I should add that sperm formed in alcohol-soaked testicles are also implicated. Birth trauma and severe epileptic seizures in infancy can also cause lasting damage to the developing brain, leading to a decline in intelligence whatever the genetic potential. This is because the human brain is born plastic and continues to develop following birth, particularly in the first year of life, only slowing down somewhat by the age of six. Any insult during this time of active brain development may have subtle or severe effects that could affect your child's function over a lifetime. Protecting your child's brain in pregnancy, birth and infancy will probably be worth more than many hours of costly private tuition later down the line. Of course, unfortunately this is not always possible.

Accepting Ability

Now that science is suggesting that a lot of our children's intelligence is out of our hands, it is important to accept this. As parents we all want the best for our children and sometimes we can get caught up in the playground hysteria when making school choice decisions; but parents should try and keep a level head and be realistic about their child's ability. You should make decisions based on what's best for your child, and not what's going to win you bragging rights. Active involvement in your child's education is the best way to assess for yourself how academic your child is (more on this in a moment). When you have a measure of this (and be as objective as you can), please try to accept it. For some reason, no one seems to want to admit the obvious, that some people are just cleverer than others – no ifs, ands, or buts about it. Around the school gates, whenever a child's exceptional reading or maths ability is discussed, someone will inevitably mutter, 'Yes, but you know what that parent is making the kid do at home . . .' There is really no point being envious of other children's ability; think about it, for all but one set of parents in the world, however smart their kid, there are always others who are more intelligent.

My gestalt realization that ability is unevenly distributed happened when I started at Cambridge University. I looked around me and thought, 'Yup, not in a million years of working 24/7 will I ever be as smart as some of these people.' You can come to the same conclusion yourself very quickly by watching old episodes of *Child Genius* on iPlayer. There are eleven-year-olds on this programme who can do sums like 6784637 x 98374685 in their heads within seconds. I can tell you quite confidently that no amount of 24/7 revision could allow me EVER to do that. Accepting your limitations and not feeling a loser about it is really satisfying, and I think we need to have the same reality check with our kids. Although having aspirations for them and pushing them to achieve their potential is positive, not all children have the same academic potential and ultimately we need to accept, appreciate and love them – in the immortal words of Bridget Jones's Darcy – 'just the way they are'.

Competitive schools are not for everyone

My personal view is that if my children do not get into the most prestigious school then they probably would not have flourished there. If I did not think that my kids had a very good chance of being accepted at a particular school, they would not even hear about it from me. I would much prefer that my children perform well in a less academic school, where they can feel 'clever' enough and remain confident in their academic abilities than flounder in the bottom half of a more academic school feeling 'dumb'. The same basic principles apply here as those I discussed in Chapter Two about choosing the right primary school for your child: choose an appropriate pond. I have seen many people at my school and university suffer crises of confidence (despite being exceptionally bright), due to being in the bottom half of an insanely competitive environment. Some of the negative effects lasted well into adulthood, and some may be lifelong. In my professional and personal experience, confidence, security, self-assurance and happiness are the solid foundations that children need to build successful lives; academic excellence is definitely welcome, but should never be at the expense of the former. That said, if you have already established in your child a base of personal and emotional security and social skills, why not go for the cherry on the cake and support your child's intelligence too, whatever their level.

Assessing and Supporting Your Child's Intelligence: Babies (up to Four Years)

As I have explained, the plasticity of your baby's brain and its vulnerability to negative environmental factors peaks in early infancy. This time (up to the age of four) is also the optimum time for parents to actively modify their child's brain development, whenever possible. This also coincides with the exact time that many parents decide to leave their children to their own devices to play, or send them off to be supervised by others. Although I am a great believer in free play, I am ultimately a child psychiatrist: I study child development. It was probably impossible for me to observe my own children without probing their intelligence alongside their attachment, social ability and empathy. I believe that monitoring and reinforcing the precursors of intelligence (language, attention, memory, spatial awareness and processing speed) during this time can at least inform me of their skills in these areas and hopefully help to improve them.

Buffer-face kids

Fundamental skills involved in intelligence include language, attention, processing speed and memory. I have mentioned how you can encourage your child's language and attention skills in previous chapters and so I will only mention processing speed and memory here. Processing speed in your child's brain works in exactly the same way as the processing speed in your computer. Some computers are faster than others. If your computer downloads a movie instantly, while others are still buffering, you can imagine who has the advantage. Clinically, one way we measure a child's processing speed is to give them a sheet of paper with lots of different symbols on it. The child is asked to cross out all the symbols of a particular shape, and timed. Their score is based on time taken, with a penalty for any false positives (crossed-out shapes that were not the specified shape) and false negatives (the correct shape was not crossed out). The task can be varied in difficulty by having all the symbols look very different or very similar.

A more basic way of testing processing speed at home, particularly with younger children, is with a sorting task. Sorting items by colour can be mastered easily by an infant and if you time this you can get an idea of processing speed (again, factoring in accuracy). Equally, the time it takes to push shapes through a shape sorter can be used. Children with good visuo-spatial skills and processing speed can do this quickly. Children who adopt a trial and error approach to the shape sorter will get there eventually, but they will be outclassed time-wise by someone who can process in their head which shape is likely to fit through which hole. Spatial ability is known to predict performance in mathematics and eventual expertise in science, technology and engineering.[7] By the time D was one year old, we had acquired so many hand-me-down toys that we had several shape sorters. The first had only three shapes (square, circle and triangle), the second had ten shapes and the third had about twenty-four shapes including complex trapeziums and parallelograms. If you are sad, like me, you can monitor your child's development through a progression of progressively harder shape sorters. Repeatedly doing this type of activity (a little a day) may reinforce their innate aptitude for spatial awareness by strengthening the brain circuitry used in these tasks, which are building blocks to more complex problems. Even if it doesn't, it is useful to know the level of ability that your child is at and spending time playing with your baby is never wasted time.

The gift of memory

Memory is another quality that is easy to assess because it is often required in day-to-day life. I used to have a very good memory and my mother has a story about me. When I was three years old, she met up with her brother with me in tow. As he left, he told my mother his new phone number and she wrote it down on a piece of paper. That night, when she wanted to ring him, she could not find the paper. However, I recited back to her the number that I had heard him say. It was correct. Sadly, following the birth of my children, I can no longer remember anything, which is highly frustrating.

Thankfully, my children have inherited my memory, and I

often joke with them that they 'stole' my memory. I first realized that my daughter had a very good memory when she was about eighteen months old. I had mislaid my keys. She watched, confused at what I was doing as I upturned the flat, until eventually I said aloud, 'Where have I put my keys?' This was a rhetorical question; I did not think that she would be able to tell me. However, Molly got up, walked to another room and showed me exactly where I had left them. It was not as if she was playing with them or she had seen them recently, as we had been together the whole time. She had seen me put them down some hours earlier, and was able to recall exactly where they were, even though I could not. These days whenever I need to remember something, I just tell Molly to remember it and I know that I need never worry about forgetting it again (or at least until she has children of her own, who 'steal' her memory in turn).

Following on from this, anyone interested in monitoring child development should play memory games with their children. Matching pairs is a good memory game that is easy to play with children. Select ten or twenty pairs of cards and place them face down in random order. Each player upturns two cards at a time and if they are a pair, they get to keep them. The winner has the most pairs at the end of the game. Other games I played were putting random objects on a tray and then taking one away and seeing if they could deduce the missing object. And the old game, 'I went on holiday and I packed in my suitcase . . .' where each person adds to an incremental list of random objects to remember. From games such as this you can get a good idea of your child's memory. You can, of course, also do the more formal 'digit recall' test, as in an IQ test, where you recite a random string of numbers and ask the child to repeat them back in order, in reverse order, or after a time delay. My telephone number trick as a three-year-old would have been an example of a time-delayed digit recall. A time-delayed seven-digit recall is pretty good for a three-year-old; I'm pretty sure I couldn't do it now.

Again, repeatedly doing this type of activity (a little a day) may reinforce their memory, and strengthen the brain connections required to do them. Again, even if it has no direct bearing on their ability, time spent playing with your child is never wasted.

Assessing and Supporting Your Child's Intelligence: Infants (Aged Four to Seven)

I enjoyed being praised for my smarts as a kid, which is why I was surprised to hear that since then there has been a backlash against praising children for being intelligent. This is largely due to some interesting work on how to praise children in order to get the best out of them, pioneered by Stanford professor Carol Dweck. Carol's highly influential theory about Growth Mindset posited that children who were praised for effort ('Well done for trying so hard'), rather than ability ('You're so clever'), tended to challenge themselves more and ended up doing better than children who were praised for innate ability.[8] Children who had been told that they were smart tended not to want to challenge themselves for fear of failure. Children who were praised for effort developed motivation and an understanding that working led to self-improvement. Carol explains to children that the brain is like a muscle and the more you use it, the stronger it becomes. I think that this analogy is great. It also holds for the elderly, because there is a wealth of research showing that elderly people who continue to use their brains in activities such as crosswords and chess are relatively protected from dementia. The idea of a plastic and evolving brain holds true even in neurology.

Effort versus ability

However, I do feel that something has gone awry with the widespread interpretation and application of Carol's work.

The segregation of 'effort' and 'ability' is a return to the defunct nurture vs nature question. This segregation is artificial; 'effort' and 'ability' are both contributory factors to academic achievement, although with differences in cultural value.

In the West, genetic intelligence is the highest aspiration. To be seen as having effortless knowledge and wit is the highest accolade. To be able to ace an exam without an ounce of revision is to engender the ultimate amount of envy. Boasting around exam time usually relates to how *little* work has been put in: the booze consumed, the parties attended are bragged about to show that the grades achieved were down to innate and 'natural' intelligence. Baby, I was born with it.

In the East, the reverse is true. He who can work hard to apply himself, to push himself single-mindedly to the limit of his ability is the most admirable. He who achieves *despite* his genetic stock, the one who rose to pull his family out of poverty, is most admired. The twat that squandered his natural intelligence by partying is just lazy. Think what *more* he could have achieved if he had had the right attitude. Rather than be admired, the cavalier academic revered in the West is pitied in the East as a 'waste of potential'. Boasting in the East is all about how *much* revision you did, as it is a marker of commitment and dedication. This cultural difference led to some unfortunate Chinese friends being mocked when they sought glory by boasting of all their hard work: 'What? You didn't get a first after all those hours of revision you told us about? You can't be that smart then!'

The thing is, just as outcomes are not down to nature or nurture alone, it is pretty obvious that it is the interaction between natural ability and hard work that drives examination results. And to end the myth of 'natural ability' I should share an Oxbridge secret: *everybody works*. When I studied at Cambridge I had a disastrous first year. Like many tiger cubs, 'Oxbridge' was my prize for a lifetime of graft. With that in mind, I basked in my glory: 'I've made it now, I can chill. Grades don't matter anymore, I've delivered and there's no more expectation.' I got to lectures late, missed the odd practical and fell asleep in supervisions. During exam term, I continued to frequent the bar and go clubbing with a fellow medic friend. After clubbing, I fell into bed. I got a 2:2 in my first year. I was happy to have passed fairly effortlessly until I found that this grade was a source of pity. Classmates would say, 'Oh dear, what happened?' Infuriatingly, I found out that my fellow clubber had got a first, having secretly *studied* and not slept after going clubbing!

At least I learnt my lesson and improved my work ethic and grades thereafter. And that's the secret of Oxbridge. The media portrayal of May Balls and gay times at Oxford and Cambridge are a snapshot in time. Had the journalists come a month earlier they would have seen the swathes of greasy-bearded, long-haired, track-suited lads (hair-cuts and shaving detract from revision time), and bespectacled, scraggy-haired lasses hiding in the library. At the highest level in any arena, innate ability *and* hard graft are both essential, nothing is 'natural'. Some crazy classmates even had the words 'Pain is temporary, glory is forever' tacked to their notice boards to spur them on. This is something the next generation is coming to understand. The culture of hard work is spreading, infecting our children with us parents as the vectors. As a tiger parent, I welcome this, but as a psychiatrist, it is worth reiterating a note of caution: expectations must remain realistic and ultimately, there is so much more to life than academic success.

The drawbacks of only praising effort

The main problem with the interpretation of the Growth Mindset (as described above) is that the message has become distorted and simplified to 'never praise ability and only praise for effort'. So much so, that teachers are actively telling parents not to tell their children that they are smart: 'Oh no, they'll stop trying if you tell them that!' For me, a lover of 'esteem praise', and for many parents who want to praise their children, this feels counter-intuitive. I do feel that deliberately withdrawing praise for natural talent is a bit mean. I have already described the consequences on some children who never hear esteem praise in Chapter Two; perhaps more damaging are the counterproductive consequences of *only* praising effort.

A shift of emphasis to rewarding personal effort instead of ability has been highly influential in the education sector and many schools have moved wholesale from celebrating 'achievement', 'competition' and 'winning' to celebrating 'participating', 'trying' and 'effort' instead. Certainly, at my children's primary school the prized 'Golden Certificates' are not handed out based on achievement (why just reward someone for having inherited a handful of good genes?) but for 'effort'. One danger with this is that children, and the adults they become, are often fed the unrealistic expectation that they can achieve 'anything' if they just put their back into it; that effort 'deserves' reward no matter the outcome. On the *X Factor*, scores of wannabees plead to be given another chance by Mr Cowell, not because of their talent but because, 'I've worked so hard / I've given my all / I will give 110 per cent'. I'm afraid I'm totally with Mr Cowell on this one: unless you are selling your sweat, how is that going to make any money?

Not only does this praise of effort create false expectations in children, but it also does in their parents. As a clinician called upon to assess children's learning difficulties, I have frequently encountered children with significant learning difficulties who have always had amazing school reports. Through sad experience, I have come to decipher that 'has excellent potential' and 'always gives 100 per cent effort' can sometimes be code for: 'This child is not achieving. He tries 100 per cent, but unfortunately he fails. The aforementioned excellent potential is as yet unrealized.' Whilst years of clinic work has enlightened me to this code, parents often take these school reports at face value, remaining blissfully ignorant of their children's ability or lack thereof. This only fuels unrealistic parental expectations, which can be very damaging.

This emphasis on 'only effort' has also turned some of our schools into caucus races, where all must win, and all must receive prizes. My first experience of a 'Non-Competitive School Sports Day' was rather an eye-opener. Children ran up and down with eggs and spoons against a timer, rather than a competitor. For the parents observing, it rather took the fun out of things. All the children were duly congratulated for their efforts, despite many of them obviously not going about their events at full capacity. Clearly I was not the only one who found the sports day dull; the following year, after many complaints from the parents, one competitive sprint race was allowed, tacked on at the end of the afternoon. Suddenly there were no more idling children and as far as I could see, this was the only event where all the children gave their full-on best. Even if 'achievement' and 'winning' have become taboos for educationalists, they still mean everything for children; the children's post-event analysis was all about who won that race.

Spare a thought, also, for the naturally academic child who always gets all the answers right, but is only rarely praised for this because she can't be seen to have an unfair advantage. Of course no one child should be singled out more than the others, but if that child has also worked very hard, and never seems to be noticed, they may get the subliminal message that their natural excellence isn't really valued and become demotivated.

Of course, on the one-hundred-metre sprint race track, as in the classroom, genetics will have its part to play in achievement. For me, though, that's life. I fully support schools being as nurturing and compassionate as possible, but I do think that at some point children need to learn that life is just not fair. Even with our best efforts we may never win the one hundred metres. Accepting ourselves and our own abilities and tolerating our failures are all worthwhile lessons. If our children's self-esteem is not only based on achievement (which I would whole-heartedly encourage), then as nurture and nature are equally important to outcomes, effort *and* ability should be celebrated, not either one or the other.

Encouraging hard work

At home I was always told I was smart, but this made no difference to my need to continue to work hard. I could always be *smarter*. However easy a maths problem was, there was always a harder one right behind it to make sure that I didn't get ahead of myself. It was the discipline that this instilled, along with my experience of effort leading to mastery that incubated the persistence, determination and motivation which allowed me to make use of my natural ability. What my parents praised and did not praise had nothing to do with it. The crux message of Growth Mindset is not 'Praise effort, not ability', but 'the more you practise something the easier it will become'; the analogy of the brain as a muscle. Schools and parents need to refocus on this message, rather than the red herring of praise.

The key to motivation

As I mentioned in my earlier chapter, nothing works well without self-esteem, and esteem praise in early infancy is really important for young children. Pre-school children see things in black and white; they do not have the capacity to understand nuance, subtlety, context or the abstract. Something is either a 'good choice' or a 'sad choice'. Nurseries do not mess about with, 'That was a sad choice, Sasha, to snatch the bear from Ben, but given that he snatched it from you first, we could also consider that to be a good choice in this context'. No pre-schooler is going to understand that. So during this period, 'Good', 'Smart', 'Kind' and all the positives you want to invoke in your child should be lavishly applied, because the only other alternative in their minds will be 'Bad', 'Dumb' and 'Mean'.

Once children get a bit older, by around Reception Year, it is probably safe to start preparing them for reality. This doesn't mean, 'Son, I lied. You know when I said you were smart? Well, I take it back. Boy, you dumb!' It means that we need to gently bring in the concepts of context and grey areas. My view is to always be as honest as we can with children in terms that they will understand. Instead of, 'You are the cleverest boy in the whole world,' you can probably leave it now at, 'You are a very clever boy.' If they ask whether they are the cleverest boy in the whole world, then you could gently start telling them more of the truth: 'Well, there are lots of clever boys in the whole world and I think you are one of them.' You should start to introduce Carol Dweck's idea that the brain is a muscle and that practice makes it stronger. You should start to emphasize the importance of hard work.

This is how a conversation with Molly went when she was about six years old:

Molly: I don't want to do maths today.

Me: You have to do maths, we do it every day.

Molly: I'm good at maths. You said it yourself. I get everything right at school, so why do I need to do it?

Me: You are good at maths, Molly, but hard work is also important. There are other children out there who are not as good as you at maths, but they are willing to work hard and soon they will be better than you at maths because they have practised more, and the brain is like a muscle. The more you practise, the stronger your brain gets (I'd been reading Dweck). There are also other children who are as good at maths as you are who are also willing to work hard. These children will do the best at maths because they are clever AND hard-working. Their brains were big and now they're getting massive!

It doesn't stop the tantrums or complaints about practising, but over time, this consistent message that hard work is *also* required has seeped in. Perhaps more motivating than words alone, Molly has experienced that over the time that she has been asked/encouraged/cajoled/forced/bribed into doing regular maths she has been able to master new processes. Sums she battled to do in the past are now simple for her. Mastery has given her confirmation and belief in the mantra that the more you practise something, the easier it becomes. It has allowed her to develop her own sense of motivation to master new challenges, which has meant less cajoling, coercion and bribery from me. More recently, the idea that she will probably never be 'the best' (except in my eyes) has been introduced, but this was at a point when developmentally she was robust enough to understand that this doesn't really matter, and she could tolerate the idea. The tricky part in the process is not about what to praise and what not to praise, but the initial enforcement of regular effort to achieve mastery.

The virtuous cycle goes something like this: effort leads to mastery which leads to a belief that effort can lead to success. With this mindset, difficult challenges are met with more effort and more mastery and your child starts to develop self-motivation and determination. If insufficient effort is put in at the outset then a vicious cycle develops: poor effort leads to quitting or failure, which prevents the connection between mastery and effort being made. This leads to a belief that effort is pointless and will only lead to continued failure. (The same disconnect between effort and success may also be reached if systems are designed to fail people for arbitrary factors such as gender, skin colour, and social class.) Undoubtedly, the hardest part for any parent is the first step in the virtuous cycle: convincing a disbelieving child to put in sufficient effort to gain their first taste of mastery. It takes persistence, patience, conviction and nerve. It will cause tears, tantrums and grey hairs, but for tiger parents this is acceptable, as they have been through it all themselves.

How It Worked for Me

My commitment to enforcing regular maths stems from my own experience. My mother taught my sisters and me maths that was slightly ahead of the school's curriculum up until I was eight years old, such that we always found maths work at school extremely easy. We moaned and complained about having to do maths at home, and I am sure there was a lot of hiding under tables and a fair few tantrums, but my mother insisted and so we persisted. By the time the teacher was teaching us the times tables at school, I could recite them off by heart easily. It made maths lessons at school remarkably dull, but it also meant that from an early age I experienced adulation and praise from peers and teachers for being 'naturally' good at maths. I knew full well that I had slogged over the learning of the times tables just as my peers now had to, but I liked the feeling of achievement and pride even so, and more importantly I started to identify myself as someone who was 'good at maths'. This meant that if a maths problem was presented, I would feel confident that I could do it. Or at least that if I couldn't do it, my classmates would not be able to either.

My mother later admitted to me that the reason she had taught us maths ahead of the curriculum was not because she thought that five-year-olds needed to know what twelve times twelve was, but because she wanted us to feel that maths was something that we were good at, and be motivated to stay ahead of the pack at it. It worked, because even after my mother stopped teaching us, my sisters and I continued to work hard under our own motivation, in order to maintain our identities as 'clever' children.

The transmission of this experience has been completed; I nearly choked with laughter when at her Year Three parents' evening Molly's teacher told me that she had a 'natural gift' for maths because although the class had only just started learning the times tables, Molly had grasped them 'incredibly quickly'. Little did she know that Molly had been working on them for a year at home with me – at significant cost to my sanity. I kept quiet, not just because of tiger mother recriminations but because it was worth it for me to allow Molly to be viewed in this way, and for her to learn that it is practice as well as innate aptitude that has earnt her this high praise from her teacher, just as I had done as a child. And so, just as it is for the Cambridge students who secretly study after a night's clubbing, the aura of 'natural intelligence' is created.

Parents can be hands-on

It is worth mentioning here that for most children, heavy parental support is required in the first instance to gain mastery in anything, not just maths. The most common example I can give is in learning to ride a bike. I have yet to encounter a young child picking up a bike and cycling off on their own accord. Usually it takes hours and days of practice with an adult. There are screams of 'I can't', there are tears from falls, there are cries to quit; but with persistence, sympathy and determination, most parents will eventually see their child take off, and then there is no stopping them. For some reason, most parents are happy to dedicate time to teaching a child to ride a bike, it is a boasted-about parental rite of passage, but they feel inhibited in investing the same in their children's education, lest they be called a 'tiger parent'.

In the remainder of this chapter I will write about how I tried to help my children in numeracy. I chose to share my experience of numeracy not because I do not encourage literacy, but because I think that literacy and creative writing are already encouraged and taught remarkably well in this country.

TOP TIP: HELP CHILDREN MASTER SOMETHING

I have found that the majority of children enjoy doing the things that they are good at. Some children are naturally good at certain things. However, most children *become* good at things. Once a child is good at something, they will invest more time in doing them and become even better at them. This needn't be maths; piano, dancing, swimming or drawing all require initial upfront parental investment. Once mastery is achieved, the child's own motivation will take over.

Why does nobody (in the UK) love maths?

I know; it is such a cliché – Chinese nerd banging on about boring maths. Believe me; I have fought hard to escape this stereotype. Andrew and I didn't get off to a good start because he assumed that I was a maths student. Maths meant to me geeky Asian with no social skills, so I wasn't very impressed.

However, now I'm an adult in the working world I am thankful for my maths skills, and am only regretful that they are not better. And as a mother, I positively lament the lack of emphasis on maths in the infant school curriculum. I think this is to the detriment of our children and even our country. Britain has produced some of the world's best scientists, engineers and economists, so it is not for want of genetic stock or tradition. Yet why does the Far East continue to dominate the Pisa Test League tables for maths and science? (At the time of writing, the top seven locations in the league table for maths are in the Far East, as are the top four in science; the UK stands outside the top twenty.)

From the perspective of my own upbringing, it is because education is so highly valued in Asia. Within that, maths and science are valued above all other subjects. So much so, that my parents dictated to my sisters and me that we had a choice of three A levels amongst four subjects: Maths, Physics, Biology and Chemistry. Despite having achieved better marks in Art and History at GCSE than science, I was to be a scientist. Mad and maddening maybe, but my parents had seen a national focus on science, maths and engineering education allow their country, Taiwan, to gain economic wealth and unprecedented development within their lifetime. On the backs of engineers, Taiwan is now a developed country and a world player in technology, despite being the size of Wales and having started in the 1940s from a much more disadvantaged base.

In the Far East, six-year-olds know their times tables up to twelve, a target that has been set by the UK government for children of eleven. And this target has thus far been largely unmet. Growing up, my sisters and I were ridiculed on holidays back to

Taiwan when our cousins (subject to the rigorous mathematics curriculum) performed long divisions in their head that had us reaching for our calculators.

'So what?' we would retort. 'Why bother when we can use a calculator?'

Shamefully, this is the same retort used by the new tech-savvy generation for whom spell-check and mobile phone calculators have deemed a brain unnecessary. Sure, I still agree to some extent that complex maths should be done using a calculator, but basic mental arithmetic and an understanding of mathematical concepts should be common knowledge.

From a cultural perspective, as someone coming from a country unanimous in its reverence for mathematics, I find it quite bizarre to experience the indifference to maths in the UK. Whilst engineers are admired in the Far East, they are depicted as 'anoraks' in the UK. Whilst maths is a subject that both boys and girls are expected to excel at in Taiwan, maths in the UK is for boys, and even then, only for the boys who are born with 'that logical, mathematical mind'. More damaging, though, than the stereotypical maths nerd image is the mainstream acceptability of poor maths skills. Whilst inability to do mental arithmetic would mean you were subjected to derision and sympathy in the Far East, it is expected, sometimes even boasted about, in the UK. I was shocked to find that many well-educated mums were openly admitting that they would struggle to help their children with 11+ maths revision. The reason they were openly admitting this was because they were not the least bit ashamed to be weak at maths, whereas I doubt anyone would openly admit to struggling to read or write at the level of an eleven-year-old. Why is one shameful and not the other? How has it become socially acceptable amongst the well educated to be bad at maths? This should surely not be?

Given the low national aspiration for mathematical ability, it is no wonder that Andrew tells me that the majority of banks are recruiting their quantitative skills staff from Asia. These skills are so sought after that my sister (who possesses a maths Ph.D. from a top US university) had no problem acquiring a highly paid position in the UK, within two weeks of arriving back from the USA, after quitting her job to be closer to her growing brood of nieces and her nephew. I am sure she would have found it harder to find a good job so quickly had her Ph.D. been in English Literature. At the population level, one wonders whether the average Joe and Joan Blogs could calculate their expected monthly mortgage repayment if the Bank of England were to increase interest rates by 0.5 per cent. Yet these sorts of calculations are vitally important if we want to keep roofs over heads and food in mouths. Maths is a vital and sought-after skill, so why are we not investing in it at the very grass roots?

Literacy versus numeracy – why not both?

Whilst reading is heavily pushed in infant schools, maths seems to be relatively neglected. If we are a country that truly believes that children should be allowed to flourish and become what they want to be, shouldn't this include an equal amount of encouragement for numeracy and literacy? This would give children a more balanced field of areas within which they might flourish. At this point, I reiterate that intelligence genes are generalist genes and predispose a child to ability across maths and languages. It is environment that dictates the preference.

Yet, in Key Stage One, Molly's state primary school pushes reading. As they should. All parents are expected to read with their children every night. The school challenged Molly at reading, so much so that in Reception she was given chapter books to take home to read with me. At five-and-a-half she was expected to read books containing the word 'obsessed'. Well, she may have been able to read the word but she did not have a clue what it meant, nor was she able to understand it when I tried to explain it to her. Molly began to hate reading and cried every night when I asked her to read to me. I persisted, thinking, 'If her teacher has given her this book, she must be capable of reading it.' After a few weeks of this, I gave up and trusted my own judgement that these books were frankly too hard. I must be the only 'tiger parent' to have written to the class teacher to say, 'Excuse me, but I think that you are overestimating my child's ability, can you put her reading books down three levels, please.'

At the same time, while we parents were expected to battle for advanced literacy in our children, there was no expectation for us to do any numeracy with them on a regular basis. I don't blame the school, it's just not currently in the National Curriculum. (No school that I know in the UK encourages daily numeracy in this way in Key Stage One, but I am pretty sure it happens in the Far East.) By Key Stage Two, the time that the National Curriculum suggests that children start doing the core of maths, their expertise and skill in literacy is far ahead of their mathematical ability. At one stage Molly was reading Roald Dahl's *James and the Giant Peach* but did not know her two times table – this seemed completely unbalanced to me. Literacy and English become the favoured subjects, having been given an early push by the school, while maths, which is introduced later, is seen as difficult in comparison and therefore more unloved. The opportunity to 'sell' maths to children is hijacked by literacy being given the advantage of earlier exposure and active encouragement.

Learning by rote

In the Far East, five- and six-year-olds will learn their times tables up to twelve by rote. Before you utter, 'We in the UK are not rote learners,' think about the reception classes up and down the land chanting their jolly phonics sounds, 'A, A, A'; 'Ph, Ph, Ph'; 'ee, ee, ee'; 'ai, ai, ai', and tell me that is not rote learning. I am also pretty sure that Molly is rote learning her spellings rather than delineating the spelling from its Latin roots. Once the connections are entrenched by rote learning, it is then possible to learn about the Latin and Greek from which the words are derived and so experience a higher meaning. In the same way, the meaning of relationships between the numbers in the times tables can be learnt post hoc. The rote learning is what gets you started.

When I received Molly's report card from Reception, she managed to 'exceed expectations' in literacy but was only 'meeting expectations' for maths. My initial response was, 'How is this possible? She comes from a family of scientists and mathematicians! Maths is a family tradition.' Truth be told, I would have been happier if the 'meeting expectations' scores had been for literacy. To make matters worse, when I asked Molly if she was struggling with maths, she said, 'Maths is too hard. Maths is for boys!'

Rather than accept that, 'Maths is hard, she's a girl, and so born without a mathematical mind', I thought about my own childhood and the start of my own maths journey. I remembered how regular maths practice had impacted my ability and mindset towards maths. I started to set Molly a few counting and maths problems every morning, to balance the reading that was set by the school every night. This was the start of the regular maths sessions both my children now endure. My view was that of course Molly's literacy was better than her numeracy – I was required by the school to support her literacy on a daily basis. Since then, Molly's maths has come along and by the end of Year One her scores in maths and literacy were more equal. She will now confidently say, 'I am good at maths,' and attempt maths problems rather than avoiding them. The solution was so simple. I still don't understand why schools are not breaking down maths into simple parts and pushing numeracy in line with literacy from Reception onwards. I'm not talking about differentiation and integration, but if children are encouraged to count, add sweets or pocket money, count the number of days until Christmas and so on daily, and from a young age, does this not take the stigma of 'difficulty' out of maths?

I am convinced that if I had not taken action to support Molly's maths in the same way I was supporting her literacy, she would not now be confidently declaring that she was 'good at maths'. Without a sound understanding of maths, her enjoyment of the sciences would be in jeopardy. Isn't it time that we put numeracy on equal footing to literacy in early years education? Only then can we really say that we are allowing our children an equal opportunity to select for themselves their strengths, and whether they lie in science or in the humanities.

TOP TIP: SET YOUR OWN HOMEWORK

I know that homework is a controversial area. There are those who insist that children should live free-range lives, unencumbered by imposed structured activity, and others who believe that without structure and tests, how can a child survive the competitive exams and job market they will be exposed to? It's a difficult balancing act for schools to get right. I can understand parents complaining that their school sets too much homework, but what I have never understood is why parents complain that schools do not set them enough. As a parent, more work can always be set from home. My children's school sets only weekly homework and no homework over any holidays. The homework is usually an art-based project (make a hat/volcano/mosque/spaceship/dinosaur habitat and so on) that inevitably the mums and dads will end up completing. This has been fine by me as I get to indulge my suppressed artistic temperament and I am proud to say that I have won, by proxy, many 'Golden Certificates' for my creations. I'm happy with this low level of school homework because it has allowed me to set my children my own homework, which is great. I get to teach them whatever I want, whatever I feel is important to encourage learning and love of learning, unencumbered by the opinions of Michael Gove, Justine Greening, or any other Education Minister.

Encourage a love of maths

It does seem that attitudes are finally starting to shift and that I am not the only one disgruntled by the apathy and low expectations for maths, even under the supposed target-setting new government initiatives. The number of Kumon centres spreading fast across the UK can attest to this. When posters at my local tube station are inviting me to set up my own Kumon maths centre in order to earn shed loads of money, one can only deduce that the demand for better maths education is already here. Perhaps now the government should think even harder about supplying more and better teaching, lest the gap between the Kumon-haves and Kumon-have-nots widens even more.

For those unfamiliar with Kumon, it is a Japanese system of learning maths focused on a daily practice using generic maths worksheets which will be targeted at your child's level. You attend a special 'Kumon Centre' where you get your worksheets marked and some advice on corrections; then you get set more worksheets to do at home until your next attendance at the centre. For this you pay a not-insignificant subscription fee, albeit this is significantly less than hiring a personal maths tutor.

You might think that being a maths lover I would be all for Kumon. Yes and no. Whilst I am a fan of improving mathematical ability, and am in no doubt that practising maths on a daily basis will significantly improve your child's mathematical ability, I am not convinced that you need to pay someone else for this. Here are my reservations.

Can it be in any way fun? Kumon advertising may suggest that the 'centres' are fun places of learning, and that the specially designed worksheets 'will make maths enjoyable', however, from what I have seen, the centres are just rented halls where children sit and do worksheets. The worksheets are similar to any other worksheets you can print from on-line sites or workbooks you can purchase from your local newsagent. There is likely to be an added value in having these worksheets targeted at your child's individual ability rather than their chronological age, but they are no more 'fun' than any other worksheets. Even the Kumon logo depicts an unhappy face. I always wondered if this was supposed to resemble the children going in or coming out of Kumon – neither seemed to send a particularly positive message.

It still relies on parental discipline. I could see the attraction of handing over my innumerate child and being handed back a numerate one, confident at maths, with no effort from me. However, in my observations of the Kumon parents, that's not the case. No, Kumon mums (I don't like to bring gender into it, but I have only yet met Kumon mums and Kumon nannies) are generally frazzled, as they are the ones who need to uphold the discipline to make the said innumerate child do the blessed worksheets throughout the week.

Evaluation is still teacher-led. Whilst parents are required to nag their children to complete their worksheets, it is the teacher who evaluates and monitors their progress and sets the agenda. Maybe I am just too much of a control freak, but I think that parents should have a role in this. Some parents love Kumon (and maths tutors) and actively avoid 'evaluating' their children's ability. They see it as somehow making a value judgement on their child and this being somehow unhealthy, as if they should always believe their child's ability is unlimited. Some such parents get a nasty surprise if their children underperform and can pass this disappointment on to their children; others blame the teachers for not getting the best out of their incredibly able child. I believe in the reverse. I think that evaluating and monitoring your child's ability is essential so that as a parent you have an accurate, realistic and evidence-based picture of your child. Then you can guide them into the appropriate school/university/career. There is no value judgement in this as actually your child *is amazing*, no matter what their ability.

Two-tier education. As I alluded to earlier, I believe that Kumon (and any private maths tuition) is just another way in which the middle classes can pull away from the mainstream. We shouldn't need Kumon; we should be putting pressure on the government to improve the whole of its maths education. The proliferation of 'professionals' in maths tuition undermines the very real and practical advancements that can be made with primary maths by parents getting involved and reinforcing school maths. Most parents who are sending their children to Kumon have at least primary school level education and should be able to help their children with maths at this level, without the requirement of paid professionals. If more effort was made to educate parents in supporting their child's education, children from all backgrounds would benefit. It worked for my parents and I hope it will work for me.

What did I do?

I am speaking from the middle of my maths journey with my children. I cannot confess ultimate success, nor admit to a pain- and frustration-free experience to date. Most of what I did, and am doing, is based on trial and many errors. I can summarize the best strategies that I have picked up but this wouldn't show the entirety of the experience, which contains many expletives, failures and revisions. Although both my children are currently performing pretty well at maths, I cannot deny the part that genetics plays in this. However, despite all of this, I will share my limited insights with you, in case you find them of value.

I introduced numbers to my kids at the same time as letters. Literacy and numeracy are to be given equal prominence in my book. Children are just as capable of learning a sequence of numbers as they are a sequence of letters. From when my children were a young age I carried a notebook around with me and if there was a period of 'waiting time', for instance waiting to be served in a coffee shop, I would draw puzzles (mazes, matching puzzles, counting puzzles) for my children. If they were completed easily, I would make the next one harder. If they were too hard, I would make the next one easier.

As the children grew older, these puzzles moved towards proper mathematics. Rather than only being served up in 'dead time', they started being served up every morning. This worked well as the children were fresh and my over-enthusiastic tendency to set more and more work was naturally curtailed by the requirement to send the children to school and for me to get to work on time. The children initially protested but this subsided as they came to accept that this was the routine from now on.

Friends looked at me as if I was bonkers when I told them that I wrote my own maths worksheets for the kids, but what better way to tailor work for your children? By having daily exposure to what my children found easy and hard, I could not only have an in-depth understanding of their precise ability, but also be in the best position to set and manipulate their next worksheet. If single digit additions were proving easy, then you can bet that double digit additions were thrown into the mix. If there were too many tears and frustrations, the next few worksheets would be deliberately easy to restore confidence. By writing my own worksheets, I could not only tailor my child's learning but heavily manipulate their confidence. Also, I love art, so many of my worksheets were embellished with cartoons that I knew the children would like.

When abstract problems became taxing, I found that reframing problems into applied mathematics sorted the problem. Molly struggled immensely with problems such as, 'What number is halfway between 26 and 36?' She cried. Many times. I tried to explain it many ways, unsuccessfully: 'You can either add the two numbers together and halve the total; or, you can add to the smaller number half the difference between the two numbers.' Molly's eyes would glaze over and her hands would go over her ears in a classic 'la-la-la – not-listening' pose, much to my annoyance. Then once, lashing out in desperation, I happened to say: 'I'm going to give you 26 sweets and give D 36 sweets . . .', and before I could even finish my sentence, Molly declared, 'That's not fair! He shouldn't get more than me! We should both get . . .

(counting) . . . 31 sweets each.' Bingo! The war was won. From then on, problems were made real and Molly relished calculating 'real world' problems. When Andrew ran the barbecue at the school fair, maths worksheets were laden with problems such as, 'Your friend Henry wants to buy three hot dogs from your dad. Hot dogs are £3 each, so how much does he need to spend? What change must dad give him from a £10 note?' At birthday time when Digi-birds were requested, 'How many Digi-birds can you buy with the £30 your grandma will give you?' Go figure. Self-interest really does help with maths. It was made useful, if not fun, and there were no more (or far fewer) complaints.

Once confidence was gained at maths, we moved on to shop-bought workbooks. If workbooks were a struggle, then the same book would be reworked again. They would be very easy the second time around, not only to consolidate knowledge but also to boost confidence. And push home the message that 'maths can be easy'. Also, because I am evaluating and monitoring my children's progress, nothing said at their parents' evening surprised me. I could pick up a Key Stage One Maths paper and know almost exactly which questions Molly would be able to answer correctly and which she would struggle with.

Why is this detailed knowledge important?

When the 11+ exams come around, or any other childhood milestone, and performance matters, I won't need to rely on the opinion of others, I can be (almost) confident of how my child will perform and if I do not think they have a good chance of success for a particular school they will not sit the exam. The bar will be set at achievable. Expectations can be managed in advance, disappointments avoided, and, crucially, self-esteem preserved. Self-esteem, confidence and a continued keenness to learn always matter more than the final mark at this age, and arguably at all ages, because life is a marathon, not a sprint. Contrary to the popular belief that children who are set regular work are 'pressurized', I believe the reverse. The 'pressure' comes from the weight of parental expectation (particularly if it is unrealistic), not parental preparation.

If you have the time and inclination, give Kumon and private tuition a miss, roll up your sleeves and give it a go. There will be many frustrations, and patience and discipline are required, although I may be just weird or genetically inclined (I come from a long maternal line of teachers), because I find it immensely satisfying, even delightful, when I get to see the penny drop and know I am passing on knowledge to my children. I remember with fondness the way my mother taught me maths (despite my tears and tantrums) and I hope that as adults my children will feel the same way. Indeed, as Molly's friends have now started to get tutors, I was proud when Andrew reported to me that he had heard her declare proudly to her friend, 'I don't need a tutor, I have the best one: my mum.'

EXTRA TIPS

• **Target work at your child's level** If you are lucky enough to have a bright kid, it can be tempting to let nature run its course, but if you can, you should try to challenge them, however young they are. This might seems like the ultimate tiger parent thing but if they are able to do something easily, why not? Indeed, if bright children are under-stimulated this can lead to behavioural problems. D has always had excellent spatial awareness (which is related to mathematical ability). The Christmas just after his first birthday I decided to get him a jigsaw, something a clever baby could realistically manage, like a three-piece. His aunty, who is also Chinese and so of the same 'educational toys' mindset, also bought him jigsaws; Thomas the Tank Engine ones. Only she bought him six-, ten- and twelve-piece jigsaws.

One evening I was cooking dinner so I put D at the table with the three-piece jigsaws. He wanted the Thomas ones, so I put those out as well, just to keep the peace while I cooked. The next minute I turned around and there he was, sitting with the six-piece puzzle completed. I nearly dropped my saucepan.

OK then, clever clogs, I thought, here's the ten-piece.

That was also pretty quickly done and dusted.

At two years of age, twenty-four and thirty-five-piece jigsaws were no problem. We even played 'Jigsaw-Offs – babies versus geriatrics' where D and my mother would race to see who could finish an identical twenty-four-piece jigsaw fastest. D was usually victorious. Soon I had emptied out several shops of their jigsaws. Sure enough, strong mathematical ability followed, so my worksheets and shop-bought workbooks were tailored to his ability, not to his age. Even though he is smart, and I tell him so, he is still required to work hard, my mantra being that hard work and effort work for everyone, including the smart.

The same should be applied at the other end of the spectrum. In my mind there is no shame in pitching things simpler if your child is finding things tough. The best way to encourage a love of learning is to set your child challenges that they will probably be able to meet with a little bit of effort. Whilst schools will set homework based on the average ability of the class, parent-set homework is better as it can and should be individually tailored.

• **Make learning fun** Learning, particularly in younger children, doesn't always need to involve a desk and a chair. Observation, conversation, imagination, thinking and feeling are all part of learning. The more creative and fun you can be, the more engaged and interested your children will be. And it's even better if you can link their learning topics to things they are studying at school. Then the context is already set, the learning will be relevant and can earn lots of brownie points at school.

• **Read to your children** I figured that once my children were old enough to read for themselves, the bedtime story duty could be rescinded. Then a tiger parent friend gave me a tip: carry on reading to them! Yes, children can read alone and this should be encouraged, but their exposure to books will be limited by the long time that it takes to read them and they will select books that are easy to read. On the other hand, they will be more willing to listen to complex stories with tricky vocabulary if they are being read to. In this way, their exposure to language and ideas is vastly widened. Phrases can be explained, concepts can be discussed. My children are encouraged to read whichever books they select for themselves by themselves, but I will always read to them a classic at bedtime. In this way, their horizons are broadened beyond their current ability.

- **What about the tiger father?** Since when did concern about the educational outcomes of children become the preserve of women? I am always annoyed when 'childcare and schools' are listed as the concerns of female voters, because apparently men do not care whether or not their children learn to read or write! At my insistence, Andrew is always enlisted to participate in supervising homework, drawing up worksheets, helping with maths workbooks and reading when he is at home. The ideal scenario is for both parents to set an example and repeat together the mantra that hard work is required. Of course, some parents may require more guidance than others. Having no problem selecting beloved old favourites *Anne of Green Gables, Heidi* and so forth to read with Molly, D showed little interest in these stories (sadly due to the gender-skewed book covers). My lack of knowledge of classics that might interest him meant that I asked Andrew to take D to the bookstore to select something they could read together at bedtime. They returned triumphantly with *LEGO Star Wars* . . . not quite the classic I had in mind.

A final thought on 'pushy' parenting

Imagine you want to push a stack of boxes across the room. You could give the stack a hefty push with all your might. With luck, this will work and the stack will be shifted. What might happen, though, is that the stack is unbalanced by the shove and topples over. A much more careful and cautious approach is this: invest time in sorting out the boxes. Place the larger and heavier boxes at the bottom and the smaller, lighter ones on top. Then push slowly and steadily from the secure base. With this approach, success is much more likely. Even though I am an old battle axe with my children with regards to making them work hard, I do it all in the knowledge that I have already heavily invested in the layers inside them and secured their core base, and the push they are receiving from me is a slow, steady and measured one.

Chapter Summary

By now you will see that I don't believe that academic grades are the be-all and end-all of worldly success. That said, I do believe parents can make a dramatic contribution towards the academic achievement of their children, whatever their starting levels. Although genes and perinatal health are large contributors to our children's intelligence, we can support and develop their natural intelligence through our parental actions.

In the early years, doing activities with your child that re-inforce language, memory, spatial awareness and attention can consolidate skills that are fundamental to later intelligence. When they are a little older, show them how practice and repetition can help them master early academic skills. If you couple all this with abundant praise for their ability and effort, they will become motivated to carry on learning in ways that will benefit them for the rest of their life. Finding enthusiastic, relevant and fun ways to learn always helps. Make your activities as practical and wide-ranging as possible, rather than just prepping for exams, and you will spark a lifelong curiosity and interest in learning, and your child will develop an identity of being able and learned. And ulti-mately, if it all goes tits-up, console yourself that adult intelligence is largely genetic anyway and cream has a tendency to rise.

7. Layer Five: Creativity and Conscience

You Know What They Say About All Work and No Play

Developing the final layers in your perfectly put-together child are the best parts of parenting. Shaping your children's interests and opinions are the bits most parents really enjoy and are often the first (and sometimes only) parts that parents-to-be consider when they daydream about their future children. Which mum or dad hasn't been hoodwinked into parenthood by dreams of huddling cosily together on the sofa, watching footie/ballet/rugby/rom-coms with their kids? No parent ever imagines having raging political disagreements with their teenage children, because we all start off with the egotistical ideals of spawning 'mini-mes' who will reflect us in all our interests and opinions. But as with all things parenting, things seldom go to plan. So what can parents do in terms of damage limitation? In this chapter I will talk about my successful and not-so-successful attempts to shape the extra-curricular and socio-political interests of my children, in the service of giving them those final layers of polish with which to go forth into the world at large.

Psychiatrists on the piano

Naively, I had thought that once the angst of ensuring my children's emotional stability, prosocial behaviour and academic potential were in hand, it would be great just to kick back and share hobbies with my kids. Yet somehow for modern parents, even this leisure-time aspect of parenting has become a stressful and competitive extra-curricular circus. I put my hands up to sometimes going along with this, but I am also cognisant of the ill effects this competitiveness can have on our children and I am always trying to modify my ways.

The archetypal tiger mother loves music, and a Grade Eight in piano and violin is the Chinese parent's official stamp of a job well done. My views on this are a little different. Growing up, expensive music lessons were not possible for me until I was well into secondary school. Neither of my parents, who had harder lives than me, had any musical training and so we grew up singing hopelessly out of tune and with as much sense of rhythm and pitch as a doorknob. My musical influences in childhood were more Duran Duran than Debussy. By secondary school, when piano and violin lessons became available, I had made the school netball team and this took precedence over music practice. Indeed, a year after taking up lessons in piano and violin, and two weeks before my first graded music exam, I broke my arm in a game of netball and my musical career, never particularly promising, was over before it had begun.

It was not until university, where I started to lust after musical boys, that the regret of being tone deaf and musically incompetent began to bite. If you go to a top university, you will find yourself practically alone if you are unable to play *any* instrument whatsoever. Even the most unprepossessing lost cause will have a Grade Three in xylophone. Further, there is a great camaraderie and social element to music and I looked on with envy as musical friends frequently went off to choir/orchestra/band practice together. It is fair to say that I came to begrudge a music-free existence. The genetics may have always been against me, but I do have a cousin who is a professional musician and so I have always wondered, 'If I had started music lessons earlier, when learning skills are easier, could I have made headway with music?'

It was this thought, rather than earning the 'Head Girl of the Tiger Mothers Trophy', that prompted me to start Molly on piano lessons at the age of five. My aspirations were less concert pianist and more Taylor Swift. I fantasized that at this age, when the brain is theoretically supposed to be a sponge, osmosis and an enlightened teacher would work its magic and Hey Presto! I would deliver unto the world a cool, musical, arty, intelligent girl and a rock-star-DJ son. If only it were so simple.

It turns out that although at this age the brain is indeed a sponge, it is a sponge in the head of a stubborn child who doesn't fancy having their brain soaked in whichever inspirational waters their parents may be trying to push them into. Why should they? They are not dumb, and with any musical instrument the initial effort far outweighs the immediate pay-off. For the parent, there is added pain: who could have known that the going rate for piano tuition in London was a pound a minute? Cue choking on my tea as I sat in on one of Molly's early piano lessons, where the lovely teacher asked Molly to play a refrain again and she point-blank looked at him and said, 'No.' Imagine the silent fuming as a standoff ensued, with the teacher's gentle encouragement and friendly cajoling being met with idle banter and stubborn resistance, all the while as I sat clock-watching the pounds slip through my fingers with not a single note being played. I am afraid to say that against protocol, there were post-lesson indignant shouts of: 'I could have bought you two Barbies with the money you just wasted! I'm not paying a pound a minute for you to chit-chat to your teacher! Play the goddamn piano!'

Then there is, of course, piano practice.

Where previously I may have poured scorn on 'evil' tiger parents who forced hours of piano practice on their children, I now only look on them with wonder, respect and admiration. How, oh how, do they do this? I struggle, and have run out of sweets, bribes and threats after enforcing ten to fifteen minutes – not even daily!

And this is someone who has form in getting their kids to do extra maths with little problem. I truly think that piano practice was invented as a form of torture for parents. I know there will be those that say, 'If children don't want to practise, then you shouldn't force them,' or, 'They are so young, why are you making them do this?' but the truth was that Molly was actually very good at piano and enjoyed her lessons immensely (largely due to her fantastic teacher). She just did not have the discipline to practise. Or perhaps it was to do with my involvement . . .

At the time, I remember having a cuppa with an old friend who trained with me as a psychiatrist way back when. We diverged in specialty, she to the elderly, and I to the young, so we lost touch. It was with delight that we reconnected when we found out that our children attended the same school. Naturally, our conversation turned to the kids. There was a school concert approaching and Molly and my friend's son, Jack, both played the piano.

Here is what happens when two psychiatrists talk to each other:

Me: How's Jack's piano playing going?

Her: Really good.

Me: Oh, because I am having such problems with Molly and piano. We have a great piano teacher that she really likes and she loves going to lessons, but we always end up having an argument whenever I have to help her with her piano practice in between.

Her: How come?

Me: Well, she'll start playing, and then, when she gets a note wrong, I'll tell her that she played the wrong note, and she will insist that she did not get it wrong. Even when I show her the notation on the music, and show her the correct note, she will insist that she is right and carry on playing the wrong note. It drives me nuts, as initially, I'm just pointing it out, not even being critical or raising my voice, but by the end, it's like two kids in a playground: 'That's the wrong note!' 'No – it isn't.' 'Yes, it is.' ''Tisn't.' ''Tis,' and so on, until eventually one of us storms off shouting either, 'I'm never playing piano again,' or, 'I'm never helping you with your piano again.'

Her: Ah! You should never point out when a child is doing something wrong – they will take it as criticism and you'll end up with the horrible interaction you described! Don't you remember, that's like, the first rule of psychotherapy. You should know better! They have to reflect on how they played themselves, not have you point it out. I never point out to Jack where he has played something wrong; instead I just ask him, 'Are you happy with what you played?'

Me: [ashen-faced and ashamed that I had failed to apply clinical skill to my own child – argh, but it's so much more difficult when it's your own child!] Oh bugger, you're right. Maybe I should try that . . .

Her: But my trouble is that he gets so cross with himself. He will play a piece fine, but will be dissatisfied that it was not 'perfect' and get very cross and frustrated with himself, sometimes even saying he is rubbish. In fact, I never need to be critical as he is more critical of himself than I am.

Me: OMG! That's terrible. Don't you see? He has taken your comments to self-reflect into his superego. You've made him continually judge his own performance and now he is his own worst critic!

Her: Yikes.

Me: Now that I think about it though, asking Molly to self-reflect wouldn't work. When she has coloured something in and it's all over the place, not within the lines, and I ask her if she's happy with it, she always says yes. Even when I point out that it has gone over the lines a lot, she says, 'That's how I want it.'

Her: That's so funny. Jack gets frustrated with himself a lot.

Me: D is the same; with him I am always trying to stop him from being so pedantic and accept that it's OK to make mistakes. I'm always trying to get him to colour outside of the lines without having to screw the whole thing up and start again!

Her: Hah!

Me: I spend half my time telling one child to be more careful, and the other half telling the other child to be more carefree . . .

Three things struck me from this conversation:

1) What works for one child will not necessarily work for another, as children's personalities are so different.

2) Parent–child dynamics are a two-way street. How a child behaves is shaped by how the parent behaves, but critically, the parenting style adopted is also shaped by the child. Molly's insouciant nonchalance pushes me to point out her mistakes because otherwise she would never acknowledge them, while D's pedantry is equally annoying and leads me to encourage him to live a little and tolerate mistakes.

3) Two shrinks can't share a drink without analysis coming into it.

I am pleased to report, however, that following Grade One success and lots of fabulous applause at Molly's school concert, she has now come to believe that playing the piano well is worthwhile and since then, piano practice has been less of a chore for me. Since the age of seven, with her piano ability now well beyond anyone else in her musically challenged family, practice is largely Molly's own responsibility, and she will diligently practise under her own steam (with occasional parental insistence on sight-reading exercises). So although I am against a childhood of hours of enforced music practice, I do feel that there is something to be said for a heavy push at the start to allow children to get the basic mastery, because it is this achievement of mastery that allows children to learn that effort and persistence is worthwhile and fuel their further time investment. Sometimes, if parents and children quit too soon, the lesson learnt is that 'effort is futile or irrelevant', and that is a dangerous message for children to take away.

Where the 'snow tigers' hang

If music examination centres are the haunts of Chinese tiger parents, then I have found the Mecca of the Caucasian tiger parents: ballet.

Molly recently sat a ballet exam. Now I am ambivalent on the issue of ballet although have to confess that I did arrange for Molly to start at the age of three, as who can resist the cuteness of little dumpling girls toddling about in pink tutus? I presumed that by the age of seven, she would have grown out of it (the discipline, the classical music, the strictness, didn't seem to me to be overtly appealing to a child) and would probably change to drama or street dance, which are my preferences and are alternatives that I duly moot each year. But no, Madam loves ballet. So I dutifully send her each week and give her due encouragement, and I attend the ballet shows and clap enthusiastically, all the while secretly thinking to myself: when will she get fed up of this because I don't want her pursuing ballet seriously and developing an eating disorder in adolescence? It's a prejudice, I know, and a cliché, but for me ballet and eating disorders are just linked. Given a preference, I'd like to think that Molly would be saying 'yes' to rocking out with the Skater Boy rather than ruefully going to his concert in years to come.

So when the exam came, Molly and I ran in like a pair of insane loons, because typically we were *late*. Molly's hair had been in a pony-tail, but now it was all tumbling out. Her face was sweating like a pig from having had to run like mad to avoid a telling off from a stern Russian prima donna. She was wearing white school socks instead of tights because it was a baking hot day and we'd both just stuffed our faces with chocolate digestives, so crumbs tumbled from pink taffeta as we barrelled huffing and puffing in through the doors.

On arrival, we were met by the other girls and parents. Every other girl (90 per cent of whom were tall, blonde and with thigh girths smaller than my arms) had their hair neatly pulled back into a perfect bun. Gel, wax and constellations of kirby grips took a vice-like hold on hair lest a strand fell out of place. Most of the girls sported a full face of make-up, and they all wore tights, not crumbs. Oops! Was there a memo I missed about a dress code or were we supposed to have intuited all this? Parents fussed about and guided the girls as they dutifully underwent elaborate warm-up stretches in the corridor. Meanwhile, Molly stood in the corner fanning her sweaty nose.

'Phew,' I said. 'They're running late so we haven't missed it. We were running, so now we are sweating like pigs.' I attempted to explain.

Arched eyebrows at my disorganization and pitying smiles from the other parents gave me a sense of how incorrectly I had judged the seriousness of this ballet exam. Then another thing I hadn't anticipated: The Spanish Inquisition.

'So, when did Molly move into this ballet class?'

'Are you sure she is at the correct exam? Some of her class mates were being examined in the earlier exam.'

'My daughter is doing ballet three times a week. How many times a week is Molly doing ballet?'

And so on.

'I dunno. We came at the time we were told,' I muttered, and started to feel perplexed at this excessive interest into what I felt was an irrelevant extra-curricular activity that I was forced to enthuse about because my kid found it fun. But then I began to feel a strange sense of familiarity at these questions. I, and others I know, have asked these questions before. They were just like the questions Chinese parents ask each other about maths and piano exams!

'So, how long has your child been at Kumon?'

'Which grade piano is your child taking this year?'

'How many times a week do you set them extra maths home-work?'

If and when my kids are required to sit for academic exams, you can bet your life that we would be early, camping outside the exam hall, probably swotting up on homemade exam cards of some description.

I smiled.

So, this is where the snow tigers hang! It's reassuring to feel vindicated, to know that it is not just Chinese parents who are a tad pushy. It's just that for the Chinese the focus of achievement is on academics and music, whilst for Westerners it's sport. Andrew recalls encountering similar parents at swim meets, when he swam in the junior national swim teams in South Africa. Many of his team mates rebelled against their ambitious parents and refused to continue swimming in adolescence because of it, in the same way that many Chinese children never touch the piano once they reach adulthood. I am sure that Judy Murray (and any parent of a top athlete) did her fair share of threatening, cajoling and bribing her sons to get out of bed and get to training when they didn't want to, yet she has become a national treasure, whilst a parent who uses similar parenting practices to target academic achievement would be vilified. Having initially felt intimidated and antagonized, I started to feel serenely at one with these other parents.

TOP TIP: EXTRA-CURRICULAR FUN

Make sure that the things your children do for fun are just that. Fun. Not all extra-curricular activities should be educational, or status-driven. For me, I think that balance is the key. I am lucky enough to have been able to give my children varied opportunities over the years including: tennis, football, chess, skiing, pottery, Mandarin, street dance, ballet, piano and swimming. They are encouraged but not forced to continue in any activity (for instance they quit Mandarin which I would rather they had continued), as ultimately these life skills are for their enjoyment, not my bragging rights. We do have to put some limitations on the extra-curricular scheduling as it can all get a bit mad-cap. This is the sort of recurring conversation we have in my house:

Kid: I want to do horse riding.
Me: You can only do that if you give something else up.
    Do you want to do that?
Kid: No.

> *Kid:* I want to do gymnastics.
>
> *Me:* You can only do that if you give something else up.
>   Do you want to do that?
>
> *Kid:* No.
>
> *Kid:* I want to do karate.
>
> *Me:* You can only do that if you give something else up.
>   Do you want to do that?
>
> *Kid:* No.
>
> [Ad infinitum]

Pass On Your Passion

If there is one great thing about parenting, it is the opportunity to pass on a passion. Seeing a little person's face light up with enjoyment when they are doing something that you enjoy, and being able to do something you enjoy with the best little people in the world. Nothing beats it.

I am therefore rather bewildered by the abundance of children's clubs and classes where little ones can learn everything from swimming and yoga to decoupage and cookery. These classes are often run alongside similar classes for adults, with the children separated off into a kind of crèche area, so the parents can pursue their passions unfettered by their children. This uncoupling of parent and child 'leisure time' is great for the industry, but seems to me to be doing us a disservice. It feeds into exhausted parents' need for 'me time', and the parental desire for an 'accomplished child', but what it actually does is deny parents the simple pleasure of passing on their passions to their child.

My husband and I taught both our children to swim. I am not

the most accomplished swimmer around, but I am able to stay alive in the deep end of the swimming pool. Swimming is a potentially life-saving skill and the quicker a child learns it the better, in my book. For my husband, swimming is a passion. He dreams of holidays swimming between the Greek islands with his teenage children (I will be going in the boat, glass of wine and magazine in hand). So we have made a point of taking the children to play in water regularly since the age of three months. The tiger mother in me, of course, wanted to progress from 'play' to 'swim', and over a summer when Molly was four, I managed to teach her to swim five, then ten metres. It was a great feeling when she managed it, both for her and for me. She positively beamed and wanted to do it again, and again. I was right there next to her in the water (holding on to two-year-old D in his armbands), shouting, 'I knew you could do it!' I almost burst with pride one day when a private swimming instructor asked me who had taught my children to swim as they were both 'so confident in the water', and I was able to smugly reply, 'Me.' Now that Molly is able to swim, she is enrolled in professional lessons to learn and refine her strokes, but the pleasure of watching her gain mastery over the water was all mine.

I was sad, then, when a friend who was an excellent swimmer asked me to recommend a swimming instructor for her toddler. I asked her why she didn't teach her child herself, to which she responded, 'I can't; I'm not qualified.' I can see why you need professional qualifications to teach a group of children, or to teach children to swim technical strokes, but I was taught to swim by my dad, and my husband was taught by his parents, as were the majority of people of my generation. So why don't modern-day parents feel qualified to teach their own children to do the doggy paddle? Probably because of the many advertised toddler swimming classes advocating professional guidance and undermining our confidence in our own ability to do it. It will be a really sad day when children are sent to professional classes to learn to cycle and bake cakes, because for me, teaching and doing these things with your young children is a parental rite of passage. Or if you hate baking and cycling then snooker, oboe, tennis, skiing, poetry, jazz music – don't keep your passions to yourself and send your children out to generic classes. Pass it on.

Open their eyes to art

My own passion is for art. Having been forbidden by my parents from going to art school (which in their eyes meant a lifetime of poverty), I continue to take great pleasure in painting, sculpting, making things and visiting art galleries. From a young age, the children have always come with us to art galleries in London and abroad. Art galleries are great places for children, as they usually feature wide open spaces. Our children wake up at six in the morning, so getting to the Tate Modern at opening time is never a problem, and at that time on a weekend morning, when sane people are still tucked up in bed (or even just going to bed after the night before – ah! those were the days), the gallery is quiet and the children can be let loose. Their attention span is short, so we are never able to take the thoughtful meander that we would have done in our childless days. But many galleries are free, so you can literally pop in to see one picture and then leave without feeling it was a complete waste of money. Most times, I ask the children to choose their favourite painting, or I will point out mine and we will look at it in detail. At other times, I bring paper and pens and they sit and copy their favourite paintings. Sometimes, we paint a picture together when we get home, 'inspired' by our gallery visit. Many exhibits are child-friendly and I can recall D aged three shouting, 'Moo!' in delight at Damien Hirst's cow, completely unperturbed by the fact that it had been cut in half, and Molly looking at Anish Kapoor's exhibit involving a wax cannon saying in hushed tones, 'Mummy, someone has made a mess in here.'

Of course, it's not always sunshine and roses and there are many times when I have had to drag sulky kids, carry sleeping kids, or bribe whingeing kids with gift-shop magnets, but when you later find that they can talk about 'Van Gogh's sunflowers' or say that their favourite artist is 'Kandinsky', it brings joy to the heart. Many galleries these days have great family days where you can work *with* your children on art projects, or at least *alongside* them, and they are usually free. I take great satisfaction in hearing my children say, 'I love art,' and seeing them embark with confidence on creating something from their own imaginations. I am also dreaming of the painting holidays in Tuscany that we will be taking together in the not-so-distant future, as a result of my taking the time to pass on my passion to them.

Checking their privilege – why children should learn to appreciate how lucky they are

Alongside extra-curricular activities and interests, our children's attitudes are undoubtedly shaped by their everyday lives. My children are fortunate enough to grow up in a desirable part of London. Designer children's clothes, designer children's shoes, designer children's toys and designer children's parties are the norm around here, which can all seem a bit mad if you spent your own childhood begging for penny sweets from your friends and making your own chess sets out of the back of a cereal packet. And occasionally I do wonder if all this privilege doesn't come with its own distorted values.

I'm thinking about the time that three-year-old Molly and her friend were on one of those children's car rides that they put outside supermarkets to extract money off parents. Her friend was delighted and declared that she was driving to the cinema. Molly pipes up with lovey aplomb, 'I'm driving to the *theatre.*' Her friend's mother raised an eyebrow at me. Ah, such mixed emotion of pride and embarrassment. To be fair, at that particular time Molly actually had gone to the theatre more times than to the cinema (but I'm talking *The Tiger that Came to Tea*, not Chekhov's *Seagull*) so it was not her fault; but, oh, the snobbery.

Then there was the time Molly and D were playing with their friends on a toy sledge. They pretended the sledge was an aeroplane, packed up belongings and were going on holiday. 'We're off to the Maldives,' one friend cried. 'No, St Lucia,' said the other. Well, why not? A fight ensued because my kids started trying to sell them food on the plane. The others said that you did not need to pay for food on planes. My kids said that you did and demanded that they pay up. I could see where the problem was here . . .

The dreaded children's parties . . .

Children's parties are another area which can get over the top. Kids' party one-upmanship seems to be the order of the day. We have been to kids' parties at health spas and with circus entertainers. My kids' parties are without exception cheap and cheerful involving Andrew dressed as a pirate or a friend bribed with alcohol to come and sing and play guitar. I'm telling you, most kids can't tell the difference! Never mind the actual parties; I don't go big on presents for children, either. Kids who invite my kids to their parties are lucky if they get a small Melissa & Doug wooden jigsaw from me. So it was rather embarrassing then that in the going-home bag of a party at which we had given said small Melissa & Doug jigsaw, was a bigger Melissa & Doug jigsaw, alongside other goodies including sweets, pencils and an anorak! What happened to a slice of cake and a few penny sweets . . . ?

I am, of course, delighted that my children are lucky enough to live in this brilliant part of the world and that they get to experience the good things in life, but I am equally keen for them to know that hard work is at the bedrock of it all, and to take none of it for granted. I believe that my less-than-privileged upbringing has 'recession-proofed' my life and that this is a big bonus. I don't see what's wrong with state primary school, budget airlines and holidays in campsites, and McDonald's is a guilty pleasure. It meant that when I earnt money, I truly enjoyed it, rather than expected it to be so. Further, having had a happy childhood, I know for a fact that happiness does not lie in material wealth. I was just as happy saving up money I'd earnt from babysitting and queueing up at five in the morning for seats to Wimbledon as a teenager, as I am now waltzing into the stewards' enclosure to drink champagne at Henley. I feel saddened when I hear stories of recession-hit families who decant Lidl produce into Waitrose packaging and play at 'Keeping up with the Joneses' when they can't afford it; not only because it assumes that being poorer somehow reflects negatively, but also because shame and cognitive dissonance are the harbingers of poor mental health.

Share Principles as well as Passions

Along with passing on our interests and passions, we (consciously or unconsciously) pass on our values too. I will address this in more detail in the next chapter, which looks at how we can help children form a strong identity. My parents taught me to be proud of myself, of where I came from and of my less than affluent roots. There were inevitably times in adolescence when it was mortifying. For instance, there was the time when my parents – who *never* buy food or snacks at museums and art galleries, even to this day, because of the 'rip-off prices' – made us sit on the steps of the Royal Academy of Art near Mayfair eating a homemade packed lunch. What's wrong with that, I hear you cry? Well, my mother packed tzungtzu (sticky rice wrapped in massive bamboo leaves). They are absolutely delicious and convenient to carry in a backpack. But imagine the looks we got – a ramshackle Chinese family sitting on the steps of the glorious Royal Academy, licking rice off ginormous greasy leaves! We probably did our bit to fuel more prejudice and hate crime.

One might have thought that as an adult I would baulk at these childhood experiences and vow never to let my children suffer in this way. On the contrary, these are some of my favourite memories from childhood – my family harmlessly doing what they enjoyed without worrying what others might think. It probably won't surprise you, then, that outside the glorious Spanish monastery at Montserrat my children ate ham and cheese rolls (siphoned from the hotel's breakfast buffet) out of sanitary towel bags. Who packs cling film on holiday? Imagine my delight when I found that the little plastic bags they give you in fancy hotels for sanitary towels were just the right shape and size for packing a mini baguette roll!

In addition, I made the conscious decision to send my children to a state primary school, although we probably could have cobbled together the money for prep schools. My reasoning was that as we may end up spending money on their education in the future, they will probably not be short of access to privilege if they desire it, but for me it was important that they experience a 'normal' childhood rather like mine. In the formative years of my children's life, I want them to learn, just as I did, that happiness is not stamped on notes; great friends are as likely to come from the local housing estate as the mansions round the corner and good times require no price tag.

So it was with concern that I listened to Molly complaining one day that, 'Our house is so small, my friend's house is much bigger and they have a big garden.' This was all the more worrying as our house is a perfectly decent size. So soon after, when we were on a holiday to visit Andrew's family in South Africa, I made a point of showing Molly and D the township shacks along the roadside. 'Do you see those children playing football? That's their house,' I said, pointing to a small tin shack. 'No it's not. You're joking,' they said. It took a while for them to believe us, but I answered all their questions and I think it sunk in. I hope this, and many similar reality-check conversations since, will cement their feet to the ground.

The value of teaching values

During the last general election, I laughed at some footage showing the shocked face of MP Tristram Hunt when he asked a primary schoolboy, 'Who are you supporting in the election?' and the boy responded, 'UKIP, because I want the immigrants to go back where they came from.' It is unlikely that a boy so young could have researched and come to an informed socio-political understanding of what he was saying; most likely, he was repeating verbatim the views of his family. What this shows is that schools and public programmes alone cannot convincingly spread the messages of tolerance and unity, they also need support from parents and families. It is because the osmosis of values between parents and children is so strong that we have a responsibility to be ultra-conscious of the messages that we are giving them. Not only will children copy our ideas if they are made explicit, but they will try and cobble together what they believe to be our ideas from what we say and do. Children do not just soak up politically correct ideas from society without explanations, often they can come to their own warped conclusions if no explicit explanation is offered, so explanation and discussion about views and values is extremely useful for children.

I am by no means dictating that people share my views and values (if the schoolboy had said, 'Because immigration is causing a strain on public services in this country,' I would have respected that view, even though it differs from my own) but only that parents examine their own words and behaviour and be conscious that these accurately represent the values that they intend to pass on to their children. My personal view is that adults and children are happier and mentally healthier if they learn values of tolerance, love, curiosity, acceptance and openness rather than prejudice, hate, disinterest, resistance and rigidity. This is how I try to teach my children.

Nelson Mandela and the green M&M

Andrew and I were driving through Cape Town one time with the kids, who were in the back of the car being kept quiet by a packet of M&Ms. At one point we drove past the Slave Lodge.

Andrew: Look kids, there's the Slave Lodge.

Molly: What's a slave?

Andrew: It's a person who has no rights and belongs to his or her master. In the olden days, there used to be people who were slaves, but it is wrong and there are no slaves now.

Me: Well, there is modern-day slavery.

Andrew: Yes, but it's not on the same scale and it's quite different.

Me: Also, in South Africa, there used to be a system called apartheid which was also wrong and unfair.

Andrew: That's something different. That's not related to slavery.

Me: I know, but it is still about oppression of people and given we are in South Africa, I think the kids should know about the country's significant recent history.

Andrew: OK. When Daddy was a boy the government used to have a system of separating people by the colour of their skin. The people with pale skin were given all the best land and all the best jobs and the people with skin a different colour had to work for the pale-skinned people.

Me: Yes, if that system was still in place, you two would not be alive because your daddy would not have been allowed to marry me, because I have different colour skin. Silly isn't it?

[We are relishing this in the front seat now. See how we can simplify complex politics into language and examples that the kids can understand?]

Andrew: Then there was a man called Nelson Mandela. Remember when he died and they talked about him in your school assembly?

Me: Yes, he is a very important and good man. Your daddy met him when he was younger.

Andrew: He stood up for the people with darker skin and eventually the silly system was stopped.

Me: Yes, but before that there was a lot of violence and atrocities and he was put into prison.

Andrew: Oh, OK. You want to go into all that?

Me: Yes, it's important that they understand the history of this country, not just the beaches and beautiful scenery.

Andrew: OK . . .

[There ensues a potted history of apartheid from Andrew, with helpful and not-so-helpful interjections and corrections from me, lasting a good half hour.]

Andrew: And that's what happened.

The front seat passengers are smug in the completion of their detailed educational politics/history lesson.

Molly to D: I prefer the green M&M. What about you?

Am I raising a fascist??!

Other attempts at influencing social conscience were equally flawed. As I was driving the children home one day, we saw a man of African ethnicity sweating profusely as he performed his job, which involved using a large hooked stick to manually dredge a pond of its dense amounts of algae and pond weed. 'What a horrible job!' I exclaimed. It was a statement, not a question, so I did not expect any response, but to my surprise, after a pause a small voice shouted from the back, 'He should go back to where he came from.'

I nearly crashed the car in horror. I am sure that those words would sear into the flesh of any ethnic minority person in this country, and many white people too. When I was growing up, 'Go back to where you came from!' was almost as popular a schoolyard taunt as 'Ching Chong Chinaman'. (Funnily though, given that my parents indulged in teaching me more science than sociology and politics, for a while I thought that people expected me to crawl back through my mother's vagina.) How in heaven had I, who prided myself on my liberal leanings, managed to raise a child sprouting this type of invective?

'What do you mean? Why did you say that?' I asked tentatively. Mental images of the sanctimonious telling off I was going to give to her friend, friend's parents, teachers, babysitters, and anyone else she might have had unsupervised contact with, who could have contaminated her with this right-wing view were flashing through my brain.

'Because of what you said.'

'What? When?' I demanded, having never held such views in all my life.

'Two weeks ago, when we were doing maths homework.'

The blood drained from my face in realization. This was the conversation that we had had two weeks prior:

Molly: Why do I have to do this anyway?

Me: Because it's your homework.

Molly: Yes, but it's so boring, why do we need to do maths?

Me: Because if you don't learn to do maths or to read, then you won't be able to get a good job. You'll end up having to clean toilets.

Molly: Does that mean Siaide can't read or do maths?

[Siaide was the school cleaner. Ferocious back-pedalling was required. I could imagine Molly whispering to classmates, 'Yes, it's very sad, she can't read or write so she has to clean the toilets.' Horrifying.]

Me: No, Siaide is very clever but she didn't grow up in this country. She can read and write and do maths very well, but only in her own language. Because she decided to move to this country, she can't read or write or do maths so well in English, which is why she has to clean the school.

Molly seemed to accept this explanation, so with relief we finished the homework.

From this innocent conversation, Molly had extrapolated that people who had moved here from another country should go back to their own countries in order to have better jobs. Seeing the

African man doing a back-breaking job, she figured that given that language was probably the barrier to him getting a 'good' job here, he would have better job prospects in his 'own country'.

From this, I concluded: IT IS SO HARD TO EXPLAIN SOCIAL PROBLEMS TO CHILDREN!

Give me scientific questions like 'What's a rainbow?' (white light split into its composite colours by prism-shaped raindrops) and 'Why is grass green?' (chlorophyll) any day. How to explain social inequality, poverty, racism? Tricky! With relief that at least Molly was not a bigot, I wimped out of going into the other difficult questions (such as, why should she assume that someone

TOP TIPS: ENLIGHTENMENT

Explain the world to your children The world is a confusing place and children will receive a variety of mixed messages from teachers, friends and the media, as well as interpreting their own life experiences. Although we may think that young children are not interested in, or should be protected from politics, things that happen socially and politically will affect them whether we like it or not, whether through their teachers going on strike, or hearing a racist slur in the playground. Helping your children understand and interpret what and why things are happening in a calm, fair and sensible way, allowing them to ask questions, and admitting to not knowing all the answers can help young children begin to understand the world and develop their own opinions and attitudes.

Give them light and let them lead the way Sometimes, we parents like to think that with our many years of life experience we know it all. Yet there are many things that our children can teach us and I hope that with age I can benefit more and more from this. My parents grew up in a very conservative time, in a conservative country where racism, sexism and homophobia were commonplace. When my grandma first visited us in the UK, she shuddered at the thought of meeting a 'black' man because she had never met one before and had only seen them depicted as hoodlums and gangsters on TV. For years, my parents insisted that Boy George was a lady. After decades of being chipped away at, being called racist, sexist and homophobic in turn by their three children, I am rather proud that my parents are now a tolerant couple who stand up for women facing domestic violence and weep in sympathy over Taiwanese-directed films about gay cowboys. I look forward to the day when my children, raised on love, unity and openness, will show me the way of the future.

with darker skin was not from this country?) and issues that might arise that would require explanation of the world's skewed distribution of wealth, immigration, asylum seeking, social class and racism. It's so hard!

I will definitely explain it all properly to the children one day. I just need to think how . . .

Chapter Summary

The outer layers of our children – their attitudes, opinions and extra-curricular interests – are perhaps the most immediately visible. As children grow, these will naturally change and develop according to their own interests and personal life experiences, but for the first seven years of life, they are ours to mould. There are no absolute rights or wrongs when encouraging our children to be creative, but I think parents should grasp the enormous opportunity that they have in these early years to imprint their own values on their children. If these become deeply ingrained, parents can influence their child forever. Although I was deeply embarrassed by my parents in adolescence (a not uncommon experience), in adulthood I am eating homemade rolls out of sanitary towel bags: I seek to emulate, rather than disown them. They have won; they have influenced me forever.

Perhaps you believe that children will reach the same end-point in adulthood whatever you do. This is difficult to refute because of the lack of any counter-factual evidence. But my view is this: if life is a journey and your outcome is your destination, genes will drop you off at the airport. If you are lucky it will be London City Airport, if you are not so lucky, Luton Airport Parkway. Parenting provides you with your backpack: it can be empty, or it can be full of maps, restaurant and hotel reviews, travel guides, good books, a compass, a thermos of cocoa and a bag of chocolate chip cookies. It might not be everything you need, but it sure helps you on the way.

Ultimately, where you go from there is up to you.

8. Layer Six: Identity, Gender and Race

Why Should Mummy Bear Wear the Apron?

Mummy Bear Wears an Apron

In Reception, Molly was cast as Mummy Bear in her class assembly and we were asked to provide the costume. I went with Molly to her dressing-up box to see what we could find. Brown, long-sleeve T-shirt, brown tights, pink skirt. Good, good. But these were just normal clothes. How about some dressing-up stuff so Mummy Bear could be more of a character?

Here is our conversation.

Me: I know, I know [excited], why doesn't Mummy Bear be a doctor and then you can carry this bag and wear this stethoscope around your neck?

Molly: But Mummy Bear wears an apron.

Me: She doesn't have to, she can be a doctor. Or, I know, you can wear this fireman's costume and Mummy Bear can be a fireman.

Molly: Mummy Bear wears an apron, because she makes the porridge.

Me: Are you sure? Maybe Daddy Bear made the porridge? Your daddy makes you porridge and pancakes sometimes.

Molly: In the book at school [insistent], Mummy Bear makes the porridge and wears an apron.

Molly wore an apron.

This was one example in a long line of unsuccessful attempts by me to break the gender stereotypes prevalent in society.

The first attempt was just before Molly's third birthday, when the nursery decided to have a whole week of fancy dress. This must have been a sadistic joke on the nursery's behalf as I saw poor children being trundled into nursery for five whole days wearing the same Spiderman pyjamas, their working parents looking very displeased. I vowed that we would at least attempt five different costumes, however crappy the results. Molly was not yet three years old, so at that time I was still winning the war on polyester princess dresses. The first day, she went as a cat. We had a foam cat-mask from some party she had been to, and she wore a black long-sleeved T-shirt and black leggings. The second day, I had decided that she could go as a pirate. She had a jumper with a skull and cross bones on, some denim shorts and she could put a handkerchief around her head. I managed to coerce her into this outfit. She was not happy.

Molly: I don't want to be a pirate. They are boys.

Me: No, there are girl pirates as well. Pirates aren't just for boys.

Molly: None of the other girls will be pirates.

Me: Well, it's nice to be something different.

I had got her to the door by now, although she resisted crossing the threshold into the outside world. Eventually, she slumped down across the doorway in tears.

Molly: Why can't I just be a princess like everyone else?

This was too much, even for a feminist like me. Was I really going to force my daughter to do something against her will based on my own ideology? I made her go as a pirate but promised that she could go as a princess the next day, and that was how the war on pink polyester was lost.

The second attempt was when Molly requested a pink stethoscope for her fourth birthday. I went to Toys 'R' Us to purchase said stethoscope, only to find that the only pink stethoscopes they had were attached to a nurse's uniform. The doctor's costume, meanwhile, was resplendent with blue stethoscope. I literally stood in front of the costumes for hours, deliberating in my mind. Should I buy the doctor's uniform and encourage her to break some stereotypes so that she might aspire to be a doctor like me, or was it too much hassle to risk tears on her birthday and screams of, 'I wanted a pink one!' There were no tears on her birthday.

The third time was when Molly and D were playing together.

Molly: You be the doctor and I'll be the nurse.

Me: Wait, why can't D be the nurse and you be the doctor?

Molly and D in unison: Because doctors are boys and nurses are girls!

Me: [in disbelief that this is happening in my own household] No, they are not! I am a doctor and I am a woman.

Molly and D: [looking at me silently for a moment as they ponder this puzzling conundrum]

Molly: Yes, but he wants to be the doctor and I want to be the nurse. Anyway the nurse's uniform has a skirt so it is for a girl.

Damn you, Toys 'R' US! I knew I should never have bought the pink stethoscope!

It was because of such incidents that I felt I could not write a book on parenting without including a chapter on gender-neutral parenting and gender-neutral parents, as this is an issue I feel extremely passionate about. As we enter a new era of dual-income families and same-sex parents, I think that we 'parenting experts' need to adapt. For starters, we need to stop the mother bashing ('refrigerator mother', 'good-enough mother', 'schizophrenogenic mother', 'maternal guilt' – all terms coined by my professional predecessors) and create a new rhetoric. Yes, it is still a fact that the majority of parenting, even in dual-income families, is done by mothers. Nevertheless child psychiatrists, psychologists and other people who have a voice in parenting should be leading the way by pointing out the lack of a scientific evidence base for the crucial role of mothers (over fathers) advocated by our predecessors. We should be leading the way in advocating gender-neutral parents, and emphasizing the individual qualities that parents of either gender can bring to their children. Equally, that boys and girls should be raised as individuals rather than identified by their gender, as our unconscious biases in parenting and education can have far-reaching consequences which curtail potential in both girls and boys. I believe that girls and boys are more similar than we think, and the era of separate parenting strategies for them should be consigned to history.

Gender-Neutral Parenting

I attribute any academic success that I have had 100 per cent to the fact that I did not have a brother. Taiwanese parents of my parents' generation had a strong preference for sons, but having none meant my parents had no choice but to put their hopes and aspirations into us girls and foster and promote our abilities *as if* we were boys, and as such, capable of anything. My parents rarely did things for us, but taught us how to do things for ourselves, from cooking to changing the fuse in a plug. We were encouraged to be independent rather than reliant. My father spent time teaching my sisters and me computer programming and electronics when we were in primary school. I was never interested, but my sisters went on to study engineering and maths at top universities. Had we had a brother, I am sure that things would have been different. He would have been the one encouraged and burdened in equal measure with the pedestal, and we girls would have been left to cultivate a pastime. Unfortunately, like me, my parents were not able to fully rebel against societal norms, and in addition to academic encouragement in traditionally male-dominated disciplines, we were, of course, still expected to cook, clean, behave modestly and serve our father.

In the West, where the gender preference is less explicit, one can almost believe that the problem does not exist, but when you examine behaviours more closely, you begin to see that gender-based parenting is still pervasive. We can blame media and society at large as much as we want, but the reality is that we are all culpable: from the toys we buy to the interests we encourage, the expectations we hold, the behaviour we accept, the activities we choose to do, the assets that we praise and our own day-to-day behaviour and language.

Even when we think we are being gender neutral, or are trying to be, often we are not, because gender bias is so subtle. How many parents of boys have actively gone out to a toy store and bought their son a baby doll, a push chair and a bottle? How many parents of girls have done this? From my inspection of the bed-rooms of the little boys I know, I would say that very few boys have been bought dolls specifically. The parents will make the justification, 'Oh, he was never interested in dolls.' Yet, from my experience of little boys with *older* sisters, the majority enjoy playing with baby dolls in the pre-school years (before peer pressure kicks in). Even more so if actively encouraged, as you would naturally encourage a girl. That's just one example of many.

How many times have you praised your daughter for looking beautiful? How many times have you done this for your son? How many times have you rebuked your daughter for spoiling their dress, but allowed your son to get mucky? How many times have you praised your daughter's social skills, whilst praising your son's mathematical ability? How many times have you persisted with a one-on-one craft activity with your daughter, even though she was bored and you ended up doing it yourself, while saying that your son does not have the patience for it and taking him out to run around in the park instead? When it's a boy's birthday party, how many times have you bought LEGO as a present, while choosing a craft jewellery kit for a girl? In answer to that last question I can reveal that at a recent joint birthday party for my kids, the total tally on craft activity for Molly was 5/20 and 0/20 for LEGO, whereas D scored a whopping 8/20 on the LEGO, 0/20 for craft. We are all guilty to a greater or lesser extent of the above perpetuations of gender stereotypes (myself included) without even thinking about it.

Unconscious gender bias is everywhere

This type of unconscious gender bias has been studied in relation to women in academia and the workplace, and their lack of advancement, and is thought to be one of the driving factors for the lack of women in science. King's College London's unconscious bias training defines unconscious bias as, 'Biases of which we are not in conscious control. These biases occur automatically, triggered by our brain making quick judgments and assessments of people and situations based on our background, cultural environment and our experiences.' One key study highlights the scale of the inequalities that can arise from unconscious bias.[1] This study asked male and female senior academic faculty members to assess the job applications for the position of laboratory manager at a science faculty. Amongst the applications, the exact same application form was sent to raters 127 times, but given the applicant name of John half the time, and Jennifer the other half. Despite having exactly the same form, selectors rated John as a significantly better candidate than Jennifer, and they also offered John more money and mentorship. Both male and female senior staff made the same decisions. This type of experiment shouts out that there is still a very long way to go before we reach real gender equality.

My view is that it is not only in the workplace that these unconscious biases are occurring. By virtue of being unconscious they permeate every aspect of our lives, including the parenting of our children. Long before 'Jennifer' was facing employment discrimination, she would have faced two decades of gender-based 'brain-shaping' by parents, schools and society which would have already limited her chances of applying for the position of laboratory manager at a science faculty in the first place. How?

In Chapter Five, I discussed 'behavioural management' as a parenting technique that uses discriminating encouragement, rewards and praise to help shape children's behaviour. In fact, this technique can be used to help a child to do anything, from concentrating longer to eating their greens. If our parenting is guided by unconscious bias that encourages, rewards and praises our children according to gender stereotypes, then we are unconsciously grooming our children into gender-based norms. Behavioural management is even more powerful if there is consistency in rewarding the same behaviour across contexts (for example, home and school). For gender-based norms, there is almost universal consistency in the take-home message.

Here are some common gender expectations:

Girls: pretty, well-behaved, obliging, modest, good listener, kind, clean, sociable, gentle, empathetic, comforting, manipulative, bitchy, bossy, creative, loves languages and communicating, sensitive.

Boys: boisterous, loud, limited attention span, active, sporty, out-doorsy, mathematical, likes rough and tumble, aggressive, cheeky, dirty, assertive, opinionated, analytical, brave, straightforward.

The consistency makes the message even more powerful, to the extent that non-conformity becomes pathological. In clinics, I have found many unhappy girls who have more of the latter qualities, and many boys with the former. These children often feel sad, lonely, bullied and ostracized because they do not 'fit in'. So common is this phenomenon that gender-identity clinics are seeing an explosion in referrals as we begin to be able to talk openly about these issues. Yet, is this a problem with the children, or is it the way we, as a society, choose to pigeonhole them? It is only by making our bias *conscious* that we can interact in a child-centric rather than a gender-centric way with our children. How different would girls and boys be if gender was irrelevant in the treatment they received from birth?

My Chinese daughter believes she's a blonde

I'm taking a detour here into racial difference. It might seem odd, but there is a point because even in our very recent history, peoples of different ethnicity were treated very differently from each other and unconscious bias today is likely to be as prevalent for race as it is for gender.

Race and skin colour is a tricky thing to talk about. I had my own (albeit mild) experiences of racism as an immigrant to the UK, which over the years prompted a fair share of ponderings regarding racial identity. I wanted my children to avoid this kind of 'identity crisis' if possible, and thought I knew how to handle matters. As with all things pertaining to children, this didn't always go entirely to plan.

Most parents naturally draw on their own experiences of childhood as a point of reference, both in terms of how to do things and how not to do things. Having emigrated from Taiwan to the UK, my race had at times been an issue for me growing up. It is well known that immigration has strong associations with mental health, due to the stress both of leaving behind a social network and of feeling like an outsider, or 'not belonging / being accepted' in the new country. The stress of leaving behind family was more of a problem for my parents than for me, but I certainly sometimes experienced the 'not belonging' feelings. Although I was largely anglicized, my outward appearance was clearly Chinese, and this bothered me for a long time. I remember one instance when I was ten: I closed my eyes tight and wished very hard that when I opened my eyes again I would have white skin. I didn't want to change who I was, or my family, just the colour of my skin. It wasn't the taunts of 'Ching Chong Chinaman' or mock martial-arts moves I was constantly subjected to, which were easily dispelled by my sharp tongue, but the pervasive stereotyping. Rightly or wrongly, I felt it was grossly unfair that all 'Chinese people' (which actually included any East Asian ethnicity from Japanese to Indonesian) were regarded as what I refer to as 'book nerds'. Every teacher and every employer I have ever had has described me as 'conscientious'. Why don't people just say 'efficient', which implies the same but without the connotations of hard working? I felt that there was a bias that went along the lines of people thinking clever white kids were 'naturally clever', while clever Chinese kids 'worked hard, but did nothing but work and were definitely a bit uncool'.

It's much better now than in the past. Susie Bubble, Jemma Chan, Alexa Chung, Gok Kwan, Mylene Klass, Lucy Liu, Devon Aoki and even my old friend Ching He Huang are regularly on television rocking the Asian cool. I don't think that I would have had such an issue with being Chinese if I was growing up in London today, but I grew up in the era where Chinese people on television were represented by Peter Sellers in fancy dress. An Indian friend described a similar stereotyping problem he had, saying how *Indiana Jones and the Temple of Doom* was his most hated film, as he was forever being mocked about eating monkeys' heads at his school, Eton. Funnily enough, it was also in the most privileged of environments, at Cambridge University, where I experienced the most ignorant, petty racial stereotyping. Frequently people commented on how good my English was and questioned where my Chinese accent was from, to which I responded, 'Norf London, innit.' Others commented on my 'strange' keenness for shepherd's pie: 'I thought Chinese people only liked rice!' I am seriously not making this up! My poor Etonian friend fared no better. He went backpacking around Nepal with a school friend, and on their return was told by his friend that his family had mistaken him in the trip photos for 'the hired native that carried the bags', proving that for some people, even an Eton and Cambridge education cannot cut through the colour of one's skin.

I remember being acutely jealous of a Romanian friend of mine, who despite also being an immigrant to the country managed to pass herself off as the quintessential English rose by virtue of her white skin, blonde hair and European name. She was never once asked about Romania, or treated to random stories starting, 'I met a Romanian once . . .' It struck me that skin colour is important here, because although second generation Eastern European immigrants will be fully accepted as British (if their names permit), my children and grandchildren may not.

This thought was on my mind at the point of naming Molly and D. I was acutely conscious that I wanted to give them the gift of racial anonymity. Being mixed race, they are a skin colour of 'ambiguous' ethnicity. I wanted them to be taken for who they were, not what their name or skin colour represented. They were given mainstream European names and took my husband's European surname, such that unless they chose to divulge their Chinese middle names, on paper, no one would be able to tell that they were not European. This was a fully conscious decision, because even though we live in much enlightened times, even in a cosmopolitan city like London I think race and skin colour still mean something.

That said, I take instilling cultural pride and identity in my children seriously. They are told that they are Taiwanese, and pitch up proudly on school cultural days in Chinese costumes, brandishing the Taiwanese flag. They regularly eat Chinese food, they have visited Taiwan, and they spend regular time with their Taiwanese grandparents in London. They identify with being Chinese.

Great, hey? My plan was working. Knowledge, awareness and pride in their ethnic roots, but also the possibility of hiding behind the mask of complete 'European-ness' when required.

What happened next, then, was rather unexpected. It started with a discussion of Disney Princesses:

Me: Which is your favourite Disney Princess?

Molly: Sleeping Beauty. Or maybe Cinderella. They are the prettiest.

Me: I like Jasmine.

Molly: I don't like Jasmine.

Me: Why?

Molly: She wears trousers.

Me: [Phew, this is related to fashion rather than race] OK, then, what about Mulan, you look most like Mulan.

Molly: No I don't.

Me: Yes you do.

Molly: No I don't.

Me: You have black hair and so does Mulan.

Molly: No I don't, I have yellow hair.

This wasn't a one-off; this sort of thing continued. At the end of Reception, Molly's Year Six partner gave her a Chinese-looking Barbie doll.

Me: That's nice; she's given you a Chinese Barbie.

Molly: How did she know I was Chinese?

Me: Because you look Chinese.

Molly: No I don't.

Me: You have black hair.

Molly: No I don't.

Me: You have yellowish, brownish skin.

Molly: No I don't, I have light skin.

Me: [What the hell?] *Silence.*

I was not surprised, then, that when Molly's Year One class produced a tea towel, with each child's self-portrait printed on it, I saw that she had depicted herself with blonde hair. What I didn't expect – and was relieved to see – was that her blonde best friends had drawn themselves with black hair. Maybe Molly's image of herself as being blonde was not about race, but something deeper about identity and wanting to belong: wanting to be the same as her friends. It struck me that I could learn from this; that difference is in the eye of the beholder and where we seek to find similarity not difference, we can find it – however improbable.

From a scientific perspective, an awful lot of energy was spent in the past looking for differences between peoples of different ethnicities. I am ashamed to say that my forebears in science were responsible for several publications regarding the intellectual and physical superiority of Caucasians compared to other races. Skull sizes and shapes, IQ testing and various other 'science-based data' was used for this endeavour. This science was given credibility by the glaringly obvious differences in skin pigmentation. Hell, even muscle structure, blood and bone marrow typing are different between races, so racial difference must be real and important and should dictate social policy. So it was thought.

Yet in more enlightened times, we are happy to overlook these minor differences. Sense, it would seem, has prevailed. Just as with Molly and her pals, when similarity rather than difference is sought, it is found in spades.

Exploding the myths around gender difference

So, why can't this be the same for gender? We no longer say, 'You can't be President because you are black,' so why do we still say, 'You can't look after children because you have a penis?'

Yes, yes, I am medically trained and am therefore well aware of the genetic, anatomical and hormonal differences between the male and female of our species. As a scientist interested in gene-environment interactions though, the questions I pose are these:

1) How much of measured difference is genetic/biological, as opposed to shaped consciously or unconsciously by society?

2) Are the differences so large that we should apply entirely different sets of rules to the way we treat girls and boys at home, school and work?

Boys and girls are more similar than you think

Gender difference is much smaller in children. For children aged up to seven years, the main effects of the sex hormones oestrogen and testosterone have not yet come into play, and girls and boys at this age should be more similar than at any other age. Boys can still hit the high notes and girls can run without hindrance from their own body parts. Yet the differences in the way they are treated (by parents, schools, media and society at large) start at birth and will already be marked by the time they reach the end of this age group.

If you look for differences, they will be found. I have it on the word of a couple of mates of mine – a Queen's Square neurologist and a John Radcliffe (Oxford) neuro-radiologist, since you ask – that if they were handed a brain or an MRI scan of a brain, they would not be able to tell if it belonged to a man or woman. Yet we are always being told about the massive brain differences between men and women. Practically every science paper on any medical condition will report sex differences. As a scientist, I know that one of the first steps in data analysis is to report the gender of the sample and to look for these sex effects. In every scientific publication involving a human sample, sex differences will be vigorously sought out. We scientists are trained like truffle pigs to sniff out and bring back to the world the sex differences that we just know are hiding there in our data sets. Sometimes they exist and sometimes they don't. If you find a sex difference it will go straight into your write-up, if you don't, then it's *boring*, and not worth mentioning. Think of it as a bad-science, Ben Goldacre-ish sort of publication bias, one that continually reports gender difference. If we were to be absolutely fair about it we should make a huge list of all the ways in which girls and boys are similar and all the ways they are different. I am pretty sure that the similarities would far outnumber the differences.

There are overlaps rather than complete differences. Whichever differences you care to cite, verbal ability, social ability, map-reading ability, speed, strength and so forth, even when these are borne out in large samples of tests between men and women, the results will show overlapping function rather than completely discriminate groups. Put simply, this means that a variable proportion of women will perform like men, and a variable proportion of men will perform like women. Even when there is a really obvious biological difference between men and women, such as muscle mass, the difference in performance is not huge. Less than fifty years ago, this difference was amplified to the extent that women were thought too feeble to run a marathon, and were thus prevented from doing so. Nowadays, I am pretty sure that Paula Radcliffe could beat more than 99 per cent of men in a marathon and female participation in marathons continues to rise year on year. Although the mean strength/speed of the average man will be faster than that of the average woman, the overlap is great.

Typical 'male' qualities, such as aggression, high sexual drive, lesser verbal/social skills, the ability to read maps, the reluctance to ask for directions, are also found in many women. The liberation of women in the last century has seen women freed to express their sexuality and their aggression, and to turn to vices previously the preserve of men: smoking, drinking, ASBOs, fisticuffs and the like. Conversely, contrary to popular belief, many men are able to multi-task.

Are these differences biologically or environmentally mediated? Do boys have a genetic predisposition for fighting, stealing and getting into trouble with the police or do we as a society encourage this? Boys are encouraged in rough and tumble play; to stand up for themselves, physically if necessary. Boys will be boys, after all. Do girls have a biological predisposition for depression and eating disorders? Or do we as a society somehow encourage this? Girls are encouraged to care about their looks and discouraged from showing anger and aggression to others. The evidence is very hard to find as no culture has yet managed to obliterate gender bias in parenting, education or society. I think that genuine biological differences are there if you look for them, but as we have seen how early environment can shape our children's brains, so it can amplify the difference between genders. Crucially, it is us as a society who decide the significance that is attributed to these minor differences.

And finally . . . Even if you think everything I have said is nonsense and believe strongly that there are overriding biological gender differences, would you disagree that the fundamentals of human security, the stuff that makes a child flourish – warmth, love, praise, affection and guidance – are universal, and not gender specific? Why, then, should girls and boys be treated differently because of their gender? Where it matters, we are the same.

What horror, then, to find that on top of the prevalent unconscious bias in the way we treat girls and boys, there has been a recent fashion in deliberately parenting them differently? I believe that drawing up parenting plans specifically led by gender-based social pressures perpetuates old gender stereotypes and that this is damaging and retrogressive. Society is moving towards equality, why should parenting be any different? We should be calling out gender bias in parenting and education. This does not mean that we always have to treat boys and girls the same. It means that we treat each boy and each girl as an individual, giving them equal opportunities to explore their own femininity and masculinity, whatever their biological sex.

The antidote

I love the recent explosion of campaigns designed to inspire girls into traditionally male fields. A glossy advertising campaign from *Sports England* showed ordinary girls and women of all shapes, sizes and colours enjoying sport. On the surface it was about sport and fitness, but ultimately it was about self-esteem. Its underlying message is that women should be confident about their bodies, which is great and why the campaign has been so acclaimed. There have been a number of other positive campaigns empowering women to achieve; to study maths and science, aim high, aspire and be ambitious. *Great!* Despite all that women have achieved in the last one hundred years, I can attest that they still underestimate their ability in the workplace and this media encouragement is totally welcome.

However, it doesn't work on its own.

How do I know? Because I, and all the other girls who were fed through an ambitious, high-expectation girls school in the nineties, have already heard this message. We were already aiming high, flying the flag. Then, like generations of women before us, we were stopped in our tracks – either when we reached the higher echelons of our organizations or when we fell pregnant. Many of us even felt bitter about the encouragement we had received as schoolgirls, because we had been fed a dream that society could not yet deliver.

The bottom line is that there is only so much that women can change. Society has to play a part too. Running advertising campaigns encouraging women 'to change' (which is code for encouraging them to become more confident and ambitious) in order to fit into pre-existing masculine organizations does not work. In fact, it perpetuates the myth that the reason equality has not yet been achieved is because women have not put enough effort into changing: 'They do not put themselves forward', 'They shy away from leadership positions', 'They choose to opt out'. These flawed arguments turn a blind eye to all the women who are put off by the sexism, bullying and macho cultures that still abound in many of the top professions. (Something that also puts off a significant number of men.) In addition, the fact is that if society wants there to be a next generation, *someone* needs to look after the children. Many of us believe strongly that this should be the child's parents. If we continue to one-sidedly empower girls and women to take on rewarding and powerful careers, what is society's solution to the issues of 'parenting' and 'family-life'? Ask any psychiatrist or psychologist: childcare is not the same as parenting. Empowering girls alone is not the solution.

What is the solution?

I believe that for every 'Girls can do what we used to only expect boys to do' advertising campaign, there should be a corresponding 'Boys can do what we used to only expect girls to do' one. Footage of boys crying, talking about their emotions, helping

TOP TIPS: FREEDOM OF CHOICE AND EXPRESSION

Mind your language Engendered language is very pervasive, which is why it is so hard to overcome. Every traditional tale and history lesson is encoded in gender stereotype. Every word we choose to use may be gender-stereotyped (ambitious men/pushy women) even the words 'to father a child' and 'to mother a child' mean completely different things (the former means to impregnate a woman, the other to mollycoddle). My view is that language is a good place to start, as it is the fabric of our culture and society. To this cause, I hope that you appreciate that in this book where I mean 'parent', I use the word 'parent', rather than 'mother', which cannot be said for the majority of parenting scientific papers, news articles, websites and media. Even then, it was harder to do this than even I, an out-and-proud feminist, imagined, as 'parent' and 'mother' are just *so* deeply ingrained as synonymous.

Offer a free choice of activities In the selection of extra-curricular activities for my children, both children have been offered the opportunity to participate in what the other (opposite gender child) wanted to do. So when Molly wanted to do ballet, D was also offered the opportunity. When D wanted to do chess and football, Molly was also offered the opportunity. As it turned out, D declined ballet but took up street dance and Molly plays chess and football. We parents can engender our children by the extra-curricular activities we set for them. Billy Elliot was offered boxing, not ballet.

Play I have no idea if this is scientifically supported, but I have found that little boys who have *older* sisters are more than happy to play with dolls and kitchen sets. However, boys who do not have any siblings or who are the older sibling usually don't. Their bedrooms are universally masculine, filled with cars, balls, LEGO sets and jungle animals. Many parents hold the view that boys should not play with dolls. Would I have bought a doll and kitchen set for my son if I had not had a daughter first? I can't honestly say. What I can say, is that many boys enjoy and should be allowed to explore these toys and develop this side of themselves, in the same way that girls should not be denied balls, LEGO and cars. If we want men to be caring and domestically engaged, they need to rehearse these skills from childhood and know that these aspects of themselves are valuable. The same goes for girls and their engagement in science and sport. The toys and environment that we parents provide in these first years of life are a large part, if not the entirety, of a child's first experience of the world. A limited milieu at this age may shape a life.

another child, reading, drawing, dancing, dressing up as a princess. Footage of men sticking on plasters, listening to the ideas of their female colleagues, talking to their daughters, nursing their elderly parents, helping children with their homework, picking up children from school, doing the laundry, cleaning the house, cooking the family dinner. These are the activities that really keep Britain going. The engines of Britain are not just the boardrooms, but the living rooms, dining rooms and kitchens across the country. Without these domestic engines, no one could get to work. As long as these activities are undervalued and represented as 'female', or lower-order, tasks, there can be no escape for women from the home and little respect for women overall.

Many boys and men already do these things and they need to

know that their efforts are appreciated. The ones who are not doing these things need to be empowered and enabled to do so, otherwise any women's empowerment programme will be futile. If we want women in the boardroom, we will need men in the nursery. As long as we continue to view ambition, aspiration, determination and ruthlessness as the only virtues worth rewarding, we are devaluing and undermining the equally valuable virtues of compassion, loyalty, understanding and sensitivity. As such, we marginalize the fantastic people (male and female) who possess these traits and we will create future generations with warped and unbalanced ideals. While empowering girls is good, we must also focus on educating boys. To balance the campaigns that seek to empower girls, we desperately need some campaigns to empower boys to truly be themselves.

Identity and parents

I have talked a lot about the importance of role-modelling as a learning tool for children. If we want children to grow up without the limitations of gender stereotyping, the best place to start is in the home. Here, many families (including my own) are already falling at the first hurdle of gender-neutral parenting: gender-neutral parents. As I said earlier, throughout this book I have used the term 'parent', a deliberately gender-neutral term, because I have written this book with both mothers and fathers in mind. However, just in case the message still hasn't quite got through, here is my tongue-in-cheek take on the issue:

Gender-neutral parents

Can a man change nappies?
  Yes He Can. (Astronauts use velcro to strap things down. They are mainly men. Sewage workers deal with excrement. They are mainly men.)

Can a man puree vegetables?

Yes He Can. (I have seen many men do this on *Masterchef*.)

Can a man bottle-feed expressed milk/formula?

Yes He Can. (Vets and farmers bottle-feed lambs all the time. They are mainly men.)

Can a man sterilize bottles?

Yes He Can. (Scientists sterilize their equipment all the time. They are mainly men.)

Can a man do the laundry?

Yes He Can. (Bachelors do this without a problem.)

Can a man cook the dinner?

Yes He Can. (Most professional chefs are male – particularly the highly paid ones. Funny, that.)

Can a man sing nursery rhymes?

Yes He Can. (Justin Fletcher, OBE: male.)

Can a man take a child to the doctor?

Yes He Can. (Unskilled task, any numpty can do this.)

Can a man drop off and pick up at a nursery?

Yes He Can. (Unskilled task, any numpty can do this.)

Can a man read the letters that come back from school?

Yes He Can. (Any literate person can do this.)

Can a man check a child's homework?

Yes He Can. (If he has the intellect to be able to do the home-work, he is qualified to check it.)

Can a man pick up an unwell child from school?

Yes He Can. (Unskilled task, any numpty can do this.)

Can a man iron name labels onto clothes?

Yes He Can. (If he can iron shirts for work, he can do this.)

Can a man sign a permission slip?

Yes He Can. (I presume he can write his own name.)

Can a man make an Easter hat?

Yes He Can. (Mister Maker is a man.)

Can a man read with a child?

Yes He Can. (Any literate person can do this.)

Can a man interview a nanny/au pair/babysitter?

Yes He Can. (Many men interview staff for jobs.)

Can a man go to a parents' evening?

Yes He Can. (Unskilled task, any numpty can do this.)

Can a man give a cuddle?

Yes He Can.

There you have it. Confirmation, with observational evidence from a medically qualified doctor, trained in medicine, genetics, psychiatry and psychology. There is no medical, genetic, psychiatric or psychological reason why men cannot do any of the above.

Where men are not doing these things, there are only two reasons:

1) Men don't want to.

2) Women don't want them to (they don't want to nag or fight with their partner/they want control over parenting and the household).

I hope that you will take all this in the light-hearted way in which it was intended. I am a feminist, but not a 'man-hating' one. Quite the contrary; I love and value men, which is why I believe that they can bring so much more to their children than a pay packet. Men are a highly skilled and under-utilized resource in parenting and deserve to step out from their supporting role. Their involvement should be actively encouraged. Just as equality in boardrooms benefits companies, equality in parenting will benefit children. Some men may not parent in the same way as women, just as some women may not lead companies in the same way as men, but new ideas and ways to do things should always be welcome.

When Andrew was tasked with looking after seven-month-old Molly during his gardening leave, he shunned the music classes I took her to. Instead he purchased a jogging buggy and ran for miles with her down to a mini-assault course where she sat and watched him do sit-ups. Not exactly what I would have done, but hey, Molly stayed alive and who's to say that the fresh air and adrenaline was any worse than being encouraged to jangle bells and shake rattles by an over-enthused teenager? If more men took an active interest in parenting, and more women allowed them to do so, equality in the workplace and society would follow.

Dads are parents too

A few months ago I attended a fascinating talk on the impact of maternal post-natal depression on children. As I've previously mentioned, for children this impact lasts not just for the duration of the mother's depression; because of the massive brain development that happens in the baby's first year of life, unfortunately it can be life-long. Many clinical trials have been undertaken to treat maternal post-natal depression to prevent negative outcomes in children, such as cognitive behavioural therapy (CBT) and anti-depressant medication, but all have had only marginal effects.

When questions went to the floor about possible solutions, people came up with the same old answers: better awareness, more resources for CBT for mothers, and a few medical innovations: a blast of oxytocin nasal spray. Oxytocin is the 'mothering' hormone released in pregnancy and during breastfeeding and when it is given to apes it has been found to increase 'maternal behaviour'.

Tentatively, I put up my hand. 'Umm – wouldn't it just be easier to ask the dads to step up and do the parenting bit?' It struck me as obvious that if the best anti-depressants were contra-indicated in breastfeeding, and CBT was taking too long, that one should look not to new and under-developed drugs like oxytocin to 'cure' the mother, but to additional support that could take over the 'warmth, love, responsive parenting, engagement and social interaction' with the baby. The clue was in the term 'parenting'. Dads are parents too.

What amazed me was the response.

Maybe I had asked a silly question. Maybe there were already piles of research, unread by me, that excluded fathers from nurturing a baby. There was an awkward silence as if I had breached some sort of sacred unspoken code of conduct. There followed mutterings from my esteemed male colleagues in the front row. The speaker, a lovely man but clearly shaped by the ideology of his generation, responded to my question thus (as verbatim as I can remember, but I cannot vouch that it is word for word): 'Yes, but there is already a large role for fathers to take to support their wives. Often fathers are at work.'

Yowzers!

I wondered if I had time travelled back to the 1960s.

Can it really be that in the twenty-first century, my esteemed, brilliant, talented, caring profession is still stuck in a time-warp? Decades after my predecessors saddled mothers with terms such as 'Refrigerator mother', 'Schizophrenogenic mother', 'Good-enough mother', 'Tell me about your mother' along with all the volumes on the paramount importance of maternal bonding and maternal attachment – can it be that we have not moved on from the primeval importance of mothers to babies?

Parental bonding: the maternal versus paternal debate

- Parental bonding and responsive parenting to babies is vital.

- Biology provides some mothers with an advantage over fathers for bonding through pregnancy, birth and breastfeeding hormones. This hormonally driven advantage is lost once mothers stop breastfeeding. In the UK, less than 30 per cent of mothers will still be breastfeeding their babies at six months.

- Some mothers lack this advantage and are uninterested in babies.

- Some mothers get post-natal depression and are completely incapable of, or are severely handicapped in, their bonding and responsive parenting.

The conclusion should be that fathers who have a strong desire to bond and care for their babies are no less capable of bonding and parenting than mothers. Once mothers have stopped breastfeeding, they and their husbands are equally placed biologically to provide the love, care and nurture that is required to support a baby's development. If a mother has post-natal depression or is uninterested or incapable of parenting for whatever reason, then the father is better placed to provide the love, care and support (provided he is not also disinterested or depressed).

And yet, there is no evidence to support this.

Just piles and piles of research on the bad outcomes for babies raised by mothers with problems. Why is that?

The myth of the 'Indispensable Mother'

In the past, it was the mother's role to nurture babies and look after the children. The body of evidence regarding mothers has built up over time. People writing research proposals and funding bodies granting money for research want to see an 'evidence base' for the work that they are funding. Very little research has been done on fathers as the main carers for babies because, up until the last few decades, this just happened so rarely. Even today, the vast majority of funded research in the parenting area relates to looking at mothers and their children. There is no evidence that fathers can care for babies, but equally, there is no evidence that they can't. There is no robust scientific evidence that maternal care is better than paternal care. Aficionados of Ben Goldacre (who writes about 'bad science') will know that in order to robustly prove this, the scientific gold standard would be a blinded and controlled study with a very large sample size taken over time. In other words, you would have to follow a large cohort of babies raised mainly by men and another cohort raised mainly by women (matched for economic, educational and social factors) and then assess the children 'blind' – without knowing whether they were raised by mothers or fathers. Guess what? This has never been done. Naturalistic studies are only now becoming possible because of the advent of increasing numbers of same-sex parents. We should soon be able to scientifically compare two dads with two mums and be able to answer the question of the necessity of maternal care; but until the evidence is out, I don't think that 'experts' should inject so much gender bias and judgement into their advice.

The future of parenting

From my experience of working with same-sex families, men have made damn good parents. The gay dads that I have met (both personally and professionally) have largely been fantastically capable of love, warmth and responsive parenting and I am still unsure why two X chromosomes are required to change nappies, puree food and sing 'The Wheels on the Bus'. If someone can find the evidence on this, please publish it. In my mind, there is nothing inherent in the Y chromosome that incapacitates good parenting; it is society, perpetuated by the experts, media, and let's face it, even you and I that hampers progress. There remain large incentives for many people *not* to produce research and data that may support equality in parenting capability.

I think it's time to start challenging the skewed evidence that was carried out in less equal times and start generating new scientific evidence on 'fathering'. My profession should be at the forefront of this research, helping to stamp out the gender bias in parenting. As we move slowly towards equality within the workplace, I don't see why child psychiatrists and psychologists can't do more to bring gender equality to the issues of parental responsibility and childcare. Meanwhile, government initiatives seem to be handing over more and more childcare to the state. We need to take back control of our own parenting. Both parents, in concert where possible; gender should be irrelevant. The advent of paternity leave is a small step in the right direction, but more still can be done.

I am reminded again of Harlow's primate experiments. The baby monkey chose to lay with the wire-frame dummy covered in faux fur that gave it warmth and comfort, rather than the wire-frame monkey that gave it milk. It is love that matters, not mammary glands, and I am confident in my assertion that mothers and fathers are equally capable of that.

The Maternal Work–Life Balance:
From Babies to Four-Year-Olds

What my esteemed colleagues failed to recognize was that in this day and age, many mothers are also working. Many mothers are breadwinners, who love and are brilliant at the jobs they do. I love children and couldn't have been happier when I became pregnant. I had always wanted children, and indeed was one of the first of my cohort of peers to become pregnant. What I totally didn't expect was to get MAD.

Maternal Adjustment Disorder

This is not a real disorder, but it should be. Adjustment disorder is a real disorder (ratified in World Health Organization mental health classifications) and I have just bunged 'maternal' in front of it to describe how I, and many other mums I know, felt when we first became mums.

The legitimate diagnosis of adjustment disorder is described as a 'state of subjective distress and emotional disturbance, usually interfering with social function and performance, and arising in the period of adaptation to a significant life change or to the consequences of a stressful life event. The stressor may have affected the integrity of an individual's social network or the wider system of social supports and values.'[2] It's supposed to apply to stressors like migration, bereavement or adaptation to illness or disability; but why not modern-day motherhood?

Having a child is a significant life change. What I found distressing was not the obvious things – the sleepless nights, the financial pressures, the breastfeeding, blah, blah, blah – but rather the subtle but seismic change in identity and power that women undergo the moment they become mothers. As much as I'd love to say that this life-changing experience affects both genders equally, unfortunately I do not think this is true. For most families, the brunt is borne by the mother. This is, of course, a modern-day phenomenon. Even one generation ago, women grew up without expectation of financial independence, or autonomy, or economic power. Thus they felt no big loss when they settled down to have a family. They came from a position of inequitable power and continued in the same position, and so little adjustment was required.

Identity crisis

Up until childbirth I had enjoyed financial independence. I was quite satisfied with my identity as a doctor and with my intelligent colleagues and friends, thank you very much. I had a healthy salary. I rented my own flat, I owned my own car; I bought whatever I wanted with my money. For a time, Andrew lived in *my* flat and drove *my* car. At another time, I lived in his flat and drove his car. We shared the household chores. Our relationship was fifty/fifty. So where is it written that once you pass a melon-sized being from out of your nether regions, the contract you had with your partner, with society, with your own identity has to be torn away with your placenta? From then on, I was no longer me. I was Mrs Andrew. Even though I had kept my own surname, once Molly and D came along with their dad's monogram, it was inevitable that I would now be referred to as Mrs Andrew. Staunch refusal to change my name on my passport led to me being interrogated at Heathrow airport for child-trafficking when the official doubted my relationship to two-year-old Molly because of our non-matching surnames. Thankfully, Molly came to the rescue. As I started my feminist rant of, 'Taking your husband's name is an outdated sexist practice,' at the official, she said, 'Why are you getting so cross, *Mummy*?'

Identity-wise, I was still a doctor, of course, and yet I was not the high-flying, arse-kicking, doctor-stroke-clinical-academic jet-setting-to-international-conferences professional I had set out to be. The toughest decision faced by many driven parents like myself is the decision between career and children and I respect the individual choices made by others even if they differ from mine, because by God I know it is a really tough one, and most of the time decisions are made because we are stuck between a rock and a hard place.

Personally, I am lucky enough to be married to someone who was able to pay the mortgage because my post-tax income would have been just about equivalent to decent childcare for two children. Andrew's salary was significantly higher than mine, so we didn't seriously consider him giving up his job to look after the children. The issue of money wasn't the main driver in the decision making: I could either work to pay for childcare or I could do the childcare myself. The former would be more beneficial to my career, the latter more beneficial to my children, but immediate financial differences were negligible. On the flip side, Andrew is often out of the house before six thirty in the morning and not back until eight in the evening, if he is even in the country, so for much of the time all the responsibility of parenting fell to me. I felt the weight of that responsibility; how our children turned out was down to me. As a child psychiatrist who has spent years listening to and helping children and families who have struggled, it seemed implausible not to at least attempt to practise what I preach: to spend time with my own children. In the battle of children versus career, children had to win out for me.

So although I worked full-time until I completed my specialist training, I decided that I would only take a consultant position for a maximum of three days a week, in order to be there for my children at least part of the time. Working so little is highly frowned upon in a profession where apparently working until ten every night, even on Saturdays, is deemed a standard working week. I had hoped that in a female-dominated specialty which focuses on children things might be different, but found that at consultant level, this was not the case. For the sake of family life, I took positions that allowed me to work three days a week, accepting that I would be over-qualified and under-paid. I stood to one side as friends and colleagues sped by in their race to the top. This period was not without its frustrations, tears, self-hatred and despair. What I had not anticipated, yet was possibly the most destructive, was the loss of identity. It was amazing how naked I felt when stripped of a prestigious job title and accompanying pay slip. Stepping back from the career I had always worked towards had eased my life, but the loss of status and identity tasted bitter.

When I reluctantly went with my post-baby fat to sign up for gym membership, I felt physically wounded to see that the lady had listened to my description of my work circumstances and written: Occupation: Housewife/Doctor.

I had never identified myself as a housewife. A mother, yes, but not a housewife. I don't and doubt I ever will darn my husband's socks (although once my mother-in-law did offer to teach me). I often joked with Andrew that I was considering giving up my profession to run a loss-making boutique that he'd have to fund to keep me quiet. I'm joking of course, but some jokes speak truth and there are myriad multi-talented, highly educated, fund-manager/lawyer/doctor/management consultant scientist accountant housewives up and down this country who are training to be nutritionists/interior designers/teaching assistants holistic-therapists/loss-making boutique owners so that they may also be mothers. (There is nothing wrong with these professions, it's just that women often turn to them because they offer more flexibility. They are not the careers that these women have trained so long and hard for.)

I argue that this stripping of identity is enough to cause a 'state of subjective distress and emotional disturbance, interfering with social function' and this 'affects the integrity of an individual's social network'. Work is not just about money, it is also about esteem, about intellectual stimulation, about friendship, about intelligent conversation. Replacing all this with discussions about faecal consistency with other MAD mums, raucous bouts of 'jelly on a plate' to a mute baby, and various rebukes, un-requested nuggets of parenting advice, raised eyebrows and generally being spoken to like an idiot, from teachers/parents/ friends/the supermarket check-out lady/any random stranger, just doesn't bear comparison. If you think that this phenomenon is just a case of women 'whingeing', not knowing how lucky they are to be able to look after their baby at home, financially sup-ported by their husbands, remember that for generations men have faced a very similar adjustment on retirement, with well-recognized negative consequences for their mental health and sometimes even premature death. Adjustment disorder is real and can be a precursor to full-blown depression.

How power shifts

Equally corrosive is the insidious shift in power in the marital relationship. The first (and last) time Andrew ever dared utter, 'What have you been spending my money on?' stuck in the gullet. Never, since graduation, had I had to ask permission to spend money. I earned money; I spent it how I saw fit. Yet with declining hours of paid work came diminished income and an inherent shift in the power dynamic in our relationship. As I was now 'at home more', there somehow passed an unspoken expectation that the days of shared laundry, cooking, cleaning and household chores were over; an unspoken expectation that money had to be 'asked for', and 'kindly bestowed'. I developed nagging worries: What if the worst happened and our relationship faltered? How would I manage financially alone, having stepped off my career track? What about my future, given my loss in pension contributions? Or worse still, would I feel I could not leave? I am fortunate in having enough stubborn resilience to be able to stand up for myself and politely tell Andrew 'where to get off' if he ever refers to 'his money' again. I start to tot up the pay that he actually owes me, in terms of lost career opportunities, childcare, housekeeping, and the education and healthcare of his children. But I could see that if I had not corrected him, my self-esteem – and with it our relationship – would have been eroded. It also served to concrete my decision that I would not give up on my career completely, even if at times it would have been the easiest thing to do.

It was with that sense of needing more purpose and identity in my life that I tentatively started writing, at first for my own sanity, but later for enjoyment. Slowly but surely, my confidence grew and I started to realize that even if the system would not support me to work alongside parenting, I could use my own skills to support myself. I started speaking to friends about work outside of the NHS which, although I loved, had rejected me for my lack of ambition, work ethic and dedication because of my insistence on limited hours. I started doing private work with some friends and this led to more confidence in my ability, along with connections and friendships which have led to more and more opportunities. These eventually culminated in a return to a prestigious NHS position on *my terms* – three days a week. Even better, my writing, which had become my means of therapy, led to the wonderful opportunity to write this book.

I am not alone. So common is this story of frustrated mums taking their destinies into their own hands that the term 'mumtrepreneur' has been coined. These are ambitious, educated and talented women. Isn't it about time the system changed to retain this talent? I know that many corporations are introducing 'return to work' programmes, which is a start, but it feels too little too late. The training costs required for companies to run these programmes is huge, and the motivation required by parents to

TOP TIP: GUILT WHERE GUILT IS DUE

One of the main burdens that mothers carry is that of guilt. I confess that prior to having children I was a perpetrator in inflicting maternal guilt. In the past, if a child was brought to clinic for an assessment by their father I would wonder, 'Where is the mother and is this a cause of the problem?' If a child was brought by their mother, I never pondered the whereabouts of the father (I assumed they had buggered off permanently or were at work). Luckily I no longer hold this prejudice, but I now know that this type of prejudice is rife amongst professionals working with children and is probably a major contributor to maternal guilt.

When Molly and D were sick at nursery, I would always be called before my husband, even though the nursery had both our telephone numbers. Andrew would only be called if I could not be contacted. Dentists, hospitals, teachers, opticians – basically any other professional dealing with our children would always ring *me* to sort out anything to do with our children, even when we were both working full-time. The implication? Children are their mother's responsibility. Father's work is more important. Why is that?

Worse still, mothers even get blamed for the sins of the father. Andrew had a spate of being late to pick up Molly and D on his nursery runs. Rather than rebuke him when he finally arrived, the nursery staff were congenial. However, the following day *I* would be given a telling off about the children being picked up late. I immediately countered that it was my husband who was late and not me. They acknowledged this and asked me to let my husband know that this was not on. Luckily, I had taken a good dose of assertiveness that morning and said, 'You know, if I tell him it will be perceived as nagging. It will be much more effective if you ring him at work and tell him yourself.' To my alarm, the nursery teacher became all bashful and said, 'Am I allowed?' This was the first time that I realized the unfairness of it all. Professionals are more than happy to criticize working women on their parenting but dare not criticize working men. 'Mrs B,' I said, 'not only are you allowed, but I would be delighted if you did!'

My top tip, therefore, is this: if you are a professional who works with children, be it teacher, nursery worker, teaching assistant, doctor, nurse, dentist, or other, please be fair and call fathers to account as well as mothers. Responsibility shared is guilt halved.

retrain to do a job they were previously competent at is a huge barrier. Companies should never have let these women go in the first place. Part-time and flexible working hours for parents (male and female) are a much better solution.

The Maternal Work–Life Balance: Four- to Seven-Year-Olds

As children grow, so the work–life balance dilemmas change. As children begin to be siphoned off to school, the parents' hands-on role diminishes as whole chunks of the day's childcare are taken care of. Unfortunately, even with school-age children this is not the end of working-parent conundrums. At my hard-won London

NHS consultant job I 'only' did three days a week, but this still meant that I could no longer drop off the children at school on a daily basis. I am not quite sure who worked out the logistics that school should start at eight fifty in the morning and work should start at nine, because who in London can get to work in ten minutes . . . ? And how many childminders want to come for just an hour of work in the morning to take the children to school?

Then there was the afterschool care. I am lucky that my mother has always taken the children after school for two days a week. I say, 'lucky', but of course, luck had little to do with it. I purposely moved home to the other side of London, even though it was miles from my job, expressly for this reason. The result is that I have to endure a seventy-five-minute commute each way to work, in order to have my mother on hand, but for me this is bearable because I implicitly trust my mother to nurture my children. I had only one afternoon that needed to be covered with paid childcare, so I wasn't considering a nanny or an au pair. And anyway, I had fought hard to get a part-time job to stave off the need for this type of childcare. After meeting a few young ladies one summer who might have been able to take the kids after school for one day a week, I settled on one and congratulated myself on solving the problem. One week before school started I texted to confirm arrangements, only to find that the chosen lady had decided to disappear off the face of the earth. I suddenly felt immensely sick; just as I was about to return to 'my career', I was struck down once again by the nagging problem, who will look after my kids?

I thought about starting a breakfast club at the school with a rota of parents, or paying the parent of another child in Molly or D's class to take them. I looked into which other parents might be interested. And as each cockamamie plan fell through, I felt the same sinking feeling. It was then that I had my revelation. The solution was so simple that looking back I cannot believe I didn't think of it immediately.

Before I tell you my solution, I want to share with you an old brain teaser.

A teenage boy who grew up never having met his father has a terrible traffic accident. He is rushed to hospital and straight into emergency theatre. The surgeons gather around, ready to operate, but just then the lead surgeon looks at the boy's face and gasps, 'I can't operate, this is my son.' What has happened?

Before you come up with some elaborate reply about how the surgeon recognized the boy to be his son because they looked so similar, I will tell you that the answer is simple: the surgeon is the boy's mother. Yes, a *female* lead surgeon.

My 'novel' solution

You can see how many of us are blinded by gender stereotypes. So you might not have deduced that the solution to my childcare problems was to get Andrew involved. He was made to drop the children at school on at least one of the days I was at work, and also told to make arrangements for the children to go to after-school club once a week. Just as I was taken aback by my realization that fathers could actually contribute to regular weekly childcare duties, rather than just at the weekend, he too was surprised to be asked. He had indeed sat through my endless rantings about how maybe we could pay 'anyone-in-the-world' to take the children, without once suggesting that part of this responsibility was his. There ensued, of course, the typical grumbles: 'important job' . . . 'impossible' . . . 'money' . . . 'promotion' . . . 'blah' . . . 'blah' . . . 'blah'.

However, I happened to know that one of his colleagues had been able to wangle a late start to drop his children off at school a few times a week. This colleague had just spent a tonne of money fighting for shared custody of his children, following a divorce. For him, it was a privilege to be able to do the school run. So I pointed out to my darling husband that I was offering him exactly this privilege, without the expense of a divorce and custody battle. Bargain!

Seriously, though, surely childcare arrangements are a shared responsibility? Why does it so often fall to mothers? Even when fathers are doing childcare, it is often because the mothers have told them to do so and given them explicit instructions of where things are and what to do. The other day, having just cleaned the kitchen, I asked Andrew to make Molly a packed lunch for her school trip. He replied, 'OK. But what goes into a packed lunch?' I did not dignify this question with an answer. A grown man earning a decent salary should be able to work this one out for himself. I, for one, would like some time off from all the thinking and planning of parenting, as well as all the doing.

The changing role of fathers

Yet, even as I moan, I know that the times they are a-changing. Gender roles are slowly evolving. As I've been saying throughout the chapter, female roles have transformed dramatically over the last fifty years. Women can reach the top in almost all professions, and girls outperform boys on all educational assessments. Now it is down to the men to face their own internal struggles and adapt to keep apace of the new world order.

Of course, there has already been significant change. A father's duty in the past was to provide for the family: the roof over the head, the food on the table. He was the head of the household, often feared and emotionally distant from his family. You only have to watch films from the last century to see the difference between fathers of the past and those of the present (try *Mary Poppins*, *Peter Pan* and *The Sound of Music* to name a few). Go even further back and you get versions of *Cinderella* where Cinderella's father does not die (as in the Disney version), but is complicit in her enslavement. Interestingly, Cinderella's father is never described as being a 'wicked' father, that adjective is reserved only for the stepmother. (Fathers in those days naturally abdicated family matters to their wives and apparently did not feel the need to get involved, even when their child is a bullied house-slave, sleeping in the fireplace.)

Unfortunately, this has led to a kind of identity crisis for some men, with the pressure to change coming as rather a shock. Brought up by a pipe-and-slippers dad and a pinny-and-Sunday-roast mum, they have been schooled to believe that their identity and self-worth lies in their career. So they work ever longer hours, citing 'It's good for the family' in their defence. They fear they'll be mocked by their peers if they settle for a less prestigious career, that they'll be seen as a 'loser', or sexually unattractive to women. However, more and more men are rejecting these traditional male norms. As a new parent, my husband popped in to our neighbour's fancy dress party with Molly in a Baby Bjorn, not bothering with the fancy dress theme. One party guest commented, 'Hey, great fancy dress idea to come as Suburban Dad,' not realizing that the baby was real, this was not fancy dress and that Andrew just *was* a suburban dad. So pervasive now is the image of the proud new father walking around with a baby strapped to his chest that it no longer has any comedy value. A baby is worn much as a campaign rosette; a badge of honour and ideology for any man. From Michael McIntyre's fatherhood repertoires to Jamie Oliver's family meals in minutes, the remote and respected father figure/salary-man is gradually being toppled, replaced with images of desirable male role models travelling *en famille* with sexy women on their arms (I'm thinking Beckham and his ilk). In fact I'm pretty sure that the strong and beautiful women of the future will be actively seeking men who are happy to roll up their sleeves to change a nappy, not someone who expects to be brought a paper and a whisky at the end of the working day.

This is great because fathers can be such great role models to their children. They can demonstrate to boys that being able to cook and clean is not beyond or beneath them. They can show that sensitivity can be a sign of strength and not weakness, they can role-model to girls the type of considerate partner we would wish to have for a son-in-law. In parenting a second opinion is often crucial. Fathers can offer a different perspective to mothers so that children are exposed to a broader world view, they can

TOP TIP: PUSH FOR EQUAL RESPONSIBILITIES

We should all be pushing for a fifty-fifty split in domestic responsibility with our partners, focusing on issues such as paternity leave, flexible working hours, job-shares, well paid, high-status, part-time positions, family-friendly policies from public sector and corporate employers, and innovations in flexible ways of working for *both* men and women.

balance a mother's weaknesses (I really appreciate Andrew's more relaxed attitude at times when I get over-anxious), and crucially, where fathers are more involved with childcare, they are more able to understand and appreciate what their wives are doing.

It's very encouraging to see young men now waxing lyrical about the right spicing for chicken, bursting into tears on *Britain's Got Talent* and actively wanting to be involved with their children. The biggest stumbling block to equality now seems to be the 'establishment'; those institutions such as the government, police, army, law, banking, large corporations and, sadly, the NHS, which are still predominantly run by old male traditionalists who have not yet scanned what is on the horizon – a future male and female workforce pushing for change in the work–life balance.

In my children's eyes, my husband and I are interchangeable parents. He is just as capable as me (although, I still like to think I am a little bit better) of soothing an ailment, of bathing them and reading them stories, of checking spellings, of watching a school play, of cooking the dinner (although he likes to think he is better at this than me) and doing the laundry. He is just as capable of making my children laugh and understanding their problems, and of asking how they are. I can sleep easy at night knowing that if I should die tomorrow, they will be well looked after emotionally, and not left to sweep the fireplace.

Chapter Summary

Helping our children build a strong identity for themselves is the crucial final layer to my Inside Out Parenting. I believe that every child deserves to be treated as an individual and not limited in any way by their gender or their race. At present, however liberal we may believe we are, we often unconsciously perpetuate gender biases and stereotypes. These are ingrained in our society and entrenched in our language. The drip-drip of our unconscious bias can silently but insidiously shape our children and limit their potential. Only by making these issues conscious to ourselves and to society in general can we start to correct our own behaviour and thereby that of our children, and allow the next generation a genuine chance at equality.

Epilogue

Over the last eight years I have been on the best journey of my life. It has had its fair share of tears, fears and sleeplessness, but the happiness and pride that I have experienced watching my two crying, pooing bundles evolve into happy, confident, intelligent and kind children more than makes up for them. It is my firm belief that good parenting is the making of a child, and within that, early parenting is the most critical. I hope that I have shown some of the many different ways that parents can support their children, not only to do their best at maths and piano, but in the areas where it really counts: self-belief, self-control, communication and kindness. I have thought about parenting every day of my life and I am sure that this will continue to be the case as once a parent, always a parent!

It has been both a revelation and a privilege to be able to share my thoughts and experiences with others and I sincerely hope that they have brought a little help, solace and amusement to you. Now that the basics are covered, I wonder what the future will hold and about the next steps of my parenting journey. There are new challenges to anticipate as my children turn to *The Wonder Years* of middle childhood, and I to the next stage of parenthood, where the intense and frankly exhausting involvement described in this book must recede and give way to the equally stressful process of 'letting go'. Having built a strong inner core and firm foundation for our children, the next stage involves supporting them as they go on to discover their own paths and identities and letting them shine for themselves.

Good luck to all parents!

Acknowledgements

This book would not have been possible without the support of the many people who encouraged me to write. Thank you. Particular thanks go to Kirsten Westlake, Lucy Peacock and Yasmin Reyal, who read the very first attempt. Thanks also to all the subscribers and commentators on my blog, especially 'Marina Sofia' who 'liked' every post and whose supportive comments were very much appreciated, and to Christel Chen, Jessica Boyde and Stian Westlake for spreading the word.

Thanks to Laetitia Rutherford and the team at Watson Little for taking a chance on my manuscript, and encouraging me to take to social media despite my ineptitude. I am also extremely grateful to Carole Tonkinson, Louise McNamara, Tania Wilde and the team at Bluebird who believed in my work and encouraged me throughout the process. I am indebted to the polish they have provided.

I would not be where I am today without the early mentorship of the late Alan Flisher who gave me my first taste of child psychiatry research. I am grateful to all the amazing professors and researchers that I have had the pleasure to work with directly and indirectly. Your work is inspirational. Special thanks to Isobel Heyman, Patricia Rios and Fiona McEwen for your friendship and personal support through tough times. Thanks to Eleni Paliokosta, Stefanos Maltezeos and Susannah Whitwell for your professional support.

Most thanks to all my friends and family for your lifetime of support and without whom there would be no story, most especially: Sue Chuan, Shinn-Chung, Wen-Lan, Chyng-Lan, May Anne, Eian, Fred, Sophie, Zoe, Jessica, Peggy, Katie, Tanya, Chat, Yuen and Anton.

References

Introduction

1 Kim-Cohen, J., Caspi, A., Moffitt, T.E., et al., 'Prior juvenile diagnoses in adults with mental disorder'. *Archives of General Psychiatry, 60,* 709–17 (2003)

2 Chichetti, D., 'Resilience under conditions of extreme stress: A multi-level perspective'. *World Psychiatry, 9,* 145–54 (2010)

1. The Fixed Core: Genetics

1 Tick, B., Bolton, P., Happe, F., Rutter, M., Rijsdijk, F., 'Heritability of autism spectrum disorders: a meta-analysis of twin studies'. *Journal of Child Psychology and Psychiatry, 57,* 585–95 (2016); van Haren, N.E., Rijsdijk, F., Schnack, H.G., Picchioni, M.M., Toulopoulou, T., Weisbrod, M., Sauer, H., van Erp, T.G., Cannon, T.D., Huttunen, M.O., Boomsma, D.I., Hulshoff Pol, H.E., Murray, R.M., Kahn, R.S., 'The genetic and environmental determinants of the association between brain abnormalities and schizophrenia: the schizophrenia twins and relatives consortium'. *Biological Psychiatry, 71,* 915–21 (2012); Gillespie, N.A., Eaves, L.J., Maes, H., Silberg, J.L., 'Testing Models for the Contributions of Genes and Environment to Developmental Change in Adolescent Depression'. *Behavioural Genetics, 45,* 382–93 (2015)

2 Gene-environment interactions are based on ideas which are widely written about by Robert Plomin. One of many references available is: Plomin, R., Rutter, M., 'Child development, molecular genetics, and what to do with genes once they are found'. *Child Development, 69,* 1223–42 (1998)

2. The Malleable Core: Self-Esteem

1 These monkey experiments of Harry F. Harlow are well known and can be read about on Wikipedia or in any psychology text book.

2 Stein, A. et al., 'Effects of perinatal mental disorders on the fetus and child'. Part of a series on Perinatal Mental Health in the *Lancet*, *384*, 1800–19 (2014)

3 See the work of Mary Ainsworth, which can be read about on Wikipedia or in any psychology text book.

4 See the work of Mary Ainsworth, as above.

5 The original paper is: Reivich, K.J., Seligman, M.E., McBride, S., 'Master Resilience training in the US Army'. *American Psychologist*, *66*, 25–34 (2011)

6 Dweck, C., *Mindset: How you can fulfil your potential*, Random House Publishing Group (2012)

7 McAdams, T.A., Rijsdijk, F.V., Neiderhiser, J.M., Narusyte, J., Shaw, D.S., Natsuaki, M.N., Spotts, E.L., Ganiban, J.M., Reiss, D., Leve, L.D., Lichtenstein, P., Eley, T.C., 'The relationship between parental depressive symptoms and offspring psychopathology: evidence from a children-of-twins study and an adoption study'. *Psychological Medicine*, *45*, 2583–9 (2012). Sadeh-Sharvit, S., Zubery, E., Mankovski, E., Steiner, E., Lock, J.D., 'Parent-based prevention program for the children of mothers with eating disorders: Feasibility and preliminary outcomes'. *Eating Disorders*, *24*, 312–25 (2016)

8 Liang, H., & Eley, T.C., 'A monozygotic twin differences study of non-shared environmental influence on adolescent depressive symptoms'. *Child Development*, *76*, 1247–60 (2005)

9 Buhrmester, D., & Furman, W., 'Perceptions of sibling relationships during middle childhood and adolescence'. *Child Development*, *61*, 1387–98 (1990); Buist, K.L., Dekovic, M., & Prinzie, P., 'Sibling relationship quality and psychopathology of children and adolescents: a meta-analysis'. *Clinical Psychology Review*, *33*, 97–106 (2013); Kim, J., McHale, S.M., Crouter, A.C., & Osgood, W., 'Longitudinal linkages between sibling relationships and adjustment from middle childhood through adolescence'. *Developmental Psychology*, *43*, 960–73 (2007)

10 Campione-Barr, N., Greer, K.B., & Kruse, A., 'Differential associations between domains of sibling conflict and adolescent emotional adjustment'. *Child Development, 84,* 938–54 (2013); Dunn, J., Slomkowski, C., Beardsall, L., & Rende, R., 'Adjustment in middle childhood and early adolescence: links with earlier and contemporary sibling relationships'. *Child Psychology and Psychiatry and Allied Disciplines, 35,* 491–504 (1994); Padilla-Walker, L., Harper, J.M., & Jensen, A.C., 'Self-regulation as a mediator between sibling relationship quality and early adolescents' positive and negative outcomes'. *Journal of Family Psychology, 24,* 419–28 (2010); Stocker, C.M., Burwell, R.A., & Briggs, M.L., 'Sibling conflict in middle childhood predicts children's adjustment in early adolescence'. *Journal of Family Psychology, 16,* 50–57 (2002)

11 Bowes, L., Maughan, B., Caspi, A., Moffitt, T.E., & Arseneault, L., 'Families promote emotional and behavioural resilience to bullying: evidence of an environmental effect'. *Journal of Child Psychology and Psychiatry, 51,* 809–17 (2010); Criss, M.M., & Shaw, D.S., 'Sibling relationships as contexts for delinquency training in low-income families'. *Journal of Family Psychology, 19,* 592–600 (2005); Dunn, J., Slomkowski, C., & Beardsall, L., 'Sibling relationships from the preschool period through middle childhood and early adolescence'. *Developmental Psychology, 30,* 315–24 (1994); Gass, K., Jenkins, J., & Dunn, J., 'Are sibling relationships protective? A longitudinal study'. *Journal of Child Psychology and Psychiatry, 48,* 167–75 (2007); Jenkins, J.M., & Smith, M.A., 'Factors protecting children living in disharmonious homes: maternal reports'. *Journal of the American Academy of Child and Adolescent Psychiatry, 29,* 60–69 (1990); Tucker, C.J., Holt, M., & Wiesen-Martin, D., 'Interparental conflict and sibling warmth during adolescence: associations with female depression in emerging adulthood'. *Psychological Reports, 112,* 243–51 (2013); Widmer, E.D., & Weiss, C.C., 'Do older siblings make a difference? The effects of older sibling support and older sibling adjustment on the adjustment of socially disadvantaged adolescents'. *Journal of Research on Adolescence, 10,* 1–27 (2000)

3. Layer One: Social Skills

1 Simpson, E.A., Miller, G.M., Ferrari, P.F., Suomi, S.J., Paukner, A., 'Neonatal imitation and early social experience predict gaze following abilities in infant monkeys'. *Scientific Reports*, Feb 1;6:20233 (2016)

2 Saint-Georges, C., Chetouani, M., Cassel, R., Apicella, F., Mahdhaoui, A., Muratori, F., Laznik, M.C., Cohen, D., 'Motherese in interaction: at the cross-road of emotion and cognition? (A systematic review)'. *PLoS One 18*; 8(10):e78103 (2013)

3 Rutter, M., Andersen-Wood, L., Beckett, C., Bredenkamp, D., Castle, J., Groothues, C., Kreppner, J., Keaveney, L., Lord, C., O'Connor, T.G., 'Quasi-autistic patterns following severe early global privation. English and Romanian Adoptees (ERA) Study Team'. *Journal of Child Psychology and Psychiatry, 40,* 537–49 (1999)

4 Lord, C., Rutter, M., Goode, S., et al., 'Autism diagnostic observation schedule: a standardized observation of communicative and social behavior'. *Journal of Autism and Developmental Disorders, 19,* 185–212 (1989)

4. Layer Two: Emotional Stability

1 Thielen, A., Klus, H., & Muller, L., 'Tobacco smoke: unraveling a controversial subject'. *Experimental and Toxicologic Pathology, 60,* 141–56 (2008); US Department of Health and Human Services, 'A report of the surgeon general: How tobacco smoke causes disease: What it means to you'. Atlanta, GA: Centers for Disease Control and Prevention (2010)

2 Lambers, D.S., & Clark, K.E., 'The maternal and fetal physiologic effects of nicotine'. *Seminars in Perinatology, 20,* 115–26 (1996)

3 Knopic, V.S., Maccani, M.A., Francazio, S., & McGeary, J.E., 'The epigenetics of maternal cigarette smoking during pregnancy and effects on child development'. *Development and Psychopathology, 24,* 1377–90 (2012)

4 Matthews, S.G., & Phillips, D.I., 'Minireview: Transgenerational inheritance of the stress response: A new frontier in stress research'. *Endocrinology, 151,* 7–13. (2010)

5 Viding et al., 'Anti-social behaviour in children with and without callous-unemotional traits'. *Journal of the Royal Society of Medicine*, 195–200 (2012)

6 Ibid

7 Webster-Stratton, C., *The Incredible Years*. www.incredibleyears.com

8 Beydoun, H., Saftlas, A.F., 'Physical and mental health outcomes of prenatal maternal stress in human and animal studies: a review of recent evidence'. *Paediatric and Perinatal Epidemiology*, *22*, 438–66 (2008); Talge, N.M., Neal, C., Glover, V. and the Early Stress, Translational Research and Prevention Science Network: Fetal and Neonatal Experience on Child and Adolescent Mental Health, 'Antenatal maternal stress and long-term effects on child neuro-development: how and why?'. *Journal of Child Psychology and Psychiatry*, *48*, 245–61 (2007); Van den Bergh, B.R.H., Mulder, E.J.H., Mennesa, M., & Glover, V., 'Antenatal maternal anxiety and stress and the neurobehavioural development of the fetus and child: links and possible mechanisms. A review'. *Neuroscience and Biobehavioral Reviews*, *29*, 237–58 (2005)

9 Van den Bergh, B.R.H., Mulder, E.J.H., Mennesa, M., & Glover, V., 'Antenatal maternal anxiety and stress and the neurobehavioural development of the fetus and child: links and possible mechanisms. A review'. *Neuroscience and Biobehavioral Reviews*, *29*, 237–58 (2005)

10 Ibid

11 Berkowitz, G.S., Wolff, M.S., Janevic, T.M., Holzman, I.R., Yehuda, R., & Landrigan, P.J., 'The World Trade Center disaster and intrauterine growth restriction'. *Journal of the American Medical Association*, *290*, 595–6 (2003)

12 LaPlante, D. P., Barr, R.G., Brunet, A., Du Fort, G.G., Meaney, M.J., Saucier, J.F., Zelazo, P.R., & King, S., 'Stress during pregnancy affects general intellectual and language functioning in human toddlers'. *Pediatric Research, 56,* 400–10 (2004)

13 Beydoun, H., Saftlas, A.F., 'Physical and mental health outcomes of prenatal maternal stress in human and animal studies: a review of recent evidence'. *Paediatric and Perinatal Epidemiology*, *22*, 438–66 (2008); Talge, N.M., Neal, C., Glover, V. and the Early Stress, Translational Research and Prevention Science Network, Fetal and Neonatal Experience on Child and Adolescent Mental

Health, 'Antenatal maternal stress and long-term effects on child neuro-development: how and why?'. *Journal of Child Psychology and Psychiatry, 48,* 245–61 (2008); Van den Bergh, B.R.H., Mulder, E.J.H., Mennesa, M., & Glover, V., 'Antenatal maternal anxiety and stress and the neurobehavioural develop-ment of the fetus and child: links and possible mechanisms. A review'. *Neuroscience and Biobehavioral Reviews, 29,* 237–58 (2005)

14 Rice, F., Harold, G.T., Boivin, J., van den Bree, M., Hay, D.F., & Thapar, A., 'The links between prenatal stress and offspring development and psychopathology: Disentangling environmental and inherited influences'. *Psychological Medi-cine, 40,* 335–45 (2010)

15 Cook, M. and Mineka, S., 'Observational condition of fear to fear-relevant versus fear-irrelevant stimuli in rhesus monkeys'. *Journal of Abnormal Psych-ology, 98* (4): 448–59 (1989)

5. Layer Three: Behaviour and Self-Control

1 Webster-Stratton, C., *The Incredible Years,* www.incredibleyears.com; Triple P: www.triplep.net; Jo Frost: www.supernanny.co.uk

2 Wass et al., 'Training Attentional Control in Infancy', *Current Biology, 21,* 1–5 (2011); Wass, S.V., Scerif, G., & Johnson, M.H., 'Training attentional control and working memory – is younger better?'. *Developmental Review* (2012) http://dx.doi.org/10.1016/j.dr.2012.07.001

3 The MTA Cooperative Group, 'A 14-Month Randomized Clinical Trial of Treatment Strategies for Attention-Deficit/Hyperactivity Disorder'. *Arch Gen Psychiatry, 56:* 1073–1086 (1999)

6. Layer Four: Intelligence

1 Amy Chua, *The Battle Hymn of the Tiger Mother,* Bloomsbury (2011)

2 Mansell, W., 'Hidden Tigers: Why do Chinese children do so well at school?' the *Guardian,* Monday 7 February 2011

3 Gottfredson, L.S., 'Mainstream science on intelligence: An editorial with 52 signatories, history and bibliography'. *Intelligence, 24:* 13–23 (1997)

4 Plomin, R., and Deary, I.J., 'Genetics and intelligence differences: five special findings'. *Molecular Psychiatry, 20,* 98–108 (2015); doi:10.1038/mp.2014.105; published online 16 September 2014

5 Plomin, R., Defries, J.C., Knopik, V.S., & Neiderhiser, J.M.,'Top 10 Replicated Findings From Behavioral Genetics'. *Perspectives on Psychological Science 2016,* vol. 11(1) 3–23

6 Plomin, R., and Deary, I.J., 'Genetics and intelligence differences: five special findings'. *Molecular Psychiatry, 20,* 98–108 (2015); doi:10.1038/mp.2014.105; published online 16 September 2014

7 Maria Grazia Tosto, Ken B. Hanscombe, Claire M. A. Haworth, Oliver S. P. Davis, Stephen A. Petrill, Philip S. Dale, Sergey Malykh, Robert Plomin, Yulia Kovas. 'Why do spatial abilities predict mathematical performance?'. *Developmental Science (Dev Sci),* on-line ahead of print (2014)

8 Dweck, C.S., *Mindset: The New Psychology of Success,* Random House, New York (2006)

8. Layer Six: Identity, Gender and Race

1 Moss-Racusin et al., C. A., 'Science faculty's subtle gender biases favor male students'. Proceeding of the National Academy of Sciences USA, 2012; published ahead of print 17 September, 2012, doi:10.1073/pnas.1211236109

2 World Health Organization. ICD-10

Index